THE JAPANESE' MOST BITTER AND BLOODY
DEFEAT—THE BATTLE THAT SHATTERED
THEIR MYSTIQUE AS NEVER-SAY-DIE
FIGHTERS ONCE AND FOR ALL...

"A fascinating account of what has been
called the greatest sea battle in history. It
grows with graphic narrative, much of it
told by the participants in their own words.

"Excellent vignettes portray the leaders on
both sides as revealed in official reports,
personal letters, oral histories, narratives,
interviews, and some published volumes.
Mr. Hoyt's re-creation dramatically covers
this far-spreading battle, after which the
Japanese Fleet never again had the power
to contest the sea. Japan was doomed, for
without the sea all other military and national power is weakened and futile."

—E. M. Eller
Rear Admiral USN, Ret.,
Past Director of Naval History

THE BATTLE OF LEYTE GULF

EDWIN P. HOYT

PLAYBOY
PAPERBACKS

To
the memory of my friend,
the late
Admiral Harry W. Hill

THE BATTLE OF LEYTE GULF

Copyright © 1972 by Edwin P. Hoyt

Cover illustration copyright © 1979 by PEI Books, Inc.

Published simultaneously in the United States and Canada by Playboy Paperbacks, New York, New York. Printed in the United States of America. Library of Congress Catalog Card Number: 79-88827. Reprinted by arrangement with David McKay Company, Inc.

Books are available at quantity discounts for promotional and industrial use. For further information, write to Premium Sales, Playboy Paperbacks, 1633 Broadway, New York, New York 10019.

ISBN: 0-872-16629-5

First Playboy Paperbacks printing December 1979.
Second printing June 1981.

CONTENTS

1

THE FIRST STRIKING FORCE

Since the bitter lessons of the Battle of the Philippine Sea, the Japanese surface fleet had been preparing as best it could for the operations to come. One positive change was the mounting of 25 mm anti-aircraft machine guns on the ships: the battleships got 120 new guns, the cruisers 80, and the destroyers 40 guns. The Japanese commanders, watching the attrition of their air forces and carrier fleet, had only too clear an idea of what was to come in the big battle they sought.

It was to be called the Sho plan—Sho meaning "victory" in Japanese. It was to be the Japanese Navy's last desperate foray to try to stop the burgeoning power of America.

The Japanese fleet at this time was basically split into two sections because of the problem of securing adequate fuel for all the ships. The carrier force and several cruisers and destroyers were stationed in the Inland Sea, under command of Vice Admiral Jisaburo Ozawa, who ranked second in the fleet to Admiral Toyoda.

The second part of the fleet, led by Vice Admiral Takeo Kurita, had gone to Lingga Roads, just across the strait from Singapore, where it could take advantage of a good fuel supply to conduct some training for the battle to come.

The training included gunnery and torpedo firing, for the Admiral wanted to move in swiftly, strike, and destroy. He did not know quite when; it was estimated that the Japanese fleet would take six to eight months after the June defeat at the Marianas to get back into fighting shape. But, of course, there was no such time available.

Admiral Kurita was a good servant of the emperor. He took life as it came. He was a distinguished, if taciturn, officer. He had been an admiral since 1938 and was now fifty-five years old. He had served in many capacities, in destroyers and cruisers and as cruiser commander and destroyer commander. He had fought in the battles of the South Pacific and was a thoroughly experienced commander. And he was ready for whatever might happen.

As the fleet trained, the planners in Tokyo laid out the Sho Operation in as much detail as they could. Admiral Kurita was not consulted—he was not on that level—but in August several members of Admiral Toyoda's combined fleet staff from Hiyoshi came down to Lingga Roads and discussed the plans with the Admiral and his key men. As was made very plain to him, and as he knew already, the seizure of the Philippines by the Americans would effectively end Japan's ability to use the fuel supplies from the southern Empire. It was bad enough after the fall of the Marianas, with the new bases acquired. Fall of the Philippines would bring disaster. So the emphasis of the Japanese training was to strike fast and *prevent* the landing of American forces in the Philippines, wherever they might happen to move. Kurita bettled his black brows and his downturned mouth stiffened at the prospects, but no one could say that he was either unwilling or unduly pessimistic about the outcome of the battle. He believed in miracles, and said so.

When the fateful days of October arrived, and Admiral Halsey moved against Okinawa and then Formosa, Admiral Kurita and his force knew that the moment of their movement was not far off. But like all the operational units of the Japanese fleet, the Second Fleet apparently believed Imperial General Headquarters' communiqués. "A dozen or more enemy carriers and many others of his ships were sunk or damaged," said Kurita's battle summary, "while gradually concentrating our air strength southward, the attacks against the task forces were continued."

On October 15 Kurita still waited, while the aerial fight went on, but messages were now filling the air, outlining the program as it was being changed to meet new conditions. The men of Kurita's force learned what would be expected of them—or part of it. They would move out soon to Brunei, and from Brunei they would sail on October 22 at 0800, passing through San Bernardino Strait at sundown on October 24. They would engage the Americans in a night action east of Samar, destroy the enemy, and break into Tacloban at dawn on October 25, to wreak havoc among the enemy convoys and put an ignominious end to the American landings.

Training was stopped on October 15 as everything waited for new orders. On October 16 two ships were scheduled to go into drydock in Singapore. The order was canceled. Workmen were still installing radar sets in the float planes of the fleet. This work was stopped. A convoy of tankers was sent ahead to Brunei for refueling; Destroyer Division Two was also sent ahead. The alert came on October 17, and the fleet sailed for Brunei at 0100 on October 18. The delay had been occasioned by combined fleet headquarters' waiting to discover where the landing was going to be. The discovery had come, initially, when American minesweepers were found in the area of Leyte Gulf on October 17, but headquarters did not definitely announce the invasion of Leyte until October 18. Already the Sho plan was in trouble in two ways: (1) its aerial support had been largely knocked out by Admiral Halsey's strikes; (2) the delay in sending the fleet meant that the Americans would be landed before the Japanese arrived, which increased the organizational ability of the Americans, and made the Japanese task that much more difficult.

It was a proud fleet that left the Singapore region that night. The new battleships *Yamato* and *Musashi* were the finest vessels of their kind in the world, the world's most powerful fighting ships, displacing 68,000 tons, and capable of 27 knots. The older battleship *Nagato* was some 21 years their senior, with 16-inch guns, and could make better than 20 knots. The old battleships *Kongo* and *Haruna* were notable for a Japanese shipbuilding oddity—their masts were shaped like tall pagodas—and they carried 14-inch guns. These ships were supported by 10 heavy cruisers: *Atago, Takao, Maya, Chokai, Myoko, Haguro, Kumano, Suzuya,*

Tone, and *Chikuma,* the light cruisers *Yahagi* and *Noshiro,* and 15 slender destroyers. In spite of the fact that there were no carriers present, as planned, it was an impressive force of ships.

When the fleet arrived at Brunei at noon on October 20, it waited for orders. They came in the middle of the afternoon of the next day, and they showed something of what had been happening on Formosa and in Japan.

The enemy, said the orders, was directing his main force to land in the central Philippines, and the combined fleet was "to direct all of its power" to destroy him, in conjunction with the army.

So much, so good. And when it came to Admiral Kurita's orders they were scarcely changed from his earlier understanding. He was to break through to the Tacloban area at dawn on October 25 "and after first destroying the enemy's surface forces, will cut down his landing forces."

But there were significant changes. Admiral Kurita could understand that he was to have no carriers, as had been the original plan so long ago. No one had told him the extent of the losses of planes in the fight against the Third Fleet, but it did not take much to put two and two together, knowing that the carriers had been left in the Inland Sea to rearm with planes and train their crews. And the northern force of Admiral Ozawa, which originally was scheduled to come on with the strength of its carriers, included at least four big new carriers that could outclass many of the American ships. But now Ozawa's force had been cut back to become a decoy, to lure the American carriers northward and keep them out of the battle.

Most disconcerting—and more than that to many of the men under Admiral Kurita—was the fact that the timing of his part in the action had been changed. Everyone had planned and trained for a night action. Now they were told to break through the Americans in broad daylight.

Most of the complaints were over the decision to stage this daylight attack; this idea was contrary to all that the officers and men had been practicing for months, and to the Japanese training program for years past. Rebellious talk became so general that Admiral Kurita pressed his lips together in his stern face and called a conference of division commanders and their staffs aboard the *Atago*, his flagship. This is what he said:

I know that many of you are strongly opposed to this assignment. But the war situation is far more critical than any of you can possibly know. Would it not be shameful to have the fleet remain intact while our nation perishes? I believe that the Imperial General Headquarters is giving us a glorious opportunity. Because I realize how very serious the war situation actually is, I am willing to accept even this ultimate assignment to storm into Leyte Gulf.

You must all remember that there are such things as miracles. What man can say that there is no chance for our fleet to turn the tide of war in a decisive battle? We shall have a chance to meet our enemies. We shall engage his task forces. I hope that you will not carry your responsibilities lightly. I know that you will act faithfully and well.

That speech by Admiral Kurita quieted the most dissident, and brought the assembled officers to their feet in a standing ovation to their admiral's patriotism and high-mindedness. The officers of the fleet, then, if not the men, knew precisely where they stood in the Japanese scheme. For this was to be the great battle, and they were to play the decisive role. Admiral Ozawa in the north was facing an even more dismal prospect, but his one hope was that by following his strange orders he would make it possible for Admirals Kurita, Nishimura, and Shima to meet and close the pincers on the Americans without the help of the American Air Force from the carriers. Under those conditions, the miracle might amount to something.

2

THE SEVENTH FLEET

When Admiral Chester W. Nimitz had taken over command of the American naval forces in the Pacific at the end of December, 1941, he had known that one of his primary problems was to organize a group of "fighting admirals" who would use the slender resources of the fleet to best advantage in striking back at the Japanese. Very quickly he began sorting them out. A man got his chance, and if he muffed it, he was transferred out.

High on Admiral Nimitz's list of fighters appeared the name of Thomas C. Kinkaid of the Class of 1908. Kinkaid was a wiry, thoughtful man who sometimes referred to his own "professorial" nature as though it were a fault, a man who sometimes wished he had more of the quality often called charisma, a quality he gently envied in Admiral Halsey. Early in the war Kinkaid commanded the cruisers in Admiral Wilson Brown's Task Force 11, one of the first to attack the Japanese in the South Pacific. The war moved, the search for fighting admirals continued, and soon Kinkaid had his own task force, built around the carrier *Enterprise* which he had "inherited" from Halsey. The force fought gamely in the early battles around Guadalcanal, and the *Enterprise* was hit and put out of action for a time; so Kinkaid knew the good and the bad of battle. In November, 1942, Kinkaid was ordered to the North Pacific to take command of the force that would oust the Japanese from the Aleutians. His success here secured for him the command of the Seventh Fleet, when General MacArthur's movement in the Southwest Pacific made it necessary for him to have more ships and a more integrated naval command than the operations with Nimitz's Pacific Fleet would allow.

Kinkaid took on a difficult job. Because he had come with the reputation of a fighting admiral, General MacArthur expected that he would be followed by a great train of ships. Such was not the case. The Pacific Fleet had its own compelling needs, and spared only what was necessary for MacArthur's movements, lending most of the vessels for one operation, then taking them back. Actually that technique was necessary, because there were not enough transports and tankers and even fighting ships to go around in the early days.

The General was very cordial, but a little testy when he learned that he was not getting the fleet for which he had been pleading for so long. Kinkaid said no, and he explained that there was no way to get at the Japanese from an Australian base. When the ships came, they would have to go to Espiritu Santo in the Hebrides. MacArthur demurred, but Kinkaid stood firm as a naval specialist, and although he did not convince his commander, MacArthur had a complete respect for the specialist, so he let the matter lie between them.

But he kept bringing it up in one way or another. "Well, if King won't give me a fleet," he said one day, "I'll get one from the British."

Kinkaid knew that Prime Minister Churchill was very eager to have strong British representation in the Pacific, because of British political interests there. Had Britain possessed more naval resources in these grim days, Churchill might have pressed for a British fleet around Australia, but the Asiatic fleet had to be kept in the Indian Ocean for the protection of India. MacArthur also felt that Kinkaid, as a fleet commander, ought to have a fleet of his own, but Kinkaid saw the picture from the navy point of view and told MacArthur that, if the British did send ships, he wanted them put under the Nimitz command. Eventually British units did come to the Pacific, and for the most part they did go into the Pacific Fleet's sphere.

Kinkaid had MacArthur's confidence, and when that situation obtained there was little a commander could not do in his own area. His problems in organizing this invasion stemmed from some lack of coordination, but that could be put down to the speed with which the Americans were moving, and particularly the rapid change of plans that had brought about the Leyte invasion in October.

"The door's always open," MacArthur had said once to Kinkaid. "Come up and see me any time you want and don't bother to telephone."

Sometimes during these sessions and during planning meetings, Kinkaid would have things to bring up that he knew would pain and might anger MacArthur. Here is how he approached such problems:

"Well, General, I've got something this morning that I don't think you'll approve of."

"All right," MacArthur would say. "What is it?"

So Kinkaid would talk, and MacArthur would pace up and down, smoking his pipe but not interrupting.

"Then, when I finished," Kinkaid said, "he'd start to talk. I knew that the General would eventually get off base if I had a good case, so I'd just let him talk until he did and then I'd say, 'General, you know darned well what you said then isn't so.'"

MacArthur would look at him over his shoulder and say, "Well, maybe not," and go on walking and talking, puffing on his pipe.

"For something that he didn't want, if I felt strongly enough about it, I felt that I could press him." (That was the basic reason for all those many brief visits over the months.) "There were two or three occasions when I did do that, when I thought I had to—when it was something of importance. . . . I had one or two rather strong arguments with him . . . but I believe that I could talk to him more than anybody down there unless possibly his Chief of Staff. . . ."

All this was important in the planning of the Seventh Fleet's new operation, for it reflected the kind of relationships in the command. The war had progressed until it was now time to attack the Philippines. The plan of July had been thrown out, and the frantic changes of September were in. But the good thing to be said about the planning, unlike that of the Japanese, is that the men who would execute the plans had a voice in laying them. By the time the plans were made, there was still time for a meeting of all concerned.

Some of the commanders involved were in the Admiralty Islands, at anchor in Seeadler Harbor. They flew down to Hollandia and Kinkaid held a meeting of some 75 officers to explain and to answer questions.

As the Seventh Fleet was organized, it involved some 700 vessels of every conceivable fighting variety from battleships to PT boats. Admiral Kinkaid and his staff, in the command ship *Wasatch,* would be with Vice Admiral Wilkinson, in the *Mount Olympus,* for Wilkinson was Deputy Commander of the fleet as well as Commander of the Southern Attack Force. Those ships were accompanied by the light cruiser *Nashville,* which would also carry General MacArthur and his staff to Leyte, and by 5 destroyers. In location, they would be with the Southern Attack Force.

The Southern Attack Force was a huge compendium of control vessels, command ships, transports, and landing ships of several varieties. It would carry the troops and put them ashore, and in this mission was protected by 24 destroyers assigned to the task groups. Besides that, the force was protected by Rear Admiral J. B. Oldendorf's Fire Support Unit, which consisted of 3 "old" or World War I design battleships, 3 heavy cruisers, 2 light cruisers, and another 13 destroyers. Southern Attack Force would put the XXIV Army Corps ashore to begin the conquest of Leyte.

To the north of them the Northern Attack Force would land, as noted in the plan. Rear Admiral Daniel E. Barbey was in command, in his ship *Blue Ridge,* and he would take in X Army Corps to begin its fighting. He would move with the Palo attack group, which consisted of more than 12 attack transports loaded with troops, cargo transports, landing ships, and a destroyer screen made up of 4 destroyers, close support vessels to smash the beaches, and 7 tugs. Rear Admiral W. M. Fechteler in the *Fremont* controlled a similar force with part of the corps in it, with its own destroyer screen. And the Northern Force was also protected by its personal Fire Support Unit under Rear Admiral G. L. Weyler: 3 old battleships and 6 destroyers. Then came Rear Admiral A. D. Struble, with the Panaon Attack Group, of transports and similar ships, protected by destroyers and two light cruisers to bombard the beaches.

Basically, air power was to be supplied this time from the sea in the manner of the Central Pacific invasions, but with reliance on escort carriers. Rear Admiral Sprague commanded the Escort Carrier Group, made up of 3 units called *Taffies*, with each of these *Taffies* divided into smaller units of 2 to 4 carriers, each commanded by a rear admiral. There were in all 18 escort carriers, each with 20 to 30 planes (an average of 28 planes per carrier) or more than 400 planes. This group was accompanied by 4 cruisers, two of them Australian, and 8 destroyers.

There were, of course, auxiliary forces, for minesweeping and hydrography, beach demolition, and service of fuel and ammunition, water and provisions. There were 2 seaplane tenders with 12 PBY patrol bombers, and nearly 40 PT boats.

And in addition to all else, for protection, the Seventh Fleet had supporting submarines—about 25 from the Pacific and Seventh Fleets—1000 planes, and the new battleships, cruisers, and destroyers of the mighty Third Fleet. Besides which, no one really expected the Japanese fleet to come out and fight.

Kinkaid's Seventh Fleet was directed to special duties, and these he laid before his commanders at that large meeting in Hollandia: they were responsible for transporting and establishing the landing forces ashore in Leyte Gulf. That done, they would provide air protection for convoys and direct air support for the landings. They would give air support to the ships by providing a combat air patrol. The submarines of the enemy would be driven off by anti-submarine patrols. They would bring in reinforcements and supplies, and prevent the Japanese from reinforcing the Leyte garrison. They would open and keep open Surigao Strait, and go into Visayan waters and provide reconnaissance by submarines and lifeguard service for airmen.

At the meeting, each group commander explained his role chronologically from the time the fleet would arrive off Leyte on October 17, Admiral Oldendorf going first. The planning had been very thorough, and most of these men had engaged in some part of it, so when all the explanations had been made, the only questions asked were by General MacArthur's representatives, who had not been in on the naval planning. At this time all were in agreement that the plans represented the best they could do.

October 10 was the day that things began to happen. A few days earlier, Admiral Kinkaid flew down to the Admiralty Islands to have supper with Admiral Wilkinson and discuss last-minute ideas. He took with him Sir Roger Keyes, Admiral of the British Royal Navy, who was in Hollandia for a visit, and they looked over the ships steaming in the heat of Seeadler Harbor. Dinner was a quiet meal. It was not Kinkaid's way to "harangue the troops," as he put it; he regarded himself as too much of an "old rain in the face" for that. Next day, Kinkaid flew back to Hollandia, satisfied that everything was going as well as it could go, and the preparations to get underway continued.

On October 10 an Army and a Navy officer flew to Leyte under cover of darkness in a PBY, and landed south of Tacloban. Their mission was to warn the people of the area that the landings were imminent, so the Filipinos would get away from the beaches and not be hurt. The warnings were delivered to the guerrillas, and were very effective. Only in Tacloban town did the people remain, and that was because the Japanese would not let them leave. But for the purpose of the landing, the people were properly warned. Samuel Eliot Morison reported in his study of the landings that not a single civilian was injured in the pre-landing bombardments.

Also on October 10, the minesweepers and hydrographic ships left Manus for the rendezvous point of the fleet at Point Fin, off the entrance to Leyte Gulf. The next day the relatively slow LST's of the southern group moved out from Manus. On October 12 the Dinagat attack group left Hollandia and the bombardment group and the escort carriers left Manus. The minesweepers, the Dinagat group, and the protecting ships would meet on October 17 and begin preliminary operations. That meant the two major protective commands, the battleships and the escort carriers, would be on hand from the beginning in case of trouble.

The carrier group, for example, left Seeadler Harbor at 0500, and two hours later moved into a special formation of two columns, six ships in each column, for gunnery practice of an hour and a half. At 1300 the ships joined Admiral Oldendorf in the *Louisville* and his section of cruisers and old battleships.

The movement was uneventful. On October 15 the group reached a point about 30 miles off the Palaus and sighted land just after midnight. Twelve hours later a storm set in with a wind of 30 knots and rain, but by the morning of October 16 the storm had subsided and the groups began to fuel.

Three islands, Suluan, Calicoan, and Homonhon, lay north of Point Fin, and Dinagat Island lay west of it. These places guarded the entrance to Leyte Gulf, and the Japanese maintained installations on them. Thus the Americans would sweep the area for mines, then a force of cruisers and destroyers would lay down a brief barrage on shore, and units of a Ranger Battalion under Lieutenant Colonel H. A. Mucci would eliminate the Japanese. It was understood, of course, that this action would alert the Japanese high command to the coming landings; that was the brunt of Kinkaid's argument for less time lapse.

The sweeping began at 0630 and within a matter of minutes the word was on its way to combined fleet headquarters at Hiyoshi. Admiral Toyoda was still grounded on Formosa and his staff was making all the difficult decisions in his name. The decision made that morning was to put the naval part of Sho-1 into effect, and order Admiral Kurita to sail for Brunei.

The Fire Support Group moved in, and at 0801 the cruiser *Denver* fired the first shot at Suluan Island. The preliminaries to the invasion were on, the *Denver* firing her 5- and 6-inch guns and the other ships firing theirs. The opposition was so light that although plans had been laid for the *Denver* to lay down fire where it might be called for by the troops ashore, there was no call.

Just after noon a high wind caused the destroyer *Rowell* to carry away a stay, which forced the mast to crack so badly it had to be thrown over the side. That, in turn, caused the loss of radio, talk-between-ships radio (TBS), and radar. The radio and TBS were fixed by re-rigging, but her radar was out of commission for the whole battle.

Carrier operations had been scheduled for this day against the Japanese airfields on the Visayan Sea islands, such as Panay, Negros, and Cebu, but the storm was so bad that the escort carrier *Fanshaw Bay*, for one, suffered damage to two fighter planes and three torpedo planes on deck. When this damage was reported to Admiral Sprague, he canceled all strikes for the day.

The mission of the escort carriers, as laid down in the overall plan for the invasion, was to provide direct air support for the landings and invasion; to put up Combat Air Patrols (CAP) over the area; and to furnish planes for special strikes, photography, and smoke laying; and, of course, to protect themselves against enemy planes and submarines.

From the beginning the escort carriers were operating on three assumptions:

1. That any major enemy force approaching from the north would be intercepted and attacked by the Third Fleet's big carriers and fast battleships.

2. That enemy surface units might approach the landing area from the Sulu and Celebes straits, or through San Bernardino Strait.

3. That it was most likely that the Japanese would try "Tokyo Express" runs to reinforce their units in Leyte, or to harry the Americans. In the battles of the Solomons these "express runs," made almost always at night, had proved very costly.

These assumptions, of course, meant that the escort carriers expected to do some fighting, but they did not expect that they would at any time become the "big guns" of the American fleet. That was Halsey's job, as laid out in the Seventh Fleet's plans for the operation.

On October 18, the weather cleared and the carriers got down to business, to make up for time lost on the previous stormy day. Combat Air Patrols were put up just after dawn, and half an hour later strikes were launched against Negros, Cebu, and Panay airfields. The weather was better, but it was not that much better, so the strikes against Panay and Negros failed to reach the target; those against

Cebu's fields were successful. At 0800 a fighter from the carrier *Chenango* was shot down over Opon Field, but the pilot managed to keep his plane in the air long enough to make a safe water landing in the harbor between Macton Island and Cebu. The alert was put out and a rescue plane was quickly on its way, but the pilot was rescued by Filipinos and taken ashore before it could get there.

The strikes continued against Tacloban, Dulag, San Pablo, and other Japanese airfields on Leyte. By the end of the day the task group had destroyed 2 Japanese planes in the air, 14 on the ground, and believed that another 8 planes had been wrecked. Besides this, the planes had destroyed an estimated 3 torpedo boats, 8 barges, 1 oil sampan, and several other small vessels, and damaged 3 torpedo boats, 5 barges, 5 luggers, and other small vessels.

Ashore, the rangers had done their work, and all the islands in the mouth of the Gulf were secured by noon on October 18. On that morning, Admiral Oldendorf led a column of his ships into Leyte Gulf, behind the minesweepers, which were still sweeping. This action was brave and unusual, but to delay would have meant a postponement of the landings, because the minesweepers had been held up in their work by bad weather. The work to be done was to bombard the southern landing beaches, bring the underwater demolition teams ashore, and make sure that any safety factor that could be gained for the troops would be gained. That afternoon, the battleship *Pennsylvania* and the cruisers *Minneapolis* and *Denver* began pounding the shore, and the ships bearing the underwater demolition teams moved to the east coast of Leyte.

The fast destroyer transport *Goldsborough* was carrying Underwater Demolition Team No. 4 which was to land at Dulag and clear a portion of the beach. The *Goldsborough* came in slowly behind the minesweepers and the big battleships and cruisers. Her captain, Lieutenant W. J. Meehan, was on the outlook for mines, because the sweepers had exploded a large number the day before, and it was nervous work moving around the Gulf before they had finished. Also, that day, several of the minesweepers had been attacked by single Japanese aircraft; that gave the *Goldsborough* something else to watch for.

It was slow work coming in, but by 1400 the destroyer transports were in position, the *Goldsborough* among them. Lieutenant Meehan ordered the ship to General Quarters, and soon the underwater demolition team disembarked in the landing craft. At 1457 the team was headed for the beach, covered by the guns of the big ships. Alongside, the teams of other transports were moving into their positions, too. Except for the noises made by the American firing, the beach was silent. For all that anyone could tell, there might not be a single Japanese there.

Then, at 1515, as the landing craft pulled toward shore, the Japanese opened up with a 75 mm gun, mortars, and machine guns. Meehan saw, and moved the ship in to about 1500 yards from shore and began firing her guns, joining the other destroyers off the beach. It was hard to find targets because the range was great and the land behind the beach proper was covered with brush. The guns blasted and the machine guns popped and the shells screamed in the air. Twenty minutes went by, and Meehan and his men could see that several of the landing craft were under heavy fire from the beach. The results showed then: a boat from Team No. 8 came alongside and transferred a wounded man to the destroyer transport. Five minutes later, *Goldsborough*'s No. 2 boat caught it—a round from a mortar—and sank very quickly. Other boats moved in to pick up the swimmers and the wounded. Luckily the UDT men were swimming, and were away from the boat when the mortar fire hit, so no lives were lost.

Meanwhile, a Japanese 75 mm gun had opened up on the *Goldsborough*. A shell landed 200 yards short. Another followed, 150 yards long on the port beam. A few seconds later in came a third shell—the Japanese gunners had bracketed the ship and this third shell struck the No. 1 stack, smashing fragments of shrapnel across the decks and wounding several members of the 3-inch-gun crew on the galley deckhouse, killing one man, and killing a UDT man who was standing on the main deck next to the stack.

It was an effective shot, smashing radio and radar lines, and damaging a forced-draft blower fan, which resulted in reducing the top speed of the ship to 20 knots. But in a moment the galley deckhouse gun crews were back in action; a few minutes later the UDT team members were back aboard ship, their job done, and 25 minutes later the *Goldsborough* ceased fire on the beach, having expended 258 rounds of ammunition.

Lieutenant J. C. May of the Medical Corps and a pharmacist's mate came aboard in short order to tend to the wounded, moving over from the USS *Talbot.* At 1830 the ships moved out into the Gulf for the night. The *Goldsborough*'s damage was not serious enough to put her out of action.

To protect the minesweepers several of the screening destroyers would move in to make smoke, as USS *Ross* did when she sighted two Japanese planes attack a hydrographic ship not too far from her at 1840. She laid a smokescreen and very shortly the air was cleared of Japanese.

The *Ross*'s mission was to bombard two sectors of a beach on Homonhon Island in the opening moves of the day, and she had done so, then moved on to her second task, which was to defend the minesweepers from antiaircraft, submarine, and surface attack. During the day she had encountered a number of Japanese planes, but not submarines or PT boats or other surface vessels of the enemy.

Half an hour later on patrol she was turning to the right when a tremendous explosion shattered her plating under the forward engine room and fire room to port. Ironically she was in the swept channel, "in the reportedly safest half."

Then, 19 minutes after she struck the first mine, the *Ross* struck another one, near the after engine room. All engineering except the after fireroom was flooded, and the list now increased to 14° to port. The *Ross* could not move herself, so the fleet tug *Chickesaw* came up and took her in tow and headed for safe anchorage south of Montoconon Island. They arrived at dawn, and prepared for a little respite. But it was not long before a Japanese plane came zooming low over the hill of Homonhon Island and dropped 2 bombs. One exploded on the beach, but the second blew up 75 yards off the port beam, and the shrapnel injured 2 men. These casualties added to the 3 killed, 21 missing, and 9 wounded by the mines.

Still, the *Ross* was not out of the fight; the damage was less than might have been expected, and with the shifting of weights her list was cut down to 10 degrees. *Chickesaw* took her under tow again and moved her to a safer place, while the crew worked on the damage of those few hours.

On October 18, the battleships and cruisers of Admiral Oldendorf's force had been pasting Leyte—his flagship *Louisville* had fired the first shot that afternoon. It was not all one-way shooting: the *Charles J. Badger* among the destroyers took time out to deliver three casualties to the *Louisville* for treatment, and one of the men died next day.

On October 19, the carrier planes were out again at 0630 over Negros, Cebu, and Panay, without observing much Japanese activity. Lieutenant F. Reiser, flying an F-6-F from the *Sangamon,* made a forced landing astern of his ship and was picked out of the water by the destroyer *Coolbaugh.* There were few enough losses so this relatively minor incident loomed large on the page of the action report of the carrier division.

Around noon a strike was launched against the Japanese fields on northern Mindanao, and twice that day the ships went to General Quarters at report of approach of "bogies," but there were no attacks on the carriers. For the day they knocked down 1 or 2 fighters and destroyed on the ground 22 fighters and 16 bombers; with 20 more listed as probables. They scoured the seas for shipping and destroyed a few small craft, damaged a minesweeper, 3 luggers, 1 schooner, and 6 barges.

Admiral Oldendorf's heavy support ships were in action again on the 19th, following planned bombardment of Leyte in the southern area to soften it for the coming landings. Late in the afternoon a Japanese plane came swooping in, was hit, and broke up about 1000 feet in the air, some 500 yards off the starboard bow of the *Louisville,* her bombs coming uncomfortably close to the destroyer *Richard P. Leary.*

October 19 was the day the softening up of the northern beaches began, too, by Rear Admiral Weyler's northern bombardment group, which was to cover the same kind of demolition activity near Tacloban. The battleship *Mississippi* and the other ships moved in behind the minesweepers long before dawn, and by 0900 that ship was in place, ready to begin firing on Red Beach, using her engines to maintain an easy position and changing batteries to cool off the hot guns. The destroyers delivering the underwater demolition teams came under sharp fire from the Japanese, and splashes could be seen around them. But the American ships were hitting hard, and the *Mississippi* claimed a small ammunition dump among other target destruction. By the end of the day she seemed to have run out of targets, had started several brisk fires, and along with the other ships retired for the night with the feeling of a job well done.

What had been seen from the decks of the *Mississippi* around midday was the action in which the destroyer *Aulick* found herself. She had moved in toward shore to cover the UDT teams and to bombard whatever targets she found on White Beach. At a range of 2800 yards she opened fire on huts that seemed to contain enemy machine guns along the beach with 5-inch guns and 40 mm guns. Just before noon, a landing craft was hit from the beach and sank. A few minutes later, some good Japanese gunners began moving in on the *Aulick* with machine gun and 3-inch gunfire from two sides—White Beach and Dio Island offshore. The *Aulick* split her fire to cover both enemy actions, but the Japanese kept on, and made direct hits, killing 2 men and wounding 12, and hitting 2 guns so that they had to revert to manual fire control.

By the day's end, thousands of rounds of ammunition had been poured into the beaches and adjacent areas, and it was known that the beaches could be secured by the troops that would come in next day. This day's work was done.

3

THE NORTHERN FORCE

"The enemy has landed. Long live the Emperor"—that was the message sent out from the Japanese advance post at Suluan Island on October 17, when the Rangers came ashore that day. Then, as far as the Japanese command in Manila was concerned, there was silence. Whatever other information would be received by the defenders of the Philippines would have to come from air observation.

Vice Admiral Kimpei Teraoka, Commander of the Fifth Base Air Force in Manila, had learned at the last that 1 battleship, 2 cruisers, and 8 destroyers were in the Gulf; he ordered an attack, in spite of his difficulties of the moment. Most of his senior officers were down with fever, and he had fewer than 200 planes with which to fight the battle. Furthermore, most of his pilots, while young and eager and patriotic, were not well enough trained to be going into battle. What happened next that day was a good indication of the problems he faced:

. . . an order was issued for an attack to be made on the enemy ships in the Gulf. Five land attack planes and eight carrier attack planes were ordered to take off from Clark. . . . The attack unit took off at 1515 and continued its flight, overcoming all difficulties, but the weather became increasingly bad [it was so bad that the American escort carriers were not operating], and just one step short of the goal the planes were forced to turn back at 1804 without sighting the enemy. Darkness overtook the planes on their return flight, and because of bad weather, the planes became separated. One plane made it back to Clark around 2200, but the rest made forced landings elsewhere, as a result of which, several planes were lost.

So, for the Japanese, only one plane out of 13 returned to base. Here was a very good indication of what the Japanese faced in all their operations in the days to come: serious aerial deficiency.

Other factors were at work, too. One was self-deception: that day, as the Americans opened the probe of Leyte Gulf, the Japanese Finance Ministry got ready to give away free sake by the barrelful "to celebrate the results" the Japanese had achieved in "smashing" the American fleet off Formosa. The President of the Imperial Rescript Association congratulated the Imperial Army and Navy both. The Emperor of Manchukuo, Henry Pu-Yi, sent a congratulatory message to Emperor Hirohito "on the great results achieved by the Imperial forces in waters east of Formosa." The Manila *Tribune* carried a five-column photograph showing "the sensational sinking of a large American aircraft carrier off the Philippine Islands," a photo taken by a Japanese plane which "participated in the attack."

On the military level, however, there was a numbness and defeatism that was new to the Japanese forces, and it grew every day. One problem was the almost complete lack of coordination on every level between the Japanese army and the navy. Basically, the one had no idea of the plans of the other.

On October 18 the Army General Staff got an inkling of naval plans when, in line with the activation of Sho-1, the navy asked for four more tankers than had been agreed on for use in the operation. Army Colonel Takushiro Hattori had some strong words for his diary:

In this operation in which land, surface and air power are uniting as one to conduct decisive battle, the fact that the Army General Staff knows nothing of Combined Fleet's operational movements is extremely deplorable, and will be the point of greatest criticisms in the study of the Sho operation by future historians. Further, in the event the use of the additional four tankers is granted as requested by Combined Fleet, the 300,000 kiloliters of fuel scheduled to be supplied to the homeland in the third and fourth quarters would be cut by half, and the self-sustaining fuel policy, seen as a ray of hope as a result of the recent intense efforts on the part of the War Ministry and the Army General Staff, would be fundamentally upset. Thus, a mortal blow would be dealt the overall war effort. . . .

Based on strategic common sense, the movement of the surface ships under present conditions, barring the possibility of a miracle, is impractical, and will only serve to increase the enemy's morale. . . .

Some of the more impracticable decisions made by the Japanese naval authorities involved air power and its use from the beginning of the Formosa and Luzon raids by Admiral Halsey's Third Fleet. When Vice Admiral Ozawa returned from the disastrous defeat at the Marianas, the carrier fleet had only 120 planes left, and the summer had been spent planning and hoping to rebuild the carrier air forces. Admiral Ozawa had expected to be ready to sail with a full carrier-plane complement about November 10, but like the Japanese leaders, he did not expect the Americans to wait for him. Thus he was faced with the problem of fragmentary and almost fairy-tale planning, certain in his own mind of the inevitability of fate. What happened next was certainly not the result of inexperience or even bad judgment on his part. There was no reason to suspect such—he was one of Japan's most experienced admirals.

Admiral Ozawa was then in his tenth year as a force in Japanese naval circles. He had been a professor at the Naval Academy in 1935, then went to sea as Commander of the cruiser *Maya*. Next year he became Captain of the battleship *Haruna*. The year after he was Chief of Staff of the combined fleet, and the year after that he had a cruiser squadron of his own.

He was a slender, thin-faced man with a bulging forehead and close-cropped hair; his eyes were dark and deepseated under prominent brows, his nose slim and aquiline, and his jaw firm and pointed beneath a tight-lipped mouth. He was very much interested in the "long-lance" torpedo and was for a time principal of the torpedo school. He had air experience—he had commanded the First Air Squadron, and in 1941 he was Commander of the Battle Squadron. When war started he had been on the staff of the navy General Headquarters in Tokyo, but he was a fighting admiral, and so in 1942 he was made Commander of the Third Fleet of Japan, and later of the task force formed with the Third Fleet as its major element. Thus he had taken the fleet out to fight the first Battle of the Philippine Sea near the Marianas.

It had been assumed, generally, that Admiral Ozawa would also lead the fleet out in the Sho operation to fight the great naval battle and defeat the Americans decisively. But it had not been assumed that the fleet would be widely separated. Ozawa had much preferred to see the fleet in the Inland Sea, but he had bowed to the exigencies of war and sent off the majority of the big surface ships to the Singapore region where they might have fuel and might train for the coming fight.

In the summer and early fall of 1944 the activity aboard the carrier *Zuikaku* was indicative of that of Ozawa's force:

The *Zuikaku* was a splendid fighting ship, and her history in this war went back to Pearl Harbor, for she was there launching her planes to bring disaster to the American fleet. She had fought in the Battle of the Coral Sea, and escaped unhurt. She had been fortunate enough not to be involved in the disaster to Japan at Midway, but had been damaged by a bomb in the Solomons, and again hit by bombers in the Battle of the Philippine Sea. This summer she was under repair, and training for new action.

Once the battle damage was taken care of, she got new personnel, and many other new pieces of armament and equipment. There were 16 new 4-inch guns, 96 new 25 mm machine guns, and multiple rocket launchers. There were new radio direction finders and new radio units, and two new radar sets and a new sonar set. There were new parts for the flight deck arresting gear and a new gasoline storage system, installed because the Japanese finally realized after the Marianas turkey shoot that they were losing carriers that might be saved if the gasoline fires could be controlled. This change also involved rearrangement of some of the inflammables on the ship, and thorough sand-bagging for protection against shell damage.

In August these preparations were carried out and stores were loaded. Then, about August 20, the *Zuikaku* went out into the western Inland Sea, leaving her base at Kure, and began to conduct training operations. In spite of the defeat at the Marianas, morale of the men of the *Zuikaku* was high that summer, and the crewmen were looking forward to the great decisive battle that would soon come.

On October 1, the *Zuikaku* and most of the other ships of the force were back in the Inland Sea, making ready and training for the coming operation. That day the *Zuikaku* loaded aerial torpedoes at Oita, then moved to Kitsuki for practice in takeoff and landing for the aircrews. On October 2 and 3 there was more training, except that the weather turned foul and aerial exercises had to be canceled on October 3. Still, they were back at it on October 4 and 5, and then sailed for Kure the next day to moor at No. 25 buoy in the harbor there. For ten days the *Zuikaku* remained in Kure, loading equipment, and giving the men shore leave (half the crew in 16-hour stretches).

Meanwhile, the other ships were assembling. The light cruiser *Oyodo*, for example, was given orders to join Ozawa's force on October 5. She would be the flagship of Destroyer Squadron 31 and also reserve flagship of the fleet. When the orders came the *Oyodo* was at dock at Yokosuka naval base, having her engines overhauled and her oil tanks checked, getting new radar, and taking on stores.

Admiral Ozawa was worried. Intelligence from the south brought even more certain indications that the Americans were on the move. If only he had until the middle of November, he would be all right; he estimated that the production lines would by then have brought his plane force up to strength, and with enough time the old hands of the *Zuikaku* and the other big carriers could teach the green fliers what they must know to fight effectively and perhaps even to survive. As it was, very few of these pilots were capable of carrier takeoff and landing.

Ozawa was resigned to losing his air force to the land bases if the invasion came too soon.

The fleet was buzzing with ideas. For example, since the summer's defeat at the Marianas, Captain Jo of the *Chiyoda* had been suggesting that he be allowed to organize a special force of fliers who would crash dive their planes into enemy ships and sink them. The matter had been brought to Ozawa's attention and he had forwarded the idea to Admiral Toyoda at combined fleet headquarters. It was not rejected, but Toyoda remarked that the time for such desperate measures had not yet come.

Then, of course, the Halsey strikes on Formosa and Okinawa and Luzon did come too soon. Whatever Admiral Toyoda himself would have done, his staff at combined fleet headquarters ordered half the planes from Ozawa's carriers sent down to fight from land bases during this battle, and the loss of those trained pilots left Ozawa with only 150 planes and crews. The planes were not the best, and the crews were the worst trained of all he had. On October 13 and 14 Ozawa conducted more training exercises, but the results were so dismal that he despaired of using these planes and crews effectively against the Americans. He sent Captain Ohmae, his Chief of Staff, to telephone combined fleet headquarters and suggest that the plan for the Sho operation be changed; he could not make effective use of the carriers as weapons; he would have to use the force basically as a decoy to draw the power of the Third Fleet away from the landing area and let Admiral Kurita rush in with his striking force.

This shortage of aircraft created a truly sad situation for the Japanese, because potentially, even now after the Marianas disaster, Japan's carrier force was something to be reckoned with. It consisted of three carrier divisions. Carrier Division One was made up of the big carriers *Unryu* and *Amagi*. But the problem was that these carriers were not yet finished and ready for sea, nor would they be until the end of the year.

Next came Carrier Division Three, which consisted of the carriers *Zuikaku, Zuiho, Chitose,* and *Chiyoda.* Finally there was Carrier Division Four, which consisted of the *Junyo, Ryuho,* and the converted battleships *Ise* and *Hyuga.* These two ships had been started as regular battleships, but after the defeat at Midway, when the Japanese saw the need for carrier strength, a year was spent in converting them to two purposes. They carried big guns and could be used for bombardment. But their main after turrets had been taken off and replaced by small flight decks, with a capacity of 24 planes.

That was all very well. The problem in the middle of October was planes, and it was a devilish problem for Admiral Ozawa. By scratching every source, he managed to find 108 planes, stealing from the *Amagi* and the *Unryu*, which could not be ready to fight within a month anyhow. In apportioning them, he gave the majority to the gallant *Zuikaku*. She would carry 24 fighters, 16 fighter bombers, 8 bombers, and 12 attack planes. The *Zuiho* would have 8 fighters, 4 fighter bombers, and 4 attack planes, as would the *Chiyoda* and the *Chitose*. There were *no planes at all* left for the *Ise* and the *Hyuga*. The whole force in the hands of Ozawa had the striking power of a single American carrier, and the Admiral knew only too well that his fliers were so ill-trained that he could not expect many of them to take off and land successfully on his ships, let alone put up effective resistance against the enemy.

The Sho operation was activated on October 18. Already much was happening in Ozawa's command. His radiomen were listening in to TBS conversations and thus learned about the landings south of Tacloban. In spite of worsening weather, the Japanese carriers were loading planes, and on October 19 commanders conferred at Yashima anchorage and at Oita airbase, getting ready for the force to move on October 20.

On October 19 matters were still so confused at combined fleet headquarters that it was considered possible to replace Admiral Shima's ships under Admiral Ozawa. Also, headquarters wanted Admiral Kurita to strike the Americans in Leyte Gulf on October 23, but Kurita could not keep such a schedule. If X Day had been October 23, then Ozawa would have sailed on October 19. Kurita said maybe he could make it October 24, but finally settled on dawn of October 25 as the moment of strike. And then Ozawa reported that he could not sail before the afternoon of October 20 because of the difficulty of loading even the few planes he had; and that he would have to operate more or less independently of the other forces, depending on where and when he found the Third Fleet. He decided to sail at 1700 on October 20.

At the Yashima anchorage, Admiral Ozawa transferred his flag and himself from the cruiser *Oyodo* to the carrier *Zuikaku* as the ships made ready to sail. Besides his carriers and hermaphrodite battleship-carriers he would have the light cruisers *Izuzu, Oyodo,* and *Tama,* 9 destroyers, 6 escort vessels, and 2 oilers.

The brave orders from the fleet called for Admiral Ozawa to lure, engage, and destroy the enemy. He could not say so to his sailors, of course, but he was under no illusions about his chances. He expected to lose all, or almost all, his force. But if he could make it possible for Kurita to move in and destroy the American landings, it seemed to be worth the disaster. Here is the way the Japanese put it:

> In cooperation with friendly forces, the Mobile Force Main Body (CarDivs 3 and 4, DesRon 31 and DesDivs 61 and 41) was to do its utmost to ascertain the enemy situation and was to risk its own destruction in a spirit of self-sacrifice in order to divert and draw the enemy carrier task forces from the waters east of Luzon to the north or northwest, thereby assuring the successful penetration of the First and Second striking forces to the enemy landing point. . . .

> It was also to seize any favorable opportunity to attack and destroy elements of the enemy strength.

> To accomplish these objectives the operational plan called for the Mobile Force Main Body to proceed south through the waters east of Nansei Shoto, maintaining a strict alert against air attack. In the waters east of Luzon or Formosa it was to close with the powerful enemy task forces and make contact. It was then to strike an effective first blow at the enemy by delivering a strong daytime air attack and at the same time, without regard for its own possible losses, make every effort to lure the enemy to the northeast. Thereafter the main body was to operate in such a manner

as to keep the enemy force just at the periphery of its air attack range, approaching him during the day and drawing away at night. By this means the main body would continue to draw the enemy into the desired area and at the same time, if a favorable opportunity should arise, would engage a portion of the enemy force in decisive battle. Also, in case the movements of the enemy's supply force could be ascertained and there appeared to be a chance of executing a successful surprise attack on this force, the main body was to make such an attack. . . .

There was the plan. Poor Admiral Ozawa, with his few score of airplanes, his three cruisers, and handful of destroyers, to take on the whole Third Fleet—and when he had disposed of Halsey and his men, to attack the American supply forces and destroy them, too.

Was it any wonder that the Japanese were praying for a miracle?

4

THE THIRD FLEET

Of all the officers in the American Pacific Fleet the best liked by far was Admiral William F. Halsey. He was Nimitz's favorite fighting admiral, and the man for whom the sailors on the ships would fight to the death. He was also, because of his constant driving attacks, the most hated of all American commanders by the Japanese.

In the air battles of October off Okinawa and Formosa, the Japanese, as noted, had claimed complete victory, and destruction of the Third Fleet.

We would certainly like to see Halsey's bulldog face [said the Japanese radio at the end of that battle]. While crying loudly to his men "Kill the Japs" . . . he, who hates the Japanese the most in the United States Navy, clearly revealed his brutality in carrying out indiscriminate raids . . . on October 10. . . . He was en route home from this attack when he received the great blow on Friday the 13th . . . this was Heaven's punishment to the Yankees who have human faces but beastly minds with an insatiable greed for world domination. . . .

This self-delusion by the Japanese almost cost them Admiral Shima's force before the Battle of Leyte Gulf could begin. For Admiral Halsey was trying, in the establishment of his "Bait Division" of crippled cruisers, to draw the Japanese fleet into battle. It was his great wish that somehow before this landing was completed he would manage to erase the strength of the Japanese fleet once and for all.

Shima came forth with his carriers and destroyers, to strike the crippled ships, but on the afternoon of October 16 a Japanese air search discovered two intact task groups, and Shima wisely turned back, ignoring the victory cries that were coming from Tokyo. He was lucky; Admiral Halsey had the Shima force under surveillance and was simply waiting. At 1435 search planes had found the Japanese 325 miles away, but because of communications difficulties the news had not come to Admiral Mitscher or Halsey for about an hour, and then it was too late to launch a strike. That narrowly did Shima miss disaster. Later in the evening, the night carrier *Independence* launched night-search planes, but they did not find the Japanese, and the next day they were out of reach.

Halsey now turned back to his mission of supporting the Seventh Fleet landings that were soon coming in the Philippines, by striking at Japanese air power in the islands. One task group hit Luzon on October 17, three groups hit hard on October 18, and two more hit on October 19. They were softening up the Japanese for the landing force.

At this time no one was really expecting much opposition from the Japanese fleet. General MacArthur's intelligence officers believed that the damage done the Japanese in the Third Fleet strikes would keep them close to Lingga Roads and the Inland Sea.

Halsey was constantly watching and testing:

Mitscher believes that trained Jap naval aviation has been virtually wiped out as a result of the June operations and our more recent strikes in the Empire-Formosa-Luzon area [he wrote Admiral Nimitz on October 22]. He bases his conclusion on the heterogeneous assortment of naval planes which participated in the last attacks off Formosa and also on the fortunate lack of skill which they demonstrated at times. I am not quite prepared to endorse that view as yet; we have no positive information concerning their current carrier group setup except evidence that some carrier-type planes appeared off Formosa. I believe that the prudent view requires withholding judgment, and also requires the assumption that the enemy still has some carrier air strength up his sleeve.

To Halsey, the big raids he had launched in September and October had shown the nature of the future use of air power with the carrier task force. He was confident that the fleet could carry out raids of two or three days' duration against any objective without too much fear of damage. As far as the inner Empire was concerned, and that included Formosa, it took the Japanese about three days to collect themselves and strike back hard. He would be willing to try strikes even closer in to home.

On October 19, even though no one really expected the Japanese to come out, Halsey began planning for the contingency. Admiral McCain's Task Group and Admiral Davison's Task Group were hitting Luzon, and then moving over next day to Leyte and Cebu. Meanwhile, Admirals Bogan and Sherman were preparing to intercept any Japanese naval units that might try to hinder the Leyte landings.

It was ". . . the policy of the commander, Third Fleet, not to wait for the clarification of enemy plans and enemy intents, but to break it up before it got started, and as early as the 20th and 21st, staff studies were being made and discussions were being held as to possible means of breaking up any counteraction which might result from the Leyte landing."

5

THE THIRD FORCE

The measure of the Japanese confusion at the time of the Leyte landings is indicated in the final conversations of the General Staffs on the evening of October 19, when it was apparent that army and navy held opposite views as to the conduct of operations in the Philippines.

The participants met at the Navy Club in Tokyo and held a discussion that grew increasingly acerbic as the night went on. The participants were four division chiefs and section chiefs of the army and one section chief and two division chiefs of the navy. Here is how it went:

NAVY: At this time we wish to carry out the Leyte penetration operation and destroy the enemy invasion convoy. Depending on the situation, we think that this may lead to a decisive fleet engagement. With regard to the above, the General Staff is of course in full agreement, and Navy Minister Yonai also agrees.

ARMY: We would like the navy to refrain from an operation which would risk destruction of the fleet. The reasons are: (1) The chances of succeeding in this operation are slight. (2) In case of failure, the enemy would gain control of the South and East China Seas, creating danger of a rapid deterioration of the overall war situation.

NAVY: If the present opportunity is missed and we

do not carry out the operation, the Japanese fleet will suffer the same fate as the Italian navy [complete loss].

ARMY: Even if this should prove to be the case, it cannot be helped. Since the fleet has no carrier air strength, if it carries out the operation it would mean that a part of our shore-based air strength, which should be attacking the enemy on Leyte, would have to be diverted to provide cover for the fleet. This would be disadvantageous.

NAVY (speaking emphatically): If the fleet does not take the offensive now, the war will be lost!

ARMY (replying hotly): Stop talking nonsense!

The discussion then broke down into name-calling, or as close to that as the Japanese could bring themselves, and soon these informal conferees adjourned without having reached any decision at all. But on the morning of October 20, the army men reported to their superiors, Chief of Staff Umezu and his deputy, and they counseled caution in complaining about the navy. "If combined fleet were to suffer defeat," said Umezu, "the consequences would be serious. However, since this matter is up to the navy, and since Navy Minister Yonai has already approved it, there is no ground for the army to put up any further opposition. . . ."

So there was no stopping the navy's plan for the Sho operation!

The plan, however, was still very much confused, and nothing showed it more clearly than the situation of Vice Admiral Kiyohide Shima and his force of cruisers and destroyers. Shima's force, in the middle of October, consisted of 3 heavy cruisers, 2 light cruisers, and 5 destroyers. In addition there were 5 troop-carrying destroyers. The fighting ships of this group had been dispatched to mop up the "remnants" of the Third Fleet after the Formosa air battle, and it was Shima for whom Admiral Halsey had laid the careful trap that never got sprung.

Nowhere is the raggedness of the Sho plan indicated more clearly than in the disposition of Admiral Shima and his force. It had been planned, when the carriers had their planes, that Shima would accompany the Ozawa force and add to Ozawa's striking power.

It was considered—until the chiefs of the combined fleet had second or third thoughts. Then they decided that it might be a better idea for Shima to take part of his force and join Admiral Kurita in his blow against the Leyte beaches. By this time Shima's force had been placed for orders under the Southwest Area Fleet commanded by Admiral Mikawa (who was not to figure in this operation at all), and had moved to Mako in the Pescadores to await further orders. Mikawa was in Manila and his strength—what there was of it—consisted of the planes of the two land-based naval air forces in the Philippines.

By radio, Mikawa's headquarters and the combined fleet discussed what was to be done with Shima's force, and on the afternoon of October 21 they agreed that Shima was to take most of his ships and join Kurita in striking. He was to go through Surigao Strait and "cooperate" with Kurita. Considering the fact that he was north of the Philippines and Kurita would be coming from the south, this cooperation was not going to be easy.

Since the army might want to move some troops into Leyte after all, the destroyer transports and part of his fighting force were taken away for transport work, leaving Admiral Shima the cruisers *Ashigara* and *Nachi*, the light cruiser *Abukuma*, and 4 destroyers. All was decided late on the afternoon of October 21, and Admiral Shima's ships weighed anchor and moved to Coron Bay on the far side of Mindoro Island, where they would move out. For the first time, then, Admiral Shima learned what was going on, but only barely, because he was not placed under the command of Kurita, but was to "cooperate," which meant that he was to act independently and hope for the best.

One reason for the difficulty in which the Japanese found themselves was the problem of assembling units that could fight together. Shima's location was an important factor in the decision to use his force as it was to be used: as a hit-and-run force to storm through Surigao Strait. Quite independently, Admiral Kurita had for two weeks been considering splitting his own striking force into two parts. Among the ships at his disposal were the two old battleships *Yamashiro* and *Fuso*, each more than thirty years old. Their 14-inch guns could wreak havoc among the American transports, if they ever got to Leyte Gulf. But the problem of traveling with new and old battleships in a train was so difficult that Kurita decided to use them independently. So the force of Vice Admiral Shoji Nishimura was created as an independent entity. It was this group that was to storm through Surigao Strait, and this group that Admiral Shima was to support.

Nishimura and Shima, as commanders, were as different as day and night. Shima was a staff man primarily, and had risen to some political power and been assigned for a time to Manchukuo. Nishimura was an old salt, a hard-bitten officer who had risen to his high rank without ever having served a tour of duty in the Naval Ministry. He was anything but a politician.

On Admiral Kurita's flagship *Atago*, the conferences continued all through the morning and afternoon of October 21, as the ships lay at rest in Brunei harbor. Kurita's plan was perfected and explained, and the decision for the pincers was handed out to all unit commanders. Admiral Nishimura's force would sail at 1500 on October 22, detour to the north, and move through Balabac Strait into the Sulu Sea, then north of Mindanao, through Surigao Strait, into Leyte Gulf.

Admiral Shima would wait—he had not so far to go—and then follow Nishimura through these waters, adding to the strength and, hopefully, the confusion of the Americans.

Admiral Kurita, with 5 modern battleships, 10 heavy cruisers, 2 light cruisers, and 15 destroyers, would move further north, just south of Mindoro Island, through the Sibuyan Sea, through San Bernardino Strait that runs between the islands of Luzon and Samar, and then cut sharply around to the right and down, meeting Nishimura and Shima early on October 25—and wreaking havoc, hopefully, among the helpless American transports in the harbor. Then he would bombard the beaches and destroy the landing forces ashore. All this would be possible, because Admiral Ozawa, from the north, was meanwhile decoying Admiral Halsey and the aircraft carriers and battleships of the Third Fleet away from the scene of action.

So it was banzai, and on into the jaws of the American naval force.

6

THE LANDINGS

On the morning of October 20, all the experience, all the wisdom, all the planning exercised by General MacArthur and Admiral Kinkaid began to pay off. This is how it would work, in the words of Admiral Kinkaid:

> On the first day it was a matter of getting the troops ashore, about 70,000 or 80,000 that first day. Then two days later about 30,000 or so more went ashore. The Army had wanted to send them up in two convoys, those who would land the first day and then those who would land two days later, but we could not do that because we did not have enough escort ships.

Thus all the troops were in the ships together, but to avoid crowding on the beaches, 30,000 men would stay aboard ship until A Day + 2. In this could be seen Admiral Kinkaid's assumption from the start, that the Third Fleet would be lurking about the area, ready to pounce on any Japanese attackers who might show up. Those transports, sitting in Leyte Gulf with the old battleships and the escort carriers to protect them, would indeed have been sitting ducks had the Japanese managed a surprise attack anytime between October 20 and October 22.

It was hot, sticky weather, and aboard Admiral Barbey's flagship *Blue Ridge* officers and men were uncomfortable; until the last they had to wear life jackets at every alert. And there was even more cause for discomfort. By October 16, at sea, Captain Ray Tarbuck aboard Barbey's flagship had the feeling that the Japanese were up to something. Perhaps, he said, the Japanese were planning to entice the carrier fleet from its mission of preliminary bombing of the airfields. This uneasiness was relieved by Halsey's return to the bombing of Philippine airfields two days before the invasion, but the general feeling of concern about Japanese intentions continued.

The Americans were looking out. Barbey's communications picked up a radiophone transmission (TBS) on October 18 which described the landing of amphibious equipment on the beaches of Leyte. Perhaps it was the same broadcast the Japanese heard. In any event, Admiral Barbey and his staff concluded that the cat was out of the bag, and from that moment on he warned his men to expect anything, anything at all.

The landings went off very well indeed. Barbey was to put General Sibert's X Corps ashore on the north. Vice Admiral Wilkinson was to put General Hodge's XXIV Corps ashore on the south: eighty thousand men—a huge undertaking. Yet, on the night before the landings, when a soldier fell overboard from one of Barbey's ships at the head of the column steaming into Leyte Gulf, there was enough compassion, enough concern with human life, that he was picked up by a small vessel at the end of the column.

Now Barbey's and Wilkinson's operations were much the same. One difference was that Wilkinson's force, originally destined for Yap Island, had been prepared to land on bad coral beaches, and actually was better prepared for the terrain discovered than Barbey's. Another difference was the attitude of Kinkaid toward his two commanders. He trusted Wilkinson implicitly. He thought Barbey a little too ambitious, but he gave the latter credit for being a very fine amphibious commander.

One thing Nimitz had not liked about Barbey's amphibious technique was the piling or storage of ammunition and other supplies on the beaches. One night during the Hollandia landings, a lone Japanese plane had come in from the west, dropped a bomb that landed in an ammunition dump, and sent hundreds of thousands of dollars worth of supplies up in smoke. Not just the money was important, but the blood and sweat that had brought those supplies onto the beach. In this invasion, Kinkaid was nervous lest it happen again.

Here was the invasion, as seen through the eyes of Captain Tarbuck:

At 0400 of A Day, Barbey's ships, some 300 of them, began entering the channel that led into Leyte Gulf. Twenty minutes later came reveille, and all hands turned out. By 0630 they were in Leyte Gulf, in clouds and showers; the Japanese land-based planes were beginning their attacks, and the destroyers around the flagship were firing. The cruiser *Phoenix* opened up, blasting some target unknown to the men of the flagship.

Just before 0800 the battleship *West Virginia* opened up on Red Beach, one of the landing areas. Spotter planes from the ships circled over the beaches, and were giving information to the gunners in the water. They passed a minesweeper in trouble, listing and pumping water overboard. The big guns of the *Mississippi* and the *Maryland* began booming, and those who watched could see the smoke plumes rising from the land beyond the beaches. They could also see the spots of smoke the Japanese anti-aircraft guns made as they fired at the spotter planes, and the popping and crackling of fire of various calibers that punctuated the booming of the big guns.

The Japanese were anything but asleep. By 0900 the flagship's radar was reporting two large groups of planes to the north, heading toward the invasion fleet. By then, the bombardment was so heavy it was growing monotonous —the men of the flagship could scarcely discern the sounds of individual guns, the booming was so incessant.

Then the landing craft began moving in to shore, from afar looking like so many little shingles pushing a bow wave and leaving a trail of wakes like pencil marks on the ocean as they moved swiftly in. Rockets by the thousands were launched on the beaches before the troops moved in, and to Tarbuck the rumble was like that of an earthquake.

Just before 1000 that morning the men moved in to shore. Within ten minutes they had penetrated to 100 yards from the beach—but the Japanese were fighting back strongly, with small arms and mortars. On White Beach two landing craft were badly hit and one was sunk. Three LST's came under fire from a 75 mm gun on Red Beach, and the Americans began to take casualties.

As the troops moved in shore, the Japanese resistance grew stronger, and the unit commanders began to call for fire from the ships on specific points. Japanese planes came over, not in great strength—there was no great strength in the islands at this time—but at about 1000 Captain Tarbuck saw one Japanese plane shot down.

Now there *was* a problem. The LST's were taking a beating because Red Beach was too flat and they could not approach near enough to shore to discharge their vehicles. They came in close, and soon three of them were blazing from accurate Japanese fire. Admiral Barbey had been unable to load pontoon units which would have bridged the shallows, and word had to be sent south to Admiral Wilkinson, whose Yap force had just what was needed. Because of this difficulty, many LST's were diverted to Tacloban airstrip. This area became a supply dump, just what Kinkaid had worried about. In a few days the beaches would be filled with ammunition and food, piled high, and the army commanders would be camped a few yards from those beaches.

"Just two cruisers loose in that gulf could have cleaned up an awful lot," Kinkaid said later. If they had destroyed the supplies on those beaches almost anytime after A Day, and had killed some of the commanders, Kinkaid believed it might have delayed the Philippines operations indefinitely.

Which, of course, was precisely the Japanese objective, although they were moving slowly toward it on this October 20.

Japanese resistance, relatively slight, had been hurt by the raids of the Third Fleet on the islands, and there was no question about it.

The low level of aerial activity is intriguing. One unit's report is very indicative of the Japanese aerial plight after Halsey's strikes of October. Here is the operations report of the 253rd Attack Unit of the 331st Air Group which was detailed to stop the Americans at Leyte:

In accordance with [order] Tenzan attack plane took off Nichols No. 1 at 1320, and another Tenzan took off at 1400 for attack on enemy ships in Leyte Gulf. Sighted enemy 1600 (8 battleships, 20 cruisers, 30 destroyers, 30 transports) and immediately went in for attack. Torpedoes released from altitude of 10 meters. One large transport definitely sunk. Attack completed 1620. One plane landed Cebu base 1705. Second plane failed to return. . . .

There *was* a successful attack at about that time. A Japanese plane torpedoed the cruiser *Honolulu*, and another attacked the *Louisville* unsuccessfully, a pair of bombs falling in the water alongside.

On October 18 the *Honolulu* had had a busy day. She was Rear Admiral W. L. Ainsworth's flagship, and he was in charge of the second section of Admiral Oldendorf's bombardment group. In the afternoon she passed safely through the Japanese minefield in the Gulf, her group picking up two mines on their paravanes and destroying them safely. There were a few problems: the *Tennessee*, for example, caught a mine in her sweep gear that had to be destroyed by the *Preble*. On the next morning the *Honolulu* had fired 31 3-gun salvos to cover the pre-landing operations, and then moved in to fire on gun emplacements and trenches under the eye of her spotter planes. All day long she had been in action against the beaches, particularly around the town of Dulag, and her planes reported hits on pillboxes and trucks in the roads, and on buildings near the beaches. On the morning of October 20, she was again involved in fire support. Early in the morning she fired on three different Japanese planes, not hitting any of them, in addition to her offensive duty; she continued her firing until noon, then began shooting only on call.

At 1559 the lookouts sighted a single low-flying plane coming in on the ship from over Leyte. Captain H. R. Thurber saw the plane.

"All engines back!" he shouted. "Emergency."

The engine room responded. The noise of the propellers began to change.

The plane bore in. When it was 1500 yards from the

Honolulu, on about a 10-degree angle, it launched a torpedo. The port 20 mm guns and the 40 mm guns began to hammer, and some of the gunners thought they had hit the plane—but it disappeared low over Leyte Gulf, into the clouds to the north.

At 1602 there was a thud and a crash. The torpedo had come home on the port side well below the waterline.

The ship was moving astern, and the transports to the east were firing on the Japanese plane. The Captain and his crew swung into action with determination. Some men were trapped below and the damage-control parties and rescue parties ran to free them. The interior ship's communication system had been knocked out, and Captain Thurber had to send a messenger to the engine room to stop all engines. Otherwise he would have been in among the transports, endangering all of them, for the transports were anchored and could not quickly get away.

Up went the signal:

THIS SHIP HAS BEEN TORPEDOED

As if anyone nearby needed to read it!

Within moments, the *Honolulu* developed a sharp list to port, and soon it stood at 13 degrees. The two turbo generators tripped out, and all electrical power was lost, which in turn caused the cruising condensate pumps to stop and steam pressure to fall. But emergency pumps were quickly started, and 13 minutes after the torpedo hit, steam pressure was back up and the engineering department reported ready to answer all bells again. Steering was moved aft, and the Captain conned the *Honolulu* toward shallow water from the 18 fathoms in which they had been working.

The *Blue Goose*, for that was her other name, was saved to fight another day. By 1615 she was moving and pumping fuel oil to correct the list. At 1625 the destroyer *Richard P. Leary* came alongside, to take off the wounded. There were also 60 officers and men dead, killed when the torpedo destroyed the ship's plotting room, a marine berth compartment, and drove a hole 29 feet long and 25 feet wide into her hull just forward of the bridge. Had Captain Thurber not backed when he did, the torpedo would have

been in the magazine, or in the engine room, and then it
might have been all up with the *Blue Goose*. As it was,
one radioman, Leon Garsian, was trapped for 16 hours in
the radio compartment before rescuers could make their
way to him with torches, cutting through four inches of
armor plate.

Admiral Wilkinson's landings in the south of Leyte were
no more eventful than those of Admiral Barbey. The destroyer *Bennion* was straddled by accurate Japanese gunfire, and several men aboard were wounded by shrapnel
from a near miss, but that was the one casualty among the
ships. Some damage was done during the night in a suspected air raid, when ships in the Gulf began firing in-
discriminately just before dark and hit the *Honolulu* again,
killing 5 more men and wounding 11. They also hit the
LSD *Lindenwald*, killing 1 man and wounding 6 others.

The quiet, in part, was because of the excellent air
cover provided by Admiral Sprague's escort carriers. The
planes had been up since 0545, a combat air patrol over
the beaches of 36 planes, another 24 planes in direct support, and more planes protecting the carriers themselves.
It was not until 0800, however, that the air strikes against
the nearby fields caught their first enemy plane in the air,
a fighter, and blasted him to the ground. Half an hour
later, three Japanese planes had attacked the carriers,
during launching operations, and they straddled the *Santee*
with bombs, but did no damage. One skip-bombed the
Sangamon, missed, and was shot down by anti-aircraft fire
from no fewer than 4 vessels. The other two Japanese were
shot down by the Combat Air Patrol. *Sangamon* was
slightly damaged by the one bomb a 250-pounder, that
glanced off her port side. For a few moments she lost
steering control. Apparently the bomb had not exploded
fully, and to that fact was attributed the minor nature of
the damage.

The Japanese pilots were not doing badly. Their luck,
however, was certainly not good. And there were not many
of them. By the end of the day the escorts had accounted
for only 5 planes. From the Japanese point of view, this
day marked a very definite change in aerial operations. The
kamikazes were coming.

The kamikaze concept was certainly not new in the fall

of 1944. As already noted, certain Japanese officers had suggested the use of suicide planes as early as the summer, when the battle of the Philippine Sea was going badly for Japan. The idea of self-sacrifice in the national interest, of "mission with no return," was an ancient Japanese concept, dating back to the beginnings of the samurai. Kamikaze referred to the Divine Wind—a typhoon-like blow that in the year 1570 destroyed a Mongol emperor's fleet as it approached Japanese waters with the very definite intent of conquering the islands. Undoubtedly some Japanese planes had dived into American ships in the past, when their pilots saw no hope of destroying the targets otherwise. But the kamikaze was a different matter entirely. Always before this time, the pilots had gone off with the intent at least to return. What was to happen now was to organize a corps of men who would use their planes as weapons and dive directly into the American ships.

The originator of the program was Vice Admiral Takajiro Ohnishi, who came to the Philippines on October 17 to take over command of the First Air Fleet from Admiral Kimpei Teraoka. For two days Admiral Ohnishi moved around the area, and he discovered the naked and frightening truth: at the time of the American invasion of the Philippines, the Japanese air forces had fewer than 100 planes to put into the air.

He was digesting this information on October 18 when the Sho-1 operation was activated in Tokyo, which meant he was supposed to mount every bit of strength he had against the enemy, thus "crushing the enemy's invasion plan," as Admiral Teraoka put it.

Ohnishi and Teraoka were completely aware of the general Japanese naval striking plan. (That is, as of October 18 they knew as much about it as anyone else did.) They agreed that the navy would be counting on their land-based air power for cover. "Just so long as the power of the enemy task force remains immense, or in other words, the enemy holds control of the air, it would be most dangerous for our surface ships to go rushing in," Teraoka wrote. So everything possible had to be done to destroy those carriers by October 25, when Shima, Nishimura, and Kurita were to close the pincers around the American forces in Leyte Gulf. It was apparent that ordinary methods would not suffice, with little time and few planes. Here, from the Teraoka diary, is the justification for the kamikazes:

Conventional methods of warfare are no longer adequate.

Since death is the inevitable fate of the young eagles [Japanese pilots] they should be allowed to die in the most worthwhile way.

We must steel our hearts in order to win the war.

It is necessary that the names of those who volunteer for this death mission be reported beforehand to the Imperial GHQ, in order that they may prepare themselves with dignity and maintain a cool head. . . .

[Teraoka and Ohnishi discussed the idea of appealing directly to the patriotism of the young fliers, but decided this would be so distinctly unmilitary an approach that it might have a bad effect.]

No, it would be better to work through their immediate superiors in view of the consequences.

If the fighter pilots can first be organized, other units will automatically follow suit. If the air forces carry this out, they will in turn inspire the surface forces. If the entire Navy is inspired with this spirit, the Army, too, will no doubt follow in line.

[Thus, perhaps one might say cynically, the leaders entrusted with the defense of the Philippines assayed their countrymen and decided on the best method by which they could secure the utmost resistance from them.]

It was finally concluded that in order to save the country there was no other method than the crash-dive tactic. Further it was agreed that Admiral Ohnishi, the incoming commander, should assume complete responsibility for the formation of the Special Attack Corps.

On October 19 Admiral Ohnishi called his staff of the First Air Fleet together at Manila, along with officers of the 761st Air Group at Clark Field and of the 201st Air Group at Mabalacat.

The admirals waited, but only the men from head-quarters and the 761st group appeared.

They arrived after noon and began talking. Admiral Ohnishi laid out the plan without delay, but he worried about the men from Mabalacat. He had decided to go to Clark Field for the night when the officers from the 201st appeared, at 1700; they missed him, headed back by plane, and in a forced landing Commander Yamamoto broke his leg. Such accidents these days were not as uncommon as they should be. The shortage of parts and the constant bombing by the Americans made plane maintenance a very iffy thing for the Japanese.

Ohnishi made his way to Mabalacat and spoke to the senior staff members. "In my opinion," he said, "there is only one way of assuring that our meager strength will be effective in a maximum degree. That is to organize suicide attack units composed of Zero fighters armed with 250 kilogram bombs, with each plane to crash dive into an enemy carrier. . . ."

He assembled the young men of the unit and spoke in a different vein. "Ministers and admirals can no longer save our country," he said. "Her salvation can only be accomplished by the sinking of the American carriers by you young men."

Commander Assaichi Tamai, the Executive Officer, spoke for the young men: "We will exert ourselves to the utmost. It is our request that you entrust the entire respon-sibility to the group itself."

Then the officers of the 201st began recruiting for the death missions. It was not hard. Nearly every flier wanted to go. When organized, the force consisted of 24 men divided into 4 units, known as the Shimpu Attack Corps or the Shimpu Special Attack Corps, a name they took from a Japanese poem:

Shikishima no yamato gokoro wo hito towaba asahi ni niyou yamazakura bana.

Which means:

"If one were to ask what is the Yamato spirit of Japan, the reply would be it is like the fragrant wild cherry abloom in the morning sun."

These young men represented the Yamato spirit, the highest form of Japanese patriotism, and they regarded themselves as brilliant blossoms of cherished flowers that would bud and dazzle the eye for a moment, then fall withered to the ground.

And Admiral Ohnishi wisely let the young men find their own way to justify what he was asking them to do. At 1000 on October 20, he summoned all those who had volunteered and made another little speech, indicating his adherence to the "one big battle" tradition:

> The fate of our nation rests on this one battle. The Divine Wind of victory in this great decisive battle of the Pacific can only be evoked by your becoming human missiles. For the glory of the Imperial Throne, for the sake of your country, this commander is requesting that you offer your lives to him.
>
> I believe that your one regret is that you will be unable to know the result of your sacrificial mission against the enemy fleet, but this will be done by having the wingmen of the close-cover unit verify the result without fail and report it to me. Then I will without fail report it to your departed spirit and to the Throne. Therefore, I ask that you resolutely carry out your mission without any regrets.

That was the end of the speeches. Vice Admiral Ohnishi shook each young man by the hand, and having established a tradition, he went back to his headquarters in Manila to await results.

As Admiral Teraoka left the scene, Admiral Ohnishi expressed himself as completely satisfied. It would be successful, he said.

Thus the kamikaze corps was born, 24 men waiting to give their lives to crash a "carrier" and delay the Americans so that their brethren in the homeland might gain time and strength to resist. Miracles were needed, and these brave young men were willing to supply them if they could.

At 0900 on October 21, the pilots of the planes at Mabalacat took off, on hearing a report of an American force east of Leyte Island, but the weather was bad and when they got to the scene they saw nothing but miles of empty sea, so they turned back and returned safely. Then, at 1500 that same day, in the operations room of the kamikaze unit stationed at Cebu Island, the telephone rang, and a voice reported an enemy task force built around 6 carriers that was sighted 60 miles east of Suluan Island. The Japanese were ready to launch a suicide mission, when a force of American fighters and bombers appeared over the mountains, swooped down on the field, and destroyed all the Japanese planes ready to take off.

Three more planes were hauled from revetments and a mission was organized to take off at 1625, led by Lieutenant Yoshiyasu Kuno. Off the 3 planes flew, into the uncertain weather and even more uncertain future they would face over Leyte Gulf.

On October 21 Admiral Halsey's Third Fleet was keeping a sharp eye out for the Japanese, for there had been sightings of major Japanese ships on the previous day, and Halsey was itching for a chance to knock off the Japanese fleet if it ventured into Philippine waters. Admiral Bogan's planes and Admiral Sherman's planes swept southern Luzon and the Visayas that day, and attacked Coron Bay. They moved out to the north and northwest, searching, but did not find anything. The pickings were slim indeed. Meanwhile, Admiral McCain's group and Admiral Davison's group fueled that day, making sure that half the fighting force of carriers was topped off and ready for anything.

The "jeep" or escort carriers were busy all day, guarding, sweeping, and fueling. They began at 0530 with a launch of combat air patrol planes, with fueling coming half an hour later. They were careful. The fueling of the *Suwannee* was interrupted by a raid alarm at 0635, but 45 minutes later nothing had happened and fueling was resumed. At 1116 came word that a "friendly" had been shot down by trigger-happy gunners in the fleet. It was a photo plane from the carrier *Petrof Bay* and the shooters were aboard an LST on the beach. Luckily, though the plane was lost, all members of the crew were rescued.

It was an easy day for the escort carriers, comparatively speaking. They struck nearby airfields and dumps and equipment and came back and landed and other planes struck some more. They shot down 4 planes in the air, and destroyed 23 on the ground, with another 8 claimed as probables. The photo plane and one other were both shot down by friendly fire—and that was the extent of the losses of the escort carriers.

The landings were going beautifully. The troops were moving steadily inland from both landing areas, Dulag and Tacloban airfields were captured this day, and Tacloban, which had dock facilities, was also captured, although here the Japanese staged a futile counterattack. The ships were unloading, and moving out, and other ships were on their way from Hollandia, bringing supplies and reinforcements of various kinds.

But there was another ship casualty that day, and it came shortly after dawn. At 0530, just as the escort carriers were launching their air patrols, 3 Japanese planes appeared out of the murk and headed for the Northern Attack Force of Admiral Barbey. They came in close, and strafed HMAS *Australia*. The anti-aircraft guns of the fleet began to rattle and pop, and one Japanese plane went down, then another, cartwheeling and splashing into the sea, oily smoke marking the graves of the pilots. Then the third plane came in, zooming. It smashed into the foremast of the *Australia*, bounced into her bridge, and killed Captain E. F. V. Deschaineux and 19 seamen. The Chief of the Australian forces present, for this was his flagship, was Commodore John A. Collins, and he and 53 others aboard the ship were wounded by the crashing plane. The bridge blazed fiercely and the shearlegs of the mast broke. She was lying near the *Blue Ridge*, and in a few minutes Barbey had his doctor aboard the Australian cruiser and was giving all the medical aid possible. But she was out of action, and later that day a little convoy was formed of the *Australia*, the *Honolulu*, the American destroyer *Richard P. Leary*, and the Australian HMAS *Warramunga*—headed for Manus and repairs.

The day went on, uneventfully as invasion days would go at sea. The soldiers were fighting fiercely on the land, and by 1600 General Sibert relieved Admiral Barbey of command of the northern troop operations. That meant he was well ashore, established, and confident of maintaining his position. The Japanese had set out to try to stop the Americans on the beaches. They had already failed on A Day + 1, October 21, to achieve that aim of their "one big battle" strategy. As for the brave sacrifice of Lieutenant Yoshiyasu Kuno, who took off late in the afternoon from Cebu, intending to crash an American carrier, it came to nothing at all.

There were air raids at 1635 and again around 1900 in the twilight—which may have been the kamikaze attackers. Planes came in 9 miles off the starboard quarter of the *Blue Ridge,* and the ships laid smoke and began firing with their 5-inch and 40 mm guns. LCI's went upwind to make more smoke. The Japanese came in again on the port side as darkness fell, and the red tracers made a fireworks display in the sky. But Lieutenant Kuno was never seen again.

7

THE FIRST THREAT

October 22 was a relatively quiet day. The escort carriers were alert to their responsibility, and it did not seem too much for them. They flew their missions, but all day long they shot down only 1 Japanese plane in the air and 9 on the ground. There was one odd report of a plane that seemed to be a TBM, an American patrol bomber, that was attacking ships in Leyte Gulf. This was written off as a captured plane being used by the enemy.

In the morning there was an enemy air raid on the beaches, and the intelligence officers felt indications of strengthening Japanese resistance. But it had not yet showed itself on the sea or in the air; rather it was in the determination of the Japanese fighters ashore. That day, at Lahug, Japanese aircraft gunners shot down 4 American planes, and 5 others were shot up but managed to make it back to their ships.

Ashore everything was going well. Reinforcements moved in and all the Army forces were making progress in moving toward their objectives. General MacArthur had made a token landing on October 20 on Red Beach, and then gone back to the *Louisville* to wait until matters were secure enough for his headquarters to be established ashore. It seemed to be just a matter of days. General Walter Krueger, his land commander, was remaining aboard Admiral Kinkaid's flagship because the communications were so good there, but he, too, expected to be ashore in a matter of hours. Admiral McCain and Admiral Davison and their carrier groups of the Third Fleet were heading for Ulithi Atoll to re-provision and rearm. They had been fighting for almost two weeks.

In fact the whole of Task Force 38 was tired. The pilots, particularly, were nearly exhausted, and the carriers needed replenishment. And just about everyone needed a few good nights of rest.

McCain's group was tired, too, and it had other problems as well. On the big carrier *Hornet*, for example:

Captain A. K. Doyle had taken aboard a new air group, Air Group 11, on October 1, and nine days later the group was in action although the weather on the way to Okinawa had been so foul that the group had averaged only one and a half practice landings per pilot. "It is doubtful," said the Captain, "if any new carrier group has ever been thrown so abruptly into such violent operations. . . . Certainly battleships are not given green turret crews eight days before action. . . ."

Another problem was the rapid expansion of the Navy air arm: the coming of ever more new carriers to the Pacific was having an effect not unlike that of the Japanese in their heavy losses.

It had resulted in what Captain Doyle called "the thinning out of experienced personnel to a point where experienced flight leaders are few." The *Hornet*'s air group commander had been killed over Formosa and it hurt— badly.

There was a problem of pilot training here, too. One day, a green pilot came in and was waved off. He had not put down his landing hook. He came around again and still did not put down his landing hook. The desperate landing officer finally ran up the deck with a spare landing hook in hand, and engaged it on a wire, so that the youngster could see what he was supposed to do. Then, and only then, did he remember to drop his hook. "While this provided entertainment for the crew," said Captain Doyle, "it indicated poor indoctrination of pilots."

The *Hornet* and the rest of the Third Fleet had had a rough time; Admiral Halsey was giving all the punishment he could to the Japanese. There had been no respite for the pilots after the Formosa fight and the strikes on central Luzon. On October 20 they had gone right in to hit northern Mindanao and the Dulag area. In their sweep they had found no opposition and only 5 Japanese planes to strafe, and in their bombing strikes they had seen so many friendly planes that they found it hard to get to the target and drop in the designated area. So it had come as a great bit of news to the *Hornet* that she was to head back to Ulithi.

In flag plot of the *New Jersey,* where Admiral Halsey held forth, there was a certain uneasiness, a feeling that the Japanese *ought* to come out and fight, but nothing very definite. The reports of Japanese ships zigzagging around the Inland Sea made them worry, and they turned over various plans of action in their minds.

In Leyte Gulf General MacArthur was waiting with as much patience as he could muster for the troops to consolidate their positions so that he might move ashore permanently. General Krueger remained on Kinkaid's flagship, and Kinkaid himself was attending to the business of keeping things moving the way he wanted them to.

Two days earlier, south in Borneo, Admiral Kurita laid his final plans for the movement that was to destroy the Americans once and for all. Because of the shortage of aircraft, Kurita's intelligence was anything but good. On October 20, with hundreds of American ships in Leyte Gulf and outside, ranging the perimeter, the Japanese combined reports listed only 41 transports, 10 carriers, 6 destroyers, and 44 other ships in the whole area. The Japanese must have known there were far more ships, but they showed a remarkable capacity for courage, complete disregard of danger, and self-deception. Vice Admiral Matome Ugaki was Kurita's commander of Battleship Division One, which centered around the big modern battleships *Yamato, Musashi,* and *Nagato,* on which the Japanese placed so much hope in this operation. If, as Admiral Kinkaid said with a shudder, a pair of cruisers infiltrating into Leyte Gulf could wreak havoc like a fox in a henhouse, then what might not battleships with 18-inch guns do? Admiral Ugaki had high hopes.

Of all the Japanese commanders, few were closer to the conduct of the naval war than Admiral Ugaki had been. He was Admiral Yamamoto's Chief of Staff from the outbreak of the war until the day that Yamamoto was ambushed in the South Pacific. Now he held a command with as responsible a job as he could have wished.

On October 20, in spite of what had happened at Formosa in the air battle, in spite of the confusion that Ugaki must have sensed in the Philippines and at home, he was determinedly optimistic. Here is his view of the war situation at that moment:

> In view of the present situation, First Air Fleet has organized the Kamikaze Special Attack Units with the 26 fighters (the entire present strength, with 13 to be employed for crash attacks) of the 201st Air Group. These planes, which have been divided into four units, will in the event the enemy carriers appear east of the Philippines, destroy the carriers (or at least make them unusable for the time being). These battle results, it is said, are anticipated before the surface ships penetrate. What exalted spirit! Not even an enemy who is a million strong or has a thousand carriers need be feared. This is because all forces are equally of this spirit. Yesterday it is reported that a mass victory rally was held at Hibiya Park [Tokyo] for the purpose of strengthening the unity of the homeland. If the 100 million citizens should immediately firmly adopt this sacrificial spirit and apply it to production and defense, who would have fears about the future of our Empire? At present the United States is engrossed in the presidential election. Dewey supposedly has a slight edge. There is no need to fear an enemy whose war objective and operational direction are motivated by self-interest.

Buoyed by such thoughts, Admiral Ugaki boarded the *Atago*, Admiral Kurita's flagship, for last-minute discussions. He was calm and confident. On the day before, heading for Brunei, the weather had been fine. Even better, just after announcement of the activation of the Sho plan, his seamen had captured a hawk which alighted on the main battery control station. It was a good omen, and it was announced over the public address system of the ship to raise the morale of all. The bird had been placed in a cage on the bridge, and would be kept as a symbol of victory for the Sho operation. And then, on the evening before entering Brunei, the ship had been bathed in a sea of phosphorescence. Such brilliance augured well for victory!

As Admiral Ugaki moved to that flagship in his barge, the destroyers and cruisers were around his battleships fueling. This was the Japanese system, particularly now in the third year of the war, when the shortage of tankers and trained crews was so great that refueling from tankers at sea was all but impossible. Thus the big ships kept their smaller companions fueled, and took on resupply from the tankers in port. The tankers were due in on the 21st to refill the battleships.

The friendly Zeros and seaplanes of the fleet and the land-based air force at Singapore flew overhead, the red rising sun on wings and nacelles giving a comforting feeling to those below. There had been two submarine scares during the day, but only one of them was apparently real; the admirals worried lest a force of big bombers from the Marianas might appear and smash them at anchorage.

Admiral Kurita's conference lasted until 2000 and then the ship commanders and force leaders moved back to their own vessels. Admiral Ugaki went back to the *Yamato,* his flagship, and had his dinner. Then he began his own staff preparations.

That evening Admiral Ugaki called the commanders of his ships to the *Yamato.* They discussed the coming sailing and the operation, until he was sure that every commander knew exactly what he and Kurita had in mind. A staff officer of the Japanese 14th Area Army appeared before the group and gave a map briefing on the situation in the Tacloban area after the American landings. It was true that the Americans had come ashore against virtually no opposition, but the 16th Division was held back for just such a defense, said the staff officer, and was planning counterattack as soon as the Kurita force could cause havoc among the ships on the beach and cut off the American resupply and line of retreat.

During the night the refueling continued. The oilers *Makko Maru* and *Yuho Maru* came in from Singapore and were put to work. Then, at 0800 the Kurita force moved out.

Admiral Kurita had many problems on his mind. He had very little concept of what kind of air defense he could expect from the land-based forces in the Philippines. He expected to meet a very strong surface force, no matter whether or not Admiral Ozawa was successful in luring the enemy north, and it was quite conceivable to Kurita that he could lose half his force of 32 ships in the coming engagement.

There were three possible routes for Admiral Kurita to take, and he considered all of them. The first was the southern route, from Borneo up near Morotai, but this would bring him under possible air attacks from land-based planes of the American air forces. The second route was to go north, and cut around down into the Philippines, but he rejected this plan as too expensive in fuel —for in everything he did he had to consider the problems of fuel and fuel resupply. The tankers available to him were at Brunei, and at Coron Bay (if they had not been sunk by this time). Two tankers were coming from the Singapore base to the Sulu Sea.

The third approach, the one Admiral Kurita chose, would take him through Palawan Passage. He knew the dangers, and they were great. The Americans were operating submarines in the region, and he was quite likely to come under attack before he ever reached the passage. But he chose this route as the greatest in opportunity and the least in danger as far as the overall picture went. He headed for that narrow body of water between Palawan Island and the region known as the Dangerous Ground, because of its reefs and shallows, which extends into the South China Sea.

Kurita was not wrong in his estimate of the American coverage of the central area of approach. As of October 20, the American submarine forces of the Seventh Fleet were very much on the alert for the possible coming of enemy ships.

The *Cod*, which had expended all its torpedoes in recent days, still remained at sea instead of going back to base as would normally be expected, for she was to make reconnaissance north of Lingayen Gulf.

The *Bream* and *Guitarro* covered the west and northwest approaches to Manila. The *Angler* and *Bluegill* covered the southwest approaches to Manila and Verde Island passage. The *Rock* and *Bergall* patrolled on a line between Cape Varella and the northwest corner of the Dangerous Ground. The *Darter* was covering the southern entrance to Palawan Passage, and the *Dace* was covering the western approaches to Balabac Straits. The *Hammerhead* was covering the southwest approaches to Brunei Bay, and the *Gurnard* was moving up to help her; the *Lapon* was east of Coron Bay, waiting for those tankers, and the *Raton* was southbound in the Sulu Sea, where she might catch the other tankers. The *Paddle* was assigned to Balikpapan on lifeguard duty to save American airmen who might be downed; the *Batfish* was headed for patrol in the eastern Sulu Sea; HMS *Tantivy* was patrolling the lower Macassar Strait; HMS *Stoic* was in the Java Sea, and HMS *Storm* patrolled east of Saleier Strait, while HMS *Sirdar* was patrolling the southern approaches to Sunda Strait.

What Admiral Ugaki and his compeers did not seem to understand was that, if at home in the United States Mr. Roosevelt and Mr. Dewey were competing for control of the American government, out in the Pacific thousands of dedicated young men had nothing more important on their minds than the destruction of this Japanese fleet; in fact *all* Japanese vessels that might come within sight.

As for the assistance the Japanese might expect from land-based air, it was not developing as the fleet's admirals had hoped. An example is the conduct of the Fifth Attack Unit of the 752nd Air Group. In line with plans for the Sho operation, this unit was to move to the Philippines lock, stock, and barrel, and to make the move on October 22. But as the planes began arriving, the commanders discovered that the expected arrangements for the landing of combat planes, and the arrangements for transports carrying the ground personnel, had not been made at all. Indeed, most of the planes got into the Clark Field area about sundown on the 22nd, and caused such serious confusion in the air traffic pattern that many of them were diverted to strange fields. Some of the ground crews were then diverted in their transports, and consequently, what was supposed to be an orderly move to the front became a confused mess, which had to be sorted out before the unit could begin operating as a unit again. Since the Sho operation depended for its success on miraculous timing, the operation was already in trouble in the Philippines on October 23. The mess had not been sorted out by midnight of that second day.

Nevertheless, not knowing that he could expect very little from his own air forces—although he would probably have moved on inexorably in any case—Admiral Kurita sailed with his force at 0800 on October 22 from Brunei Bay. It was a cloudy day, and the wind riffled the whitecaps on the waves, no help at all in visual submarine watch. But the big ships had radar and sound gear to track the enemy if he came.

They moved out at 18 knots from the broad reaches of the beautiful bay, and they began zigzagging independently within their formations. Admiral Kurita had to make another difficult decision regarding routes: there were three possible ones in the Palawan region. One would take them down the west side of Palawan Island and near the Dangerous Ground to Mindoro Strait. A second would go through the Dangerous Ground, and a third, down the east side of Palawan Island. The most dangerous route as far as possible submarine attack was concerned was the approach via the west side of the island, because the supply ships could not reach the other approaches in time to be of any use to the fleet.

On they moved, between 16 and 18 knots, the weather changing, growing better for a time, and then clouding up again.

The intelligence they were receiving was still far from accurate. They had heard that enemy forces had landed on Rapu Rapu Island, north of San Bernardino Strait. If that report was true, their plans were torn asunder; the Americans would know as soon as they passed by and give the warning so there could be no chance of achieving the surprise pincers attack. But before more than fright than the plans would have to be junked could set in, there came the comforting news that the landings had not occurred, that faulty intelligence had been at work again. Admiral Ugaki heaved a sigh of relief. "The effect of such erroneous reports at a time like this is not little," he said. Obviously, the tension was growing.

In the morning, intelligence from Leyte indicated 80

ships in the Gulf, while a later report put the figure at 100. The Japanese realized they would face a strong force, and the land fighting indicated it, too, for reports came in of fierce fighting around Tacloban and heavy Japanese losses there.

But any wavering in the fleet was silenced by a message from the Emperor: "Our Army and Navy forces, working in close unity, have intercepted the enemy fleet and inflicted heavy losses on the enemy by engaging him in fierce battle. I hereby express my deep gratitude."

The admirals and the lesser officers did not need to delve beneath the surface of this uninformative message; the reason for it was apparent in the second half:

"The situation is becoming increasingly urgent by the day. The Army and Navy forces will strengthen even further their unity and endeavor to fulfill my faith in them."

There it was, the demand by the Emperor that they succeed on behalf of the people of the homeland. Brought up to worship their emperor as a god, the men of the navy needed no more than this message to tell them that they must come back with their shields or on them—i.e., come back with their ships or not come back at all. Nothing further need be said. No more heroics than the final toasts aboard the flagship on the evening before departure were needed to remind the captains and the admirals that their responsibility to the Emperor transcended life itself.

Poor Kurita! This day he was feeling the need for air cover, and he had been stripped of his float reconnaissance planes which had been transferred to base at San Jose in the Philippines. As long as they were within cover distance by the air group from the south, everything was as satisfactory as could be expected. But a time would come when they would be naked, unless the Japanese air force in the Philippines performed better than seemed to be indicated at the moment.

That afternoon, the light cruiser Noshiro and the cruisers Takao and Atago all reported sighting submarines, but in each case the sighting turned out to be a false alarm. The nervous seamen of the Yamato and Musashi also reported sighting mines, which were equally nonexistent. But the sightings were enough to make anyone nervous, so Admiral Ugaki put in an order for aerial reconnaissance for the next day. On the ships, gunners opened up from time to time on pieces of flotsam in the water, mistaking them for mines or submarine periscopes. Dedicated or not, the mighty fleet was nervous, and it remained that way. With the coming of darkness in the afternoon, the air cover from Borneo turned back, and the fleet slowed to 16 knots for the night, zigzagging. By midnight they were approaching Palawan Passage.

There they were soon to come under the eyes of two American submarines, the *Darter* and *Dace*, and the first engagement of the great sea battle would be fought.

The *Darter* and *Dace* had been on patrol for more than three weeks. The *Darter*'s patrol had begun on September 1 at Brisbane, and had not amounted to very much. They had been assigned to scout north of Celebes Island during the Palau and Morotai landings and had been unlucky, finding nothing to scout for. At the end of September they had moved into Mios Woendi for refueling and some minor repairs that could be handled by the submarine tender *Orion*, anchored there. They sailed from this port in Biak on October 1 along with the *Dace*, bound for their respective patrol areas for the forthcoming invasion of the Philippines.

At this point in the war, the only method by which American submarines could be assured of relative safety was through the establishment of "safety lanes" marked out in longitude and latitude on the charts used by ships and planes and submarines. The submarines were very careful when operating around American bases or within range of land-based air to stay in the safety lanes. But it did not always help them much, because the planes and ships had eager crews, looking for Japanese, and perhaps their navigation was not always all it should have been. In any case, the *Darter* on October 3 was in the safety lane and ran afoul of a hunter-killer group of planes and destroyer escorts. They gave all the proper signals, but had great difficulty convincing the Americans they were friendly. That same day another submarine in the lane, *Seawolf*, disappeared, but the *Darter* stayed on the surface, put on all the speed she could manage, and with a sigh of relief

Commander David H. McClintock, her captain, slid away from "friendly" ships that day.

A few days later the *Darter* was in its patrol area, extending about 100 miles west of the southern half of Palowan Island and to the northwest coast of Borneo as far as Brunei Bay. In other words, the *Darter* had been placed by Admiral Christie, Commander of Seventh Fleet Submarines, in a position where, with a little luck, McClintock might find the big Japanese fleet that was coming to fight the battle. On October 10 McClintock was joined by the submarine *Dace*, under Commander B. D. Claggett, to form a two-ship wolfpack.

For a week they cruised. One convoy escaped them in shallow water for a time, but they managed to sink two ships and damage two (*Darter* and *Dace* together) inside the Borneo barrier reef. On October 14 came orders to cover Balabac Strait and Palawan Passage, and they did so until the night of October 18, when word came about a convoy southbound, about halfway up the west coast of Palawan Island.

The *Darter* raced north to join the *Dace*. The two captains sighted one another on the morning of October 19 and moved close enough to hold a megaphone conference.

As they were talking, two Japanese destroyers suddenly began to bear down on them. The conference was adjourned, the submarines dived hastily, and each captain sent off four torpedoes toward the enemy. They were greeted with embarrassing silence.

The Japanese destroyers each dropped a handful of depth charges and then headed off, apparently with more important matters on their minds. This action must have accounted for one of the many submarine sightings the Japanese reported in these days to Admiral Kurita, and also for his realization of what he risked by moving into Palawan Strait.

October 20 was a quiet day for the *Darter* and *Dace*, except for the news of the invasion of the Philippines which they picked up from a news broadcast. They headed, then, for Balabac Strait; that was the shortest distance from Singapore, en route to Leyte. They did not know that Kurita had moved to Brunei Bay.

At midnight on October 21, the submarines were in

contact with two heavy ships and one escort northwest of Balabac Strait. The *Darter* began moving in, but the ships went through the Dangerous Ground at 22 knots, and they got by before the submarine could get into firing position. McClintock tried to guide the *Dace* into position, but there was no luck; the Japanese made a mighty turn to the west, and at dawn all they could see were masts to the northwest while radar gave a range of more than 20 miles.

On the 22nd, as the Japanese moved toward Palawan Passage, the *Darter* and the *Dace* navigated the Dangerous Ground carefully, toward Balabac Strait again, and around midnight came close enough so that the captains could have another megaphone talk. Commander Claggett said he was low on fuel and he thought he had best leave the area and head back for replenishment.

At that moment the *Darter* and *Dace* were 50 yards apart, moving slowly at 5 knots on batteries. Two reports were received, indicating two separate convoys, and each submarine decided to take on one of the convoys. The captains were about ready to part company, when from the *Darter*'s conning tower came the report: "Radar contact, 130 degrees T, 30,000 yards—contact doubtful—probably rain."

McClintock started, and one thought flashed through his mind: "The Japanese Fleet."

Almost immediately the radar operator stated that the contact was ships. The *Dace* was given the range and bearing by megaphone. The answer back: "Let's go get them." By twenty minutes after midnight [it was now October 23] both the *Darter* and the *Dace* were chasing the contact at full power. The ships were in Palawan Passage, headed north. We were on the left flank. . . .

It quickly became apparent to Commander McClintock that they were chasing a task force, not just a convoy. He began sending contact reports, three of them, and estimated finally that the force included at least 11 heavy ships. [Actually the force included 15 heavy ships, if one drew the line between heavy cruisers and light cruisers, so it was a pretty good guess for midnight.] McClintock hoped this was the main body of the Japanese fleet, and he decided it was imperative to identify the force before attacking. He would wait until dawn.

Whatever the Japanese were doing before, they were not zigzagging while negotiating the passage, McClintock noted. They were moving at about 15 knots, radars sweeping, but that was all. The *Darter* began to move ahead.

From the left, the Japanese were disposed in five lines, moving up the passage. On the far left were *Noshiro* and 2 destroyers, 500 meters apart, then a space of 3000 meters and 3 more destroyers in line. Next, to the right, was a line of heavy ships, led by the fleet flagship *Atago*. Then came the *Takao* and the *Chokai*, the battleship *Nagato*, and behind by 3000 yards, the cruisers *Kumano* and *Suzuya*, and the battleship *Haruna*. In the center were 3 more destroyers, and to the right of them the longest line of ships, Admiral Ugaki's line, led by the *Myoko*, followed by the *Haguro*, *Maya*, *Yamato*, *Musashi*. Three thousand meters behind these ships came the *Tone*, *Chikuma*, and the *Kongo*. On the outside were 3 destroyers, the light cruiser *Yahagi*, and 2 more destroyers.

From his vantage point Commander McClintock did not see the destroyer column on the left, but his eye was caught by the second column of capital ships. The last ship seemed to be a battleship, from the size of the pip on the radar screen. He assigned himself to this column of ships, and asked the *Dace* to move around and attack from the starboard side.

The *Darter* moved into position; by 0425 she was 10 miles ahead of the Japanese and off to their left, waiting. McClintock slowed to match the speed of the target and waited for dawn. The *Dace* passed and crossed her bow and headed for a position on the right, waiting also for dawn when they would make periscope attacks.

McClintock went below to check radio reports, and found that most of the men off watch were clustered in the messroom. They were skeptical when he told them he thought they would soon make an attack on the Japanese fleet. They had been suffering a run of bad luck.

"I didn't blame them," said McClintock, "I wasn't absolutely sure myself. I had a small fear that the ships might be high-speed transports, and *not* the fleet."

But he kept moving.

At around 0430 all hands were called for coffee, before the expected attack. Twenty minutes later the order came for the men to go to battle stations, and twenty minutes after that McClintock ordered the course reversed, heading down the throat of the column of big ships. From the east the light was beginning to come up on the sea, and he could see through the periscope that there was not a cloud in the sky. He submerged to 300 feet, to check depth and density, and returned to periscope depth.

Now the first look showed one long gray shape; it was the whole column seen bows on. What was it? cruisers? or battleships? He swung around to the southeast where the light was better; he could see battleships, cruisers, and destroyers.

The sound gear was silent, and apparently the Japanese were not even in echo range for submarines. As McClintock swung the periscope, his executive officer, Ernie Schwab, kept asking questions.

McClintock would swing the periscope and mutter.

"What's there?" asked Schwab.

"Battleships."

Another swing.

"What's there?"

"Cruisers."

Still another swing, and then another mutter.

"What's there?"

"Battleships."

It *was* the Japanese fleet. No doubt about it now.

The gray ships kept getting larger. We were a little to the east of the column's track. We would pass on almost parallel courses. At 5:25 the first ships in column could be identified as heavy cruisers, with huge bow waves. There were sighs of disappointment throughout the conning tower that the targets were not all battleships. A beautiful sight, anyway. They were in close column. We could imagine the Japanese general quarters, watertight doors closed, the officers in white service pacing the bridge. I hoped the lead ship would be the flagship. It was! At 5:27 the range to the leading cruiser was under 3,000 yards. All tubes were ready.

The Japanese ships then zigged. It could not have been a better-timed maneuver for the *Darter*. It gave a perfect torpedo range of just under 1000 yards, and the profiles of what were obviously *Atago*-class cruisers could be seen perfectly.

Commander McClintock prepared to shoot on the new target course. He had the periscope up for what seemed like several minutes and the leading cruiser looked huge; she had a bone in her teeth, and the forward slant of her bridge accentuated her speed. *Atago* class: it had been his favorite target on the attack teacher in practice. How many times in the past had he estimated the angle on the bow of her flat bridge, using models. Now it was real. The angle on her bow grew: 55, 60, 65! Range was *under* 1000.

"Shooting bearing," he shouted.

"Mark," he shouted again.

"FIRE ONE!"

He fired again, and four more times, and watched through the periscope. From the bridge of the cruiser came signals from a searchlight pointed east. The cruiser was not even zigging, apparently sending some routine message to the fleet. The surprise was complete.

"Shift targets to second cruiser," said the captain.

"Bearing mark."

"Give me a *range* . . . give me a range . . . give me a range!" cried Dennis Wilkinson, the TDC operator. "You can't shoot without a range."

McClintock looked and gave him a range. 1500 yards. They were in a line of bearing.

"TDC ready."

"Bearing mark."

"FIRE SEVEN!" he shouted.

Off went the first stern torpedo, and just as it left the tubes, there was a heavy explosion.

"Depth charge!" shouted Executive Officer Schwab.

"Depth charges, hell," yelled McClintock. "Torpedoes!"

"Christ, we're hitting them, we're hitting them," shouted

Walter Price, who was punching the torpedo firing keys, and jumping up and down after each explosion.

The tenth torpedo swished on its way; they had fired six "fish" at the first cruiser and four at the second ship in the column. There had been five explosions on the first target and now Commander McClintock swung the periscope around to take a look.

"I will never forget what I saw," he said later. "She was belching flame from the base of her forward turret to the stern; the dense black smoke of burning oil covered her from forward turret to stern. She was still plowing ahead, but she was also going down by the bow. Number One turret was cutting the water. She was finished."

(According to Japanese sources, the fleet was on a highly modified zigzag course, involving relatively few turns, for the night movement. That accounted for the apparent lack of zigzagging.)

Commander McClintock expected the avenging angels of the fleet, the destroyers, to come charging after him now, and to cross and crisscross his position and course with depth charges. He headed deep. As the submarine started down, four more torpedo explosions could be heard.

The depth charging was not effective. McClintock called it sketchy. But they stayed down, for safety's sake.

Meanwhile, on the other side of the 5 columns of ships, Commander Claggett was watching with pleasure. He saw the first cruiser and the explosions and then the total envelopment of the ship in smoke so black he could not actually see the ship sink. He also saw the second cruiser smoking badly; and watched as the destroyers converged on the spot where the *Darter* had gone deep.

By this time, Claggett was beginning his firing approach in the *Dace*. He had expected the formation to scatter into some defensive grouping when two of its leading members were hit, but to his surprise nothing like that happened. On second thought he remembered that they were in highly confined waters and guessed that the Japanese did not wish to risk the danger of going aground, and would take their chances with the submarines instead.

The Japanese ships did turn slightly to the right, which

brought them toward the *Dace*. Claggett picked one large cruiser as his target—the front ship on the starboard line of capital ships. He began his approach.

The target moved nicely toward him in the growing light of early morning, and as he waited Claggett turned the periscope "rubbernecking around" and looked in awe at the big fleet. With such a plethora of targets he grew greedy, and decided to change his shot. He particularly liked the looks of the third ship in the starboard line; perhaps she was a *Kongo*-class battleship. He decided to let the first two ships go by and take a crack at her.

"I never thought the time would come when I would let two heavy cruisers go by," he said, but the larger ship had a definitely heavier superstructure.

On the column came, and it was time to fire. He got off the six bow tubes, then dived deep because a battleship was charging down on him. As he dived he heard four of the torpedoes explode.

Soon after the torpedo hit there was a terrific explosion which was undoubtedly the magazines blowing up. For twenty-five minutes thereafter, there were terrific breaking-up noises that were the most gruesome I have yet experienced in all my patrols. At this time my Engineer Officer, Lieutenant Jones, said, "Let's get the hell out of here." I agreed, but I didn't know how to do it. It sounded like she was coming down on top of us as a matter of fact, and it was one of the worst experiences I have ever had. We received a severe depth charging that kept us deep for several hours. Two destroyers made perfect runs on us as heard through the hull without the use of sound gear, but for some reason did not drop.

The first ship that Commander McClintock had selected was indeed the *Atago,* the fleet flagship. She was particularly notable because, while her second funnel was straight, her first was raked sharply back, and her mast was placed just in front of the raked funnel. There was a definite rake to her bridge, too, which gave the ship a streamlined appearance. Her overall length was more than

203 meters; she displaced nearly 15,000 tons, was powered by 4 turbines with 12 boilers, and made a speed of 34.2 knots. She bristled with guns, from her 5 20-centimeter guns to 42 25-millimeter anti-aircraft guns, and she carried 24 torpedoes and 3 airplanes (except at this point when she had been stripped of her planes for the slender Philippines air defense).

All night long the Japanese had been aware that they were being stalked by submarines. At 0250 that morning, Admiral Ugaki had a report that radiomen had overheard a submarine transmitting a special signal on a frequency of 8470 kilocycles, and the signal was extremely strong. So they knew. But in the restricted waters of Palawan Passage there was relatively little maneuvering to be done. Admiral Ugaki, for one, looked for trouble.

As the dawn came up, Admiral Ugaki was on the bridge of the *Yamato*, fourth ship in the starboard line of heavy ships. One hour before sunrise the ships had moved into this attenuated formation, specially designed for anti-submarine defense. Their course was 035. Their speed was 18 knots.

While Commander McClintock would have sworn that the ships were not zigzagging, the formation was doing so, and just before 0630 all the ships were beginning a simultaneous turn to port.

There was a violent explosion on the port column. "I suddenly spied off the port bow on the dawning horizon the flames from an explosion and what appeared to be a widening water spout," said Admiral Ugaki.

Briskly he ordered an emergency turn to starboard.

In a few moments Admiral Ugaki saw that 2 ships had been hit, and a destroyer had rushed to the side of each to stand by and rescue survivors.

Aboard the *Atago*, the mortal wounds were felt as huge shocks, one after the other. The lookouts estimated, quite wrongly, that the attack had come from nearly 2000 yards away, and so their fix on the submarine was faulty to begin with. Four torpedoes hit on the starboard side (because of that turn to port in the zigzag pattern), and they were nicely spaced, if you could call it that, forward, amidships, and aft. Immediately the ship listed to starboard by about 8 degrees. The Captain ordered the counterflooding of the port engine and boiler rooms, but there was no time, the watertight compartments on the starboard side had been blown right out of her. In a few moments the list increased to 18 degrees and then to 25 degrees.

"All hands on deck," ordered the Captain, and the men came rushing from the compartments below, if they could make their way to the top.

The torpedoes had indeed been deadly. The first had struck on the bow in the vicinity of the bread lockers, damaging all the storerooms on the starboard side, forward. The officers had ordered the manning of the pumps, but it was a futile gesture.

The second torpedo had hit on the side of the No. 1 boiler room; the boiler room had begun to fill with steam, and the damage was so severe that steam and flames began erupting from the air intake on the port side of the bridge and the port and starboard intakes on the middle deck. The junior officers' quarters near the main battery control station began to flood through cracks in the hull that appeared now. Steam pressure fell, the lights flickered, dimmed, and went out. The telephone on the bridge died, and the rest of the ship's telephones were out.

The Captain had ordered full right rudder, but with the failure of the electrical system the rudder did not respond. The list increased.

The third torpedo entered the No. 6 boiler room with such speed that the voice tube began whistling, and the center bulkhead between No. 6 and No. 7 boiler rooms cracked, and flames shot through into No. 7. At the same time the No. 3 torpedo mount, directly above the No. 6 boiler room, was showered with water and oil spray, and the crew of the mount were blown from their posts to the after control station. The damage was severe. Still the torpedo officer ordered the jettisoning of torpedoes and heavy objects on the starboard side, and 7 torpedoes went over. The eighth could not be budged.

The fourth torpedo came late, after the others had struck near the after generator room, making a hole in the rear bulkhead of the starboard after engine room. This

was a terrible hit; it caused leakage into the after generator room, which flooded almost instantly. The control
board room bulkhead cracked, and the men could not stop
the flooding. Water entered the starboard shaft alley and
the after transformer room. Fuel oil and water spouted up
through the after seamen's compartments, water flooded
into the No. 5 turret powder magazine, and five magazine
crewmen were killed.

As that last torpedo struck, the ship's list had increased
to 32 degrees. Admiral Kurita and his staff left the flag
plot and slid overboard to be rescued by the destroyer
Kishinami which was standing by. The assistant medical
officer and the chief clerk of the staff were entrusted with
the responsibility of transferring the Emperor's picture to
the destroyer. They set about their task. The list of the
ship was now about 42 degrees to starboard.

"Approach the side," was the order to the *Kishinami*.

"Prepare to lower the ensign," said the Captain.

As the water entered No. 5 turret, the list increased to
54 degrees, all communications except the voice tube were
cut off on the bridge, and the water was lapping just a
few feet below the No. 2 turret dome.

The order came to abandon ship, and the men who
could make it went over the side, to be picked up by the
Kishinami and the destroyer *Asashimo*.

The cruiser sank, leaving men fluttering in the water.
The destroyers rescued the Captain, 43 officers, and 667
petty officers and men. But the Chief Engineer, 18 officers,
and 340 petty officers and men went down with the ship.

Before the sinking, the officers on the bridge had destroyed classified materials, code machines, and books,
either putting them in weighted sacks or locking them in
the code rooms. They had moved fast to lock up the map
room and wardroom cabinet. The destroyers stayed in the
area, searching for any flotsam, but there was nothing important. The Emperor's secrets, his ship, and 359 of his
men were deep on the ocean floor below.

As to Commander McClintock's second target, she was
the sister ship of the *Atago*, the cruiser *Takao*, and she
took two torpedoes about a minute after the hits began on
the *Atago*, in spite of the fact that her alert captain had

ordered left full rudder seconds before. One torpedo struck the starboard side below the bridge and a second hit below the after deck on the same side. The *Takao* still had her seaplanes aboard, and they were damaged. One hole in the hull was nearly 12 by 24 feet, and the second was 12 feet high and nearly 50 feet long. There was considerable physical damage inside, but relatively few casualties: 33 were killed and about 30 were injured. The ship took a list of 10 degrees to starboard and the steering went out immediately after the torpedoes struck; the engines slowed and stopped and she went dead in the water. The Captain ordered counterflood and the list decreased; the ship stabilized. The crew set to work rigging an emergency rudder. The destroyers *Asashimo* and *Naganami* came to her side, and began an anti-submarine screen operation as the repairs continued.

Meanwhile, over in the starboard column of capital ships, the *Maya* had been torpedoed by Commander Claggett's *Dace*. She was still another sister ship of the *Atago* and the *Takao*, fast, modern, and dangerous. The first torpedo hit her on the port side near the chain locker, the second opposite the No. 1 gun turret, the third in the No. 7 boiler room, and the last in the port after engine room. The *Maya* immediately took a sharp list to port and began to break up.

Destroyers *Akishimo* and *Shimakaze* came alongside as she sank, to pick survivors out of the water. For the speed with which she went down, the Japanese were very lucky: out of a crew of 1000 officers and men, 769, including the Executive Officer but not the Captain, were saved by the destroyers. All that was done to save lives took place in four short minutes.

Faced with this disaster, the Japanese fleet held together remarkably well, and although command was not passed at that moment, when Admiral Ugaki ordered his rudder change, the other ships followed. Yet when the *Maya* went up, confusion did set in. Admiral Ugaki described it later from his point of view as senior officer present, now that Admiral Kurita was drying out on a destroyer with his staff.

"If other submarines are present, not only would it be

dangerous to effect a radical retirement," Ugaki said, "but as the senior commander present, a radical separation would not be feasible from the standpoint of visibility."

When the *Maya* went up he shuddered, for the cruiser was directly in front of his flagship, the *Yamato*.

"If the *Yamato*'s position had been a little more one way or the other, she would inevitably have been hit by three or four torpedoes. This is really dangerous—evading the above sub by turning to starboard and moving up. . . ." (It was this maneuver that caused the *Dace* to dive and perhaps saved more of the fleet.)

Now the Japanese began seeing periscopes everywhere, although both American submarines were on their way to deep water. Admiral Ugaki saw one to port, and reversed course.

"It is no exaggeration to say that for a time the first section was in utter confusion," he said. He was absolutely *positive* that he saw at least 4 submarines at one time or another, although, of course, only the *Darter* and the *Dace* were in the area.

Gradually the confusion sorted out, with no more unpleasant surprises for the Japanese, and Ugaki assumed command. At first he learned only that he was to take over communications command, because the *Atago* was sunk. This came by visual signal at 0700. When he learned that the Admiral was safely aboard the *Kishinami*, he breathed a sigh of relief. Then he learned, at 0830, that he was to take command. Already he had done so effectively. When he saw the mountains of southern Palawan off in the eastern sky, he realized where he was, and that only a 20-mile span was available to him between the shallows and reefs of the island and the Dangerous Ground, much of which was still uncharted. He speeded the fleet to 24 knots, even though the speed before had been 18 knots; it could not be helped. The signal flags went up and the blinkers began working, and by 0915 the fleet knew that Ugaki was, temporarily at least, in command. He sent off messages to combined fleet and to Tokyo, asking for rescue forces to bring the *Takao* back to safety, and assuring his superiors that the operation would continue in spite of this blow.

The busy crew of the *Takao* began doing what they could to put their ship back into operation. The *Naganami* and the *Asashimo* were detached from the fighting force and left behind with her.

By 1050 the engineers were starting the engines from time to time. At 1100 five crewmen who had been blown overboard by the torpedo explosions were returned by the *Asashimo,* which had rescued them. Forty minutes later, combined fleet radioed that help was on the way from Brunei.

At noon the nervous crew of the *Takao* "saw" a submarine, but the destroyers could not make any contact with it. By 1400 the damage control parties were optimistic that they would be able to bring the ship to port under her own power; it would take a jury-rigged rudder, but the engineers thought it could be done. By 2100 the *Takao* was moving under her own power, and by midnight she was heading for Brunei at 6 knots, expecting to reach port by midnight two days later.

Meanwhile Admiral Ugaki was exercising command. Few Japanese officers were more capable of taking over in an emergency, for Ugaki's experience had been among the greatest in the fleet. At Midway, when he was Chief of Staff to Admiral Yamamoto, he had been instrumental in persuading Yamamoto to retire after the loss of the 4 big carriers—and thus probably saved the fleet. He was a man of excellent judgment.

Judgment, however, was impaired by necessity this day. He wanted a speed of 24 knots but soon realized that the fleet would be short of fuel if he did this, and reduced speed to 20 knots. It was this same problem of fuel that had dictated many actions the fleet was taking. For example, the selection of this passage, west of Palawan, had been caused by fuel problems. The selection of the zigzag method—they had taken the easy zigzag instead of the more expensive complex zigzag. And any commander should have known that he needed a destroyer screen in front of the fleet, particularly when approaching a narrow passage—but there were problems of fuel again.

Admiral Ugaki led the fleet through the narrow waters with three more submarine scares, and then he changed course to north. At 1540 the *Kishinami* pulled alongside the *Yamato;* Admiral Kurita and his staff began to transfer from the destroyer to the battleship. At 1620 all was done. Admiral Kurita's flag was raised above the battleship and he took command of the force once again. Ugaki's moment of glory was over. ("This I suppose is fate," he said.) He turned over all responsibility for the Battleship Division and the fleet, and instructed his staff to do whatever could be done to help Kurita and his men. And the force steamed on for San Bernardino Strait.

Kurita issued his new orders: the force would rely on sonar searches from sundown until 30 minutes before sunrise on the morning of October 24.

The Japanese continued moving at 20 knots toward the big battle they expected in less than 48 hours, while the American submarines which had caused them so much damage were having new troubles of their own, and very serious ones, too.

By 0800 the rumpus above had died down enough so that Commander McClintock felt it was safe to move up to periscope depth and take a look. He saw the *Takao*, then dead in the water, with planes flying around her and a strong screen of three destroyers standing by. He made two approaches, but the destroyers drove him off each time; then he desisted, deciding to wait for night so the tired crew could get some rest. They had been in contact with the Japanese two nights in a row now, and many men were exhausted.

That night he surfaced after dark, within sight of the *Takao*, and made a radio report to Brisbane where his base was located, telling of the fighting of the morning and the sinking, and the composition of the force as best he knew it.

The *Darter* and the *Dace* separated to try and get the crippled *Takao* when she began to head southwest. The *Dace* went east to move "around the end" and the *Darter* headed west, passing through a large expanse of fuel oil, so large it took them an hour to get out of it.

At midnight Commander McClintock decided that the time had come to move. He figured he had about an hour to get into position for an attack. It was a pitch-black night, but once in a while they could catch a glimpse of the cruiser, wobbling, her speed varying as much as 4 knots, indicating that she was in great difficulty.

Lieutenant Ed Skorupski, Officer of the Deck, and the Captain were on the bridge, and they were making 17 knots, hurrying along to get into position. The navigator was plotting in the conning tower, and all officers were at battle stations, although most of the crew, except for the watch and plotting party, were sound asleep. He later told his story:

At about 0005, it was now the 24th, we hit a shoal, rode up over it, taking a large up angle. The officer of the deck and myself thought we were gone. I thought we had been torpedoed. I watched the stern go under water . . . as far as the engine room hatch. We seemed to be going down quite rapidly. Then all of a sudden the stern rode on up, and after several seconds we came to rest, high and dry. Still, we couldn't see the reef. After two or three minutes we were able to make out that the water was very light colored around us.

The navigator came running to the bridge.

"What was that?" he said.

"We are aground."

Quick as a flash he disappeared into the conning tower, apparently to check the chart. Very shortly thereafter he was back up on the bridge.

He said, "Captain, it can't be that we are aground. The nearest land is nineteen miles away. . . ."

Now the Americans began seeing danger. McClintock was sure that the Japanese had heard the crash as the ship went on the reef, and he was also sure that one of the destroyer screens was coming over to them. The destroyer moved to within 12,000 yards. "That may not sound close . . . but it sounded close then to us sitting there on the reef with no arms but one four-inch gun and a couple of smaller guns."

But the destroyer went about, just before high tide, which was to come at 0140. McClintock knew that he must get off at high tide or he would not get off at all, because they were so close to Palawan that they were within 100 miles of a Japanese airfield at Puerta Princesa.

Down on the main deck there was great activity. The gunner's mates, with some help from the rest of the crew, were throwing all the ammunition overboard except for about 20 rounds which we were saving for the destroyer at daylight if he should come back. The commissary officer, Don Miller, was busy with part of the crew, throwing overboard all of the commissary supplies. The engineer was having all fuel oil and fresh water blown over the side. The torpedo officer was trying to get rid of our torpedoes up forward, but we were afraid to fire them in that position for fear that they would explode as they hit the reef, as they dropped from the tubes, and our efforts to get off would have been to no avail. We were not able to get the 6 torpedoes left out of the tubes.

By high tide they had done everything they could think of, and still they were stuck. They tried to back off, but the suction valves were plugged with coral. They could not use the engines. They tried "sallying" the ship—the crew would run forward and then aft, while the engineering officer ran the battery. No good.

So they ordered the *Dace* to come and rescue them. Or rather, they made the decision that they would take the *Dace*'s help, because they had ordered her up at midnight —just as *Dace* was getting into position to torpedo the *Takao* once again. The *Dace* had broken off her approach, "a heartbreaking decision," and had come to the rescue.

By 0230, with a falling tide, the tops of the screws of the *Darter* were thrashing air—they were that dry—and McClintock gave up.

Down below activities of another nature were going on. All equipment down below was being destroyed. In the conning tower the TDC was being wrecked with a sledge hammer, also the radars. In the forward battery, particularly in the officer's shower, fires were burning where all registered publications were being destroyed.

After I gave up trying to get her off I had little to do except walk around down below to see what was going on. The air down below was so full of smoke that in fact it was all I could do to stay down there more than five or ten minutes at a time. I remember seeing one mess attendant, a six-footer named Lewis, who was having the time of his life. He had a sledge hammer and he was destroying things, and he really was enjoying it.

At about 0300 they began to abandon ship, moving to the newly arrived *Dace*. Claggett brought the *Dace* right up to the edge of the shoal, so close that McClintock worried about him and kept telling him through the megaphone to get clear. But Claggett held the ship close to the reef, sent a line from the bow to the *Darter*'s stern, and managed to stay 50 yards off the stern of the *Darter*.

Ernie Schwab, Executive Officer of the *Darter*, was on the stern directing the abandonment of the ship, and by this time (0300) the tide was so low that there was a 20-foot drop from the fantail to the life rafts. Luckily the waves were not severe.

Finally they were all off the ship except for the Gunnery Officer, the Executive Officer, the Chief of the boat, one gunner's mate, and the Captain. The enlisted men were rigging demolition charges, and McClintock went below for one last moment. He picked up a suit of blues to take with him, wandered about in the smoke for a few moments, took an ash tray with *Darter* engraved on it, and went back on deck. The ash tray was his only souvenir of a proud ship.

Everyone went off then, the Captain last; they were aboard the *Dace* at 0435. The demolition charges were supposed to go off at 0440; they exploded but did not seem to do any damage. The *Dace* backed off and tried to torpedo the *Darter*, but 4 torpedoes exploded high on the reef.

Claggett then broke out his gun, and fired 21 rounds of

4-inch shells. One round hit an oil tank forward, and that blew up, but still did not seem to do much damage. There were many hits on the conning tower, and the gunners were continuing. Suddenly, as the 21st round went out, the lookouts reported a Japanese plane overhead.. The plane zoomed in, and the gun crew leaped for the hatch, making it down before the bombs began to fall. The bombs seemed to fall closer to the *Darter* than to the *Dace*—hitting neither—and McClintock wished the Japanese could have finished his demolition.

The coming of the Japanese plane meant they had run out of time. They stayed around the area (they discovered the submarine was ashore on Bombay Shoal) as they hoped to get back aboard the *Darter* that night and finish the job.

No such luck.

At 0900 the wounded *Takao* had word from an air base that an attack plane had sighted a grounded American submarine, and the destroyers *Naganami* and *Hiyodori* were dispatched to investigate, dispose of the submarine, and recover any material of value. At 1100 they found her and shelled for three minutes. When there were no signs of life the *Naganami* sent a boarding party to finish her off, but she was too high in the shoal. They tried to pull her off. No good. They set her afire, took what documents they could find, and retired in disgust.

The *Takao* then returned homeward to Brunei as best she could, picking up support ships to accompany her on the way. In the middle of the afternoon of October 25 she entered Brunei Bay, thanked her escorts, and picked her way to her resting place. The first cripple from the big battle had come limping home.

As for the *Darter* and the *Dace,* that night (October 24) the two captains in the *Dace* approached the *Darter* to destroy her, not knowing precisely of the Japanese attempts earlier in the day, although they had seen the Japanese destroyer come up. But about 200 yards from Bombay Shoal, when they were moving in, Claggett and McClintock were on the bridge when they heard beeping as from their sound gear. They thought it was *theirs,* but were told it was not, and came to the uneasy conclusion that a Japanese submarine was lying in wait for them. They got out of the area in a hurry, and that night were ordered to Perth. From that point on the voyage was uneventful, except that the double crew caused the *Dace* to run short on supplies and everyone ended up eating vast quantities of the two staples aboard: mushroom soup and peanut butter.

8

HALSEY'S DECISION

The submarines of the American fleet were the first to
sense the movement of the Japanese fleet. *Darter* was the
very first on October 21, when Commander McClintock
reported to Brisbane that three unidentified large ships
were in view, and then confirmed this at 0200 on October
22. This was not the task force, but may have been the
cruiser *Aoba*, which had been detached from the force
earlier, to be used to back up troop transports moving in
the Philippines. (She was torpedoed and damaged in
Manila harbor that very day, October 23, by another submarine, USS *Bream*.)

McClintock's report had alerted the Seventh Fleet that
something was going on, and his second report at 0800 on
October 22 indicated seeing the ships again. The *Dace,* in
the same general area, had not been able to confirm the
sightings, so the Japanese ships disappeared into the ocean
somewhere around the Dangerous Ground. Then came the
Darter's electrifying message of the early hours of October
23, first reporting three battleships, then reporting at least
nine big ships, and a short time later excitedly noting
eleven ships.

In the morning the *Dace* was first to report the strike on
the Kurita fleet, and Commander Claggett believed at the
time that he had hit a *Kongo*-class battleship. But what was
important to the Third and Seventh fleets was the report
of the course and speed of the Japanese force—then
course 040 degrees, speed 15 knots. That report gave the
Americans on the other side of the Philippines an indica-

tion that the Japanese were moving in, and that an attempt was being made to interdict the landings at Leyte Gulf.

Early that morning of the 23rd the *Bream* reported on her torpedoing of the *Aoba*, and of the presence in the Manila area of another such cruiser and a destroyer. That evening the *Darter* indicated McClintock's belief that this was indeed the "Japanese first team," and he told of strikes on the *Atago* and the *Takao*.

Then came other reports. The *Angler* reported a task force of 4 large ships with escorts, and the *Guitarro* reported an enemy task force, "probably three battleships." Both these submarines were on patrol off Manila. *Angler* came back to report the force moving south through Mindoro Strait—and, of course, this is the route a force would follow to make its way into the Sibuyan Sea, then through San Bernardino Strait, around Samar Island, and down into Leyte Gulf from the north.

What is in a way remarkable is the fact that at this time there were no fewer than 4 Japanese naval forces at sea, 5 including the *Aoba* group, and that only 2 of them were detected by the morning of October 23.

One of these forces was that of Vice Admiral Shima, who had 3 cruisers and 4 destroyers that were supposed to conduct the hit-and-run raid from the south, along with the Nishimura force. At the beginning of the Sho operation, Admiral Shima was in port at Amami-o-Shima, an island of the Nansei Shoto chain north of Okinawa, lying on a line with the Japanese homeland. Shima had ducked in there after his dispatch on October 15 to chase the "remnant" of the American fleet and then finding, as Halsey said in a dispatch to Admiral Nimitz, that those remnants were retiring rapidly in the direction of the enemy, and further discovering that the claims of the high command were so many fairy stories. Shima was lucky to escape the Halsey trap with his skin, and at Amami-o-Shima the force fueled, and waited.

The word came on October 18, and at 0530 Shima sailed. He had refueled, and although the effort had cost the homeland dear in vital oil supplies, he was ready to fight for the Emperor.

Probably there is no greater indication of the confusion in the Sho operation than the whole situation of Shima.

Shima was responsible to Tokyo, and to Tokyo alone. As it turned out, so was Nishimura. Neither was responsible to the other, although they were supposed to work together in Surigao Strait, and both were to work with Admiral Kurita. The problem was a matter of seniority. Nishimura should have been in command; he knew the plan as a whole (which Shima did not) and he had the larger force. But Admiral Shima was six months senior to Admiral Nishimura. In the American Navy in this war, senior admirals served under juniors with good will— Nimitz made very certain of that—for it was understood in the Pacific Fleet that winning the war was the job and nothing would be allowed to interfere with it. But in the Imperial Japanese Navy seniority was a very touchy matter. In the case of Shima and Nishimura, who were anything but the best of friends, the matter was more complicated by the fact that they had been at the Naval Academy together—classmates—and that Shima got his political promotion through his Manchukuo experience. He had been junior to Nishimura. With seniority of such short standing, it is small wonder that there was a problem, but after they became captains, Shima forged ahead, as politicians do, while Nishimura was content to stay at sea. But Nishimura was not content to let his old acquaintance with the smaller fleet lord it over him.

On October 18, then, Shima set out for Bako in the Pescadores Islands, which lie between Formosa and the Chinese mainland. As if life were not complicated enough, the brass changed plans while he was at sea. Shima had had the *Aoba* and that group under his command and now, on the afternoon of October 18, they were taken away from him and he was assigned to transport duty, the object being to take troops from Luzon around the back of Leyte. So Shima was reduced to his 3 cruisers and 4 destroyers and still expected to do a big job. But that job was now changed: the *Aoba* and her group at that point were assigned to Kurita.

Shima and his ships arrived at Bako on October 20 and refueled. At 1600 on October 21 they sailed, Shima believing that he was to go to Manila, load troops, and escort them to Leyte, with his 3 cruisers and 4 destroyers! Then the combined fleet headquarters changed plans again.

Shima was not to go to Manila; the *Aoba* was. Shima and his ships would go to Coron Bay in the Calamian Islands, north of Palawan Island. There they would find a tanker waiting. They would refuel the destroyers (which had a dreadfully small capacity) and would join in the attack with Nishimura. At 1800 on October 23, Shima entered Coron. As with everything else that had been happening for the past few days, this turned out to be not quite as ordered, either. There was no tanker, so Shima had to fuel his destroyers from his cruisers.

The Sho operation was obviously less a plan than a patchwork of plans, and at one point Admiral Ozawa had the idea that he would send poor Shima out to broadcast dummy radio traffic, and then divert his battleships to bring about a surface action in a different area. It was all quite confusing, and it must have sapped Shima considerably. But at least on October 23 he had arrived at Coron Bay, and while the *Darter* and the *Dace* were struggling with the *Darter* on the reef, he was not very far away.

Meanwhile, the force with which Shima was to co-operate, that of Admiral Nishimura, was also at sea: the battleships *Yamashiro* and *Fuso*, the cruiser *Mogami*, and 4 destroyers. More confusion: although Vice Admiral Shoji Nishimura was a real sea dog, whose only shore duty in twenty-two years had been a stint of less than a year at the Naval War College, his fighting force could hardly be called a well-trained unit. Nishimura had been assigned to this force in the fall and had arrived to take it over at Lingga Roads on October 10. He did not even know his captains by sight or bother to meet with them. When a meeting of his force was held on the night before sailing from Brunei, he did not attend.

The Nishimura force sailed from Brunei Bay at 1500 on October 22, seven hours after Kurita had sailed. First he headed northwest, toward the Indo-China coast, to avoid American submarines that were supposedly lurking off the north coast of Borneo, and then he cut around, and headed for Balabac Channel, which he reached at about 1000, on October 23, without being observed. By noon of the 23rd he was in the Sulu Sea, and he changed course, heading northward, to avoid search by long-range land-based airplanes from Norotai to the south. He was heading for the western entrance to the Mindanao Sea.

The fourth major force at sea was that of Admiral Ozawa, who with his staff was aboard the *Zuikaku*. He had his 3 carriers (besides the *Zuikaku*), 2 hermaphrodite battleship carriers, 3 cruisers, 8 destroyers, and 116 planes with which to fight. The Captain of the *Zuikaku* put as good a face on the training and readiness of the ship as he could: "By the time of sortie technical skill had reached the level required for combat. The morale of all crew members was exceedingly high, and the command faced the operations with strong confidence."

Perhaps that was true of the captains and crew of his ships, for they did not know what Ozawa knew, that he was taking this force out to sacrifice itself on the altar of Japanese pride and nationalism. Without an adequate force of planes, Ozawa was under no illusions about what he might accomplish. With fliers trained so poorly that he considered them "one-way ducks"—who could take off from the carriers but would have to land in the Philippines—the Admiral had very little hope, indeed.

On October 20, at 0600 the *Zuikaku* sailed from Oita harbor in the Inland Sea, and began to draw her ships around her. By 1400 the force was moving out of the Inland Sea into the Bungo Suido. Under normal conditions it might have been caught right there, and several of the ships torpedoed, or at least the presence and movement of the force radioed to the Americans in the Philippines. But, by a combination of circumstances, no American submarines were in the area, although there had been a pack of them there a few days earlier. The wolfpack had patrolled the area for a week, but on October 18 its senior officer had decided that all the traffic was going in—and none coming out—and that if they were to have any hunting before they ran low on supplies, they had best get going elsewhere. The commander of the *Besugo*, the leader of the pack, decided to move off and hunt for shipping, and Admiral Charles Lockwood, Commander of Submarines in the Pacific, thought it was a very good idea.

So the Ozawa force moved out undetected, and began its voyage, practicing combat-noise discipline measures, and moving along in what the Japanese called No. 1 Alert Cruising Formation, at 18 knots.

In spite of the absence of American submarines, the Japanese airplanes covering the force (seaplanes from Japan) claimed to spot an enemy submarine at 1755 that day, and moved in to attack. Four minutes later the lookouts from the *Zuikaku* said they saw it, too, and three-quarters of an hour later they were disturbed by another radar vision.

October 20 was a cloudy day, and to avoid the submarines Admiral Ozawa moved the force eastward, along the coastline. The diversion satisfied him, and by 2100 he felt it was possible to turn to the southeast and begin the voyage in earnest. The weather was growing nastier, with heavy cloud and squalls, and the seas were running higher —which was all the better as far as he was concerned. Shortly after midnight the force headed south.

On the morning of October 21, the Ozawa force was steaming along at 18 knots, and came to action stations for practice at 1715.

The *Zuikaku* launched 6 search planes at 0700 and recovered them just before noon. A few minutes later someone in the fleet thought he heard torpedo noises, and the nervous Japanese sent the destroyers into an attack pattern, expending a large number of depth charges without any result. (American records indicated no submarine, nor any discovery of the Japanese at this point.) Admiral Ozawa decided, however, to continue the search for submarines, and launched one plane at 1219. It went out, completed a short sweep, and returned to land less than twenty minutes later, having found nothing, nothing at all. The embarrassed fleet moved on, but now with an almost constant air patrol above.

Small wonder that the Japanese were alert for submarines, because in the past year the submarine menace had become so great that Japanese commanders must have dreamed of American subs in their sleep. The plight in which the Ozawa fleet found itself this day was attributable to the abominable American submarines, because of their constant sinking of tankers, that carried the precious oil to Japan. Had there been enough tankers and enough oil, the fleet would be operating as a unit. But that was impossible. Thus Ozawa was heading south to throw away his force, sacrifice his carriers, so that Kurita could move in swiftly, demolish the American beachheads, and give the Japanese time to build planes to man those carriers still back in the Inland Sea, and to smash the Americans with land-based air from the islands of the homeland and the inner Empire.

There was another submarine alert after 0400 of October 22nd, when the ships were steaming in night formation. They changed the zigzag pattern, upped the speed of the evasive action, and then the *Zuiho* spotted a periscope —or her lookouts said so, anyhow. The sirens rang and the ships went to battle stations. Seven search planes were launched at 0549, and before they were recovered another search was put up. At 1153 someone swore he saw a torpedo track off the *Zuikaku*'s side, to port. The fleet went to battle stations again. But again it was nothing, nothing at all.

The poor young men who flew the planes, without adequate training, were doing the best they could, but at noon that day one of them came in hard on the *Zuikaku* and smashed up his plane in landing. That meant that instead of 116 fighting planes, plus a few float planes on the cruisers, the Ozawa air force was reduced to 115.

At noon, and for several hours afterward, Ozawa refueled his fleet, as the hungry ships drank the precious oil from the bigger tankers.

The fleet moved at 16 knots the rest of the afternoon, heading south, having taken a jog to the east while fueling. Course was changed to the southeast, heading directly for the northern tip of the island of Luzon. That afternoon and evening the ships were particularly alert for submarines. They wanted to be spotted—but not by the subs. They wanted to engage Admiral Halsey's Third Fleet carrier forces, not go down without getting into aerial action. The lookouts of the cruiser *Tama* thought they saw torpedo tracks again at 2000, and the destroyer *Wakatsuki* spent a good long time running and depth charging the empty sea once again.

Thus it went. On the morning of the 23rd the *Izuzu* reported the submarine threat, and at 0500, the crews of the fleet were returned to battle stations once again. The

Zuikaku's Captain ordered hard right rudder, the zigzag pattern changed, and the planes were launched.

On the morning of October 23 the Ozawa fleet was directly east of Formosa, heading southwest, when a plane on the search pattern reported an unidentified aircraft 60 miles ahead of the formation. Battle stations again. Again nothing.

Two more alerts came before 0800, but actually by 1100 Admiral Ozawa had to admit that he was puzzled. He did not know where the enemy was; for all the submarine scares and this new aircraft scare, he had not yet made contact, and was beginning to understand why. Early in the afternoon the *Zuiko*'s lookouts again said they saw a periscope. It was a mark of the Japanese discipline that, although they had not yet had a real scare, the fleet responded, the search was on, and the evasive actions were taken. Ozawa was carefully doing what Admiral Kurita had so badly neglected. But they were coming ever closer to the scene of action, and Admiral Ozawa knew it. Proof came that afternoon around 1600 when the radiomen of the *Zuikaku* announced that they were picking up a radiophone message from the Americans in English. The subject was not important but the clarity of the reception indicated a great deal about their nearness to the American fleet. It was frustrating to be so near and yet so far. What Ozawa wanted now, any time, was to begin drawing the Americans of the big carrier fleet away from Leyte, to keep them just far enough away so that they must chase him, and to keep them engaged long enough for Kurita and his assisting forces to do their job at dawn on October 25.

Ozawa hoped the time was coming for action. Before dark there was another submarine scare, and it was accompanied by the same skillful maneuvering. At 1730, Ozawa made preparations for an engagement; he ordered the fleet to make 24 knots and be prepared to make 30 knots on an hour's notice. That order set the engineers scurrying on all the ships. It also delivered a severe blow at the fleet's oil supply, but Ozawa must risk his fuel now at all costs, for it was essential to his plan that he be able to maneuver at high speed when he aroused the suspicions of the Americans.

That night, as the fleet steamed rapidly on the same

course—which, if not changed, would run them into the northern tip of Luzon—again they picked up a radio broadcast. This time the radio officers were sure it was a submarine making contact with its base. Three hours later came another submarine contact of the same kind. Ozawa knew that he was moving into the action zone, and next morning he would be ready for anything.

The Americans were becoming ever more alert to the possibility of some unpleasantness. On the morning of October 22, the escort carriers of the Seventh Fleet fueled and launched their morning strikes against the Japanese airfields, to keep the enemy's head down, so to speak. They were doing a good job of this, so much so that in the Third Fleet Halsey was not really worried about the air potential of the Japanese in the islands, and was hoping to continue his plan of sending two task groups to Ulithi for replenishment. When they came back filled up with spirit and matériel, he would send the other two groups to do the same job. There was a good deal of relaxation in the jeep carrier fleet as they fueled the destroyers, and that attitude continued on October 23. But the fleet was alert: the destroyer Edmonds reported a sound contact ahead of her carrier, 1600 yards away at 0800 on October 23, and the formation turned away to avoid the "enemy." The Edmonds went into action, her sonar blipping. She crossed and crisscrossed the area—and found nothing. She dropped a dye marker, and then went back to the formation, her captain having drawn the rueful conclusion that he had been hoodwinked by a school of fish.

One thing became apparent to the pilots of the escort carriers this day: from somewhere the Japanese were pulling in a lot of planes. The evidence was all around them. The Americans set out to hit fields on the Visayans and Mindanao, and on Negros. On the latter at noon on October 23, they hit Bacolod, Alicante, Fabrica, and Carolina fields, and accounted for 25 planes on the ground, shooting down one Japanese in the air. This was a considerably different story from the one the pilots had been encountering during the past few days. They lost 2 fighters to antiaircraft, and when they came home from the strikes they reported at least a dozen Japanese planes left operational on those fields of Negros. That evening of the 23rd, the jeep carriers kept their planes in the air late to protect the beaches and the ships in the harbor.

Rear Admiral T. L. Sprague was following a plan that he had worked over very carefully in his mind. "Tommy" Sprague was a careful commander; for one thing, he had made sure his men knew why they were fighting and what was going on in this Philippines operation. Before the invasion began, he had sent a message to the men of the jeep carriers, going back a little bit into history and giving his men some background. He went back to the beginnings of the Japanese fleet as a modern weapon of warfare:

For 50 years the growth of the Imperial Japanese Navy has been watched with increasing concern by the government of the United States. A successful naval war with China in 1894 and '95, a successful war with Russia in 1904 and '05, a successful naval war with Germany in 1914 to '18, have marked the progress of the Japanese toward domination of the Western Pacific. The ruthless lust for power of the military, naval, and business leaders of Japan led them to overestimate these successes.

At first secretly and later openly, they violated the provisions of the Treaty of Versailles and of the arms limitations conferences. Contrary to their solemn agreements they fortified their mandated islands and built more vessels than were permitted by the treaties. Three years ago Japan had the unbelievable effrontery to challenge the position of the United States in the Pacific Ocean. On December 7, 1941, they made their infamous attack on Pearl Harbor. The first Japanese bomb that burst shattered forever our patient efforts to live in peace with the present leaders of Japan and it abruptly awakened the fighting spirit, the courage, and the resources which must inevitably destroy this Imperial Japanese Navy.

There was a statement of aim that would have made Admiral Kinkaid proud, and Admiral Sprague was doing his best to live up to it.

The escort carriers, eighteen in all, were divided into three groups of 6 each, with destroyers and destroyer escorts to protect them largely from submarine attack, and to lay smoke in case of serious aerial attacks. Generally speaking, all the carriers were disposed to the northern end of the operating area, about opposite the middle of Samar Island. Rear Admiral C. A. F. Sprague was farthest north, with a third of the carriers; Rear Admiral Felix Stump was in the middle; and Rear Admiral Tommy Sprague's group was farthest south, operating at the entrance to Leyte Gulf.

Since the beginning of the landings, Admiral Tommy Sprague had been pasting the Japanese airfields regularly, and even though they felt the new pressure, they planned to do more of the same on October 24.

There were other signs of increasing action by the enemy noted by Admiral Sprague and his carriers. For one thing, dispatches indicated a concentration of enemy surface craft in the western Philippines. Some 50 enemy boats up to 50 feet long had been observed camouflaged in the mouth of the Agusan River, in northern Mindanao. The escort carrier planes had destroyed 7 luggers and damaged another 12 ships that day. That night of the 23rd the American PT boats were out, with the dual purpose of acting as night eyes for the fleet, guarding the approaches to Leyte Gulf against sneak attack, and smashing anything of the enemy's that moved. Usually on such nights the Japanese made some attempt to reinforce or resupply with small boats.

For example, take the activity of PT 128 that night, a boat commanded by Lieutenant G. J. Azarigian:

At 1700 PT 128 left Liloan Bay, on Panaon Island, in company with PT 130 (Lieutenant I. D. Malcolm) to patrol Ormec Bay and destroy any enemy craft they might encounter.

It took them five hours to reach the station point, a mile off Manalian Point. There they began to follow the coastline, making 9 knots, their mufflers closed to eliminate noise, and operating their radar to find the enemy if he moved. Fifty minutes later their radar made contact with enemy vessels, eight barges bringing supplies. At 2305 the boats began a firing run, circling the barges and damaging all but one, which escaped to the south.

Another run and 3 of the barges sank, 2 more were dead in the water, and the rest were creeping along. The boats then made two figure-8 runs on the barges, firing all the while, and taking small arms and machine gun fire. The Japanese fired a 3-inch shell from the island, and managed only to hit one of their own boats, nearly sinking it. The Americans kept after the other barges until they sank a 110-foot pontoon barge and most of the others, five in all of the A type and one SD sea truck. The type-A barges were carrying troops, and the SD sea truck was carrying trucks. There were perhaps 200 soldiers and several tons of supplies that would never get to the Leyte front.

The Americans had done a lot of shooting to accomplish this: 2500 rounds of .30 caliber ammunition, 4000 rounds of .50 caliber, 1100 rounds of 20 mm, 180 rounds of 37 mm, and 220 rounds of 40 mm.

But it had been a successful night. "All runs were successful," said Lieutenant Azarigian with obvious satisfaction.

This reinforcement of Leyte, and the efforts of the Japanese at sea, was coming under the eyes of the superior American commanders more and more as the hours passed. They learned of the little tragedies, the successes, and the question marks. USS *Suwannee,* for example, lost a fighter on one sweep that day, and did not know the fate of its pilot, Lieutenant Helwig, who parachuted from his plane just 300 feet above the ground. His friends saw the parachute open just before the pilot hit a rice paddy. Had he lived?

The admirals of the fleets, of course, could not know or —so cruel are the fortunes of war—could they pay any official attention to the plight of a single flier.

The concern of Admiral Kinkaid, quite properly, was the success of his landing operation. Although command of the troops ashore had now been transferred to the army, General MacArthur was still afloat, and Kinkaid's responsibility would not end until the success of the landing was assured. He had taken all the precautions he could.

He had disposed the submarines of the Seventh Fleet so they would give early warning of the movement of the enemy, particularly any movements from the Brunei Bay area, where the major battle units of the Japanese fleet had been observed earlier. He had submarines off Makassar Strait, in the entrances to the Celebes and Sulu seas, and off Hainan and Luzon, in cooperation with the Pacific Fleet submarines. As noted, the Seventh Fleet submarines caught the Kurita force, and had already reduced it, certainly doing their job. Unfortunately, the Pacific Fleet submarines were off stalking targets and had missed the Ozawa force. As for the area east of the Philippines, this was where Admiral Halsey was expected to operate with his carriers of the Third Fleet, and his efforts were to be supplemented by land-based planes from Palau and Saipan.

The *Darter*'s message of 0200 on the 22nd had given the alarm with the report of three large ships off the southern entrance to Palawan Passage. But the contact had been lost and air searches made that day had been unsuccessful in reestablishing it.

The next morning, a stream of submarine messages came to Kinkaid on his flagship. The *Darter* began again, reporting eleven combat ships. Then came the *Bream* with her report of the *Aoba* and its companions, and the welcome news that the *Bream* had sunk one and damaged another. Then came the *Darter* again, with her report of sinking the *Atago* and hitting the *Takao*. Then came the *Dace* with her report of sinking another big ship, although no one then knew it was the *Maya*. Then came a report from the *Angler* about big capital ships.

Admiral Kinkaid was definitely uneasy. The X Corps had gone into army hands the day before, but General Hodge's XXIV Corps had just declared its "independence" at noon on the 23rd, and the situation was still very definitely in balance. The cargo ships were hustling in along the beaches to unload—all to the good considering the landings as accomplished, but quite a frightening matter if one considered the possibility of Japanese battleships ranging along those beaches. Still, from Admiral Kinkaid's point of view, everything was as it ought to be on the afternoon of October 23. He had his three groups of escort carriers, outside but ranged along Leyte Gulf, north to south, and to the east stood Halsey's 3 carrier groups, and the fast battleships of the Third Fleet, plus all the other supporting ships. Kinkaid approved. He examined Halsey's disposition:

"Well," he said, "that's exactly what I would do if I were stationing these carriers myself," and he was very pleased with what Halsey had done in his behalf.

By the evening of October 23, Kinkaid was quite sure that the Japanese were launching a major effort from the west. He sent out warnings to that effect to MacArthur, Halsey, Nimitz, and to Admiral King.

Halsey and his men were watching carefully. Task Force 38—the carrier force—conducted long-range searches southwest to northwest on the morning and afternoon of October 22, including the Sibuyan Sea and the waters west of Luzon for 100 miles. McCain was on his way to Ulithi, but the other three groups of carriers did the same on October 23, with no positive results.

By the 23rd it had become apparent from air sightings and from submarine sightings, notably in the South China Sea, that the Japs were milling around and there was a distinct possibility that large-scale countermeasures might be undertaken. Viewed from our standpoint, the hazards of such countermeasures seemed to be so great that it was difficult to believe that the Japanese would undertake them. But by the night of the 23rd it was apparent that something on a grand scale was underfoot and the decision was made to move in close to the east coast of the Philippines, to project reinforced searches across the Philippines into the South China Sea, to find out just what was going on.

Of course, Halsey had his problems, too.

"If you will remember," said Carney, "beginning with the 10th of October at Okinawa these carriers and their air groups had been fighting almost continuously for fourteen days. They needed replenishment and they needed rest in the worst way. Nevertheless, this was no time to give too great consideration to that sort of thing."

And Halsey had another problem, not known to many people. Vice Admiral Marc Mitscher, his carrier officer and commander of Task Force 38, had suffered a heart attack not long before. He was still with the fleet—which he certainly would not have been had Nimitz and King known of his condition—but a great deal of his work was now being done by his Chief of Staff, Commodore Arleigh Burke, who was trying to relieve his commander of as much detail and trouble as possible.

Halsey's staff sat around in flag plot on the *New Jersey* and considered the alternatives they might have to face. For one thing, they were sure the Japanese would somehow try to surprise them; this was the Japanese tactic all through the war, and Halsey had become familiar with 't —sometimes bitterly so—in those hectic days in the South Pacific. One thing Halsey was certain of: the Japanese were going to try to use their carriers, and they would be very likely to use a technique that involved the Luzon airfields as points of shuttle to and from those carriers. This seemed particularly likely because, as Mitscher had noted in the Formosa air battle, the Japanese planes were so varied in type that the air forces must be hurting. It would be logical for the Japanese to take off from carriers, and then continue fighting from land bases, under the conditions that seemed to prevail. After all, that was precisely what the Japanese had tried to do in the June battle off the Marianas. It was a carrier war, and had been from the time of the black December 7 at Pearl Harbor. In recent months it had become even more of a carrier war as the Americans received the new big fleet carriers, improved light carriers, and supplementary escort carriers which could guard convoys and supply planes to the carrier fleet.

Halsey's staff, like Kinkaid's but with more strategic responsibility, had to make some estimates of possible enemy action, and then make plans on the basis of the estimates.

"The normal reaction of the Japanese commander faced with an emergency was to send an operation order to his command saying 'Attack with all forces available and destroy the enemy!'" said Commander Gilven M. Slonim, Halsey's assistant intelligence officer. "Frequently such stereotyped operation orders were intercepted. When analyzed in the light of available forces many were meaningless because the commander did not have sufficient forces to come anywhere near destroying the enemy."

Soon a decision would have to be made. Right now, on October 22, more information was needed.

It was 2345 when the messages about the Japanese fleet began to come in to the Third Fleet. The first message, for example, had been the *Darter*'s first sighting of the 3 ships; that message had been sent at 1725. But even in modern warfare, communications sometimes leave something to be desired. Messages piled up in code rooms and radio rooms, and this was the bane of the commander of a force. It would play a part in the actions to come, too.

On the basis of the *Darter*'s message, Admiral Halsey extended the search of his planes into the Sibuyan Sea for the next day. Admiral Bogan's group was fueling on October 23, and then was ordered to move into position to make searches to the west on the morning of October 24 that would include Coron Bay. That decision was made and the message sent out just after midnight of October 23, as Admiral Shima was heading for Coron Bay, following his own orders.

At 0830 on October 23 Halsey received a message that Kinkaid and his staff had composed the night before, indicating just how seriously Kinkaid regarded the Japanese threat against his landings.

It was "the first phase of the buildup of the magnified Tokyo Express runs against Leyte," said the message. The Seventh Fleet believed a tanker group had gone to Coron Bay to fuel the enemy force, and he regarded it as serious, referring to

. . . major task force of enemy fleet which has been assembling for several days in southern Formosa. Submarine reports indicate three probable battleships approaching from the southern position to arrive Coron Bay tonight Monday. Another group of 11 enemy ships with many radars could arrive about the same time. There are indications of a concentration of large number of enemy aircraft in the Luzon area. It is extremely important that early preparations for enemy operations be DISLUIBED [disturbed?] Com 5th Air Force and 13th Air Force requested continued thorough reconnaissance Coron Bay and approaching routes and to strike as practicable day and night. Com

3rd fleet requested strike Coron Bay earliest practicable and extend search as far as practicable to westward and northwestward. Primary objective enemy
combat ships and aircraft. It is possible that enemy
carriers will support surface forces and strike from
west on Palawan. . . .

As far as Coron Bay was concerned, Halsey was already
on record as ordering a strike as quickly as possible. He
still thought it possible to continue with the plan—letting
McCain's group reach Ulithi and rearm and rest until
October 29.

Would it be possible?

Not long after receipt of Kinkaid's worried message
about the buildup, Halsey heard from the Fifth Bomber
Command that one of their planes had sighted 4 destroyers,
2 heavy cruisers, and a light cruiser. Was this still another
force?

Halsey continued his planning for strikes on Luzon and
Lingayen Gulf, using Admiral Sherman's force for the
purpose. But the aerial search reports continued negative,
while the submarine reports became ever more exciting
that afternoon and evening, with talk of the *Dace*'s sinking
of her heavy ship, the *Bream*'s exploit off Manila, and then
the *Darter*'s message about the Kurita force.

The night carrier *Independence* was ordered to launch
night search planes. But tomorrow would tell the tale.

9

ATTACK!

On October 23, while the Americans were searching out the Japanese fleet and finding three of the units that were at sea, at least tentatively, the Japanese air forces in the Philippines were getting ready for their big effort. According to the Sho plan, the land-based air forces would exert maximum effort beginning on the morning of October 24, and the Second Air Fleet had been ferried down from Formosa for that purpose, a group of 196 planes of all kinds.

The Japanese air commanders were well aware of the importance of their mission. "The success or failure of this attack was to have a tremendous effect upon the breakthrough of the naval surface units into Leyte Bay."

The Japanese were not in a position for several days to conduct the most effective air searches, pinned down as they were by the planes from the Third Fleet and the escort carriers, and holding their air strength until the last. Thus, between October 20 and 23, the Japanese were unaware of the whereabouts of Admiral Halsey and his fleet. But at night on the 23rd it was imperative that they know, so the Japanese commander, Admiral Shigero Fukudome, ordered night search by flying boats, and two waves of dawn scouts. The pilots were told to be ready to man their planes at dawn.

Just after midnight the Japanese sighted a large force of ships at 90 degrees, some 250 miles off Manila, and Fukudome decided to launch a pre-dawn attack. The weather was vile, unfortunately, but there was nothing else to be done. It was imperative, the Emperor's wish in fact, that the Americans be destroyed. The planes took off in two waves and attacked. But the weather stopped them, and only one bomber even caught sight of a ship before they were forced to turn around and go home.

At 0630 the attacks were resumed, and this time the Japanese found three groups of Task Force 38 lined up along the eastern shore of the Philippines, 150 to 200 miles from shore.

They moved in to attack, and the aerial battle began. Here is the way the Japanese saw the battle:

At 0853 hours a group of surface craft with four regular aircraft carriers and two light aircraft carriers as its nucleus was discovered at 80 degrees and 160 miles off Manila. At 0900 hours another group with 2 carriers was found 50 to 60 miles north of the first group and at 0940 hours the third group with 3 aircraft carriers was spotted east of the San Bernardino Strait.

The first and second waves of attack planes converged upon the first group of surface craft and made a direct hit with 250 kg bombs on a large regular carrier. They set fire to one battleship, set fire and inflicted considerable damage to a cruiser, and shot down at least 32 enemy planes. Our losses were 67 planes missing. The third [3 carrier bombers] took off in the afternoon but returned owing to bad weather. Following this, 24 planes in three groups took to the air in search of the enemy's third group with carriers. . . .

What had actually happened was that the Japanese during the day did damage the destroyer *Leutze*, the oiler *Ashtabula*, and *LST 552*, and caused the sinking of the light carrier *Princeton*. Thus the Japanese claims were not so ridiculous, giving them credit for mistaking a destroyer for a battleship; in fact they did more damage than they claimed.

The story of the *Princeton* and the Japanese attack is a sad but poignant one; it shows the bravery of the enemy, his luck for a moment, and the bad luck of the American forces.

The morning had begun with dawn search teams launched by the American carriers. They headed aloft and then spread out to cover the west side of the island of Luzon, the Sibuyan Sea, which lies in the middle of the Philippines, and the Sulu Sea, which lies between Borneo and the Philippines. All three task groups had been pulled back toward the Philippine coast; now Admiral Sherman was to the north with the *Princeton* and his other carriers, just off Luzon. Meanwhile, Admiral Bogan was near San Bernardino Strait, and Admiral Davison's force was south of that, off Leyte Gulf. All carriers began flying searches that morning, and just after 0800 a plane from Bogan's *Intrepid* found Admiral Kurita's force in the Sibuyan Sea; ten minutes later, Admiral Halsey had the information. The alert was on. In flag plot the words became crisp and the thought was about the strikes to be made at the enemy force. It would all be done by air. It must be remembered that the seas around the Philippines had been Japanese waters since 1942, and were presumed to be mined effectively. The Americans had discovered in the invasion of Leyte that this was true. Thus, although it would seem a simple matter for the battleships and cruisers to move into San Bernardino Strait and trap the oncoming Japanese, Admiral Nimitz had issued strict orders that no ships were to go into the strait without his expressed permission.

While the Americans were preparing to launch their strikes against the enemy, the Japanese were coming in on Sherman's force. This also happened to be the force in which Admiral Mitscher was riding in the *Lexington,* his flagship.

During the night of October 23–24 those Japanese flying boats had effectively spotted the task group and were almost constantly over it, tracking. Night fighters were put up and kept the Japanese at a distance, but they had no intention of attacking. Their mission was to observe. A night fighter shot down one "snooper" at 0227, but they kept on buzzing around and just before 0600 the radar screens showed five separate observation planes at different points on the screens.

"The enemy," said Admiral Sherman, "was evidently well aware of our position, at least of our task group, if not of the others." He was aware of the others, and yet

Sherman's force was to bear the brunt of the big air strike called under the Sho operation.

At dawn, Sherman's carriers launched their searches. The planes, fighters and dive bombers, were armed with bombs and, in addition, the decks of the carriers were now crowded with torpedo bombers, waiting for news of the enemy so they might strike.

On the *Princeton,* operations began at 0520 with a call to General Quarters, and plans were made for a long, dangerous, and tiring day. Breakfast was prepared and served at battle stations.

The sun rose that morning at 0646. Already the *Essex* and the *Lexington* had launched their searches, which were to fan out 300 miles and report. The *Langley* was responsible for anti-snooper patrol and anti-submarine patrol, and she launched those forces, plus a 4-plane combat air patrol that would circle over the task group. The *Essex* also launched a 20-plane fighter sweep that was sent against Japanese airfields around Manila. The *Princeton*'s responsibility, which she fulfilled, was to launch a force of 8 fighters for the Combat Air Patrol.

The Japanese spotter planes were swarming around the carrier force by this time. By 0750 the Combat Air Patrol planes from the *Langley* had shot down two Japanese snoopers, and the *Princeton*'s planes shot down two more.

At about 0750 the search radar picked up a large force of Japanese planes "stacked" in the air, from 25,000 feet on down. The Japanese were about 75 miles west of the task group. First came the report of one enemy group, and then a report of a second. It was an exciting moment because the Japanese planes were discovered just after a contact report from search planes which indicated the presence of Kurita's force in the Sibuyan Sea. Admiral Sherman was ready to send his torpedo planes against these forces, so they were on deck. Then he had to put up more fighters to join the Combat Air Patrol from the carriers. That was the next order of business: the planes in the air were directed toward the enemy, and then the *Langley* and the *Princeton* each launched a dozen more fighters, and the *Essex* launched seven.

It was not enough. A few minutes later even *more* Japanese planes were spotted coming in from the west,

60 miles away. At 0831 the *Lexington* launched her remaining dozen fighter planes. The Japanese, by coming in such strength, had already accomplished one thing: they delayed the Sherman force.

What was now at stake was the life of the group, and Sherman prepared for radical sea maneuvers. Fortunately the weather was very spotty, and he could run in and out of a number of rain squalls in the vicinity. It was in the squall to escape the Japanese, out to launch and recover, and back in again.

"We were kept pretty busy with the attack for the next several hours," said Admiral Sherman.

The first planes headed toward the enemy, and soon the radar screens on the ships became confused. The largest raid of all was the third reported, and Commander David McCampbell, the *Essex* Air Group Commander, took on this one.

McCampbell had been spotted in his fighter plane on the catapult, fueling for the strike against the Sibuyan Sea force of Admiral Kurita. He was to lead the fighters. But with the coming in of this third force of enemy planes, Admiral Sherman's orders changed all that. McCampbell said:

". . . we got word of this raid coming in, had already closed to about 45 miles and so I was launched in a scramble. In other words we scrambled all the fighters who were available at that particular time, . . . we got seven off."

Even though his plane was not completely full of gas McCampbell took off and headed toward the enemy.

> . . . we intercepted them about 30 miles from our own ships. They had altitude on us at the time, about the time we sighted them they started to turn to the left, apparently searching or having overshot the position they thought we were in. We never figured out why they turned to the left. Anyway, when we hit them as they were making their left turn, they continued on. The bombers dove on through the overcast, our second combat team was to hit the stragglers or the bombers, and I told them that I would take

my combat team up and start from the top and work down.

Due to a mixup in the communications there, we had to shift channels after we got off, for 5 of them went down on the bombers and that left only my wingman and me up topside. When the bombers went through the overcast the 5 went after them, I think they got 12 or 13 planes out of that. The Jap fighters went into a Lufberry circle. There were about 40 of them and it's a pretty difficult sort of thing. We didn't even attempt to make a run while they were in this big Lufberry circle but we had altitude on them and we just circled over them and watched them and waited for them to make a move.

McCampbell's wingman was Lieutenant (jg) Roy Rushing. McCampbell called him on the radio:

. . . and told him I thought that they must be running out of gas pretty soon and I knew that we had plenty of gas so they'd have to head somewhere and that's when we would work them over; and they circled for maybe ten or fifteen minutes and headed for Manila. These were the fighters only. The bombers had all scattered and had been pretty well taken care of.

So Rushing and I followed them back to Manila. We were engaged with them for about an hour and 35 minutes. We finally, after much screaming for help, got one other man to help us out there for a little while and he ran out of ammunition and turned off and went to the ship.

[They only got one.] He was one of the 5 that had gone down with the bombers. The ship didn't support us because they had another big raid coming in at the same time and they had launched the rest of their fighters to support the second raid. So Roy and I just took it easy and we'd wait until some joker climbed a little too high or dragged a little too far behind.

They were scissoring very nicely, they kept good formation and their weave, their tactics, were very similar to our own, and perhaps had we not been familiar with those tactics it wouldn't have been so easy for us. We just bided our time there and I don't think any of them ever got a shot at us.

He and I together knocked down 15 of them and we burned 15 and claimed a couple of more probables in there because you'd see them smoke and they'd pull off and go down, well, you didn't have to watch them to see where the hell they were going. But anyway we followed them all the way in, back in to Manila and when they dove down through the clouds apparently to go to their fields we were very low on gas and out of ammunition and we thought it was time to go home.

I got back to our own ship. They had the deck spotted for takeoff and couldn't take me aboard so I had to land on one of the other carriers. I had six gallons of gas and two rounds of ammunition when I got back. Roy had a little more.

While the fighters were doing their job, the task group was maneuvering in and out of those rain squalls, making a very elusive target for the Japanese, so elusive that no successful attacks were carried out.

By 0845 the second enemy air attack had been broken up, and Admiral Sherman ordered the carriers to get ready to make their strikes against the Japanese ships as quickly as they could. The Japanese were scattered; all that showed on the radar scopes was an occasional loner, and only one within 25 miles of the formation.

At about 0900 the carriers were busy recovering fighters who were as low on fuel and ammunition, or almost so, as McCampbell had been. He landed on the *Langley*, others landed elsewhere.

The *Princeton* and the other carriers moved to a course of 065 degrees into the wind, at 24 knots, to begin flight operations. Six of the *Princeton*'s loaded torpedo bombers were moved to the hangar deck and spotted in a fore-and-aft line on the port side. The *Princeton* recovered 10 fighters and was getting ready to recover two more. The gasoline detail was fueling the planes. Everything was moving splendidly.

At 0912 the *Essex* had reported a possible "bogey"

about 6 miles to the northwest, but that was all. Otherwise, life was very quiet.

Or as quiet as it could be on a carrier that was landing shot-up planes, some of them bearing wounded men.

At 0935 a single Japanese plane was spotted through the hazy clouds. She was diving, coming in on a shallow plane on the *Princeton*. The 20 mm and 40 mm anti-aircraft guns of the *Princeton* and the ships around her began to open up.

At 0938 the *Mobile* came on the talk-between-ships circuit.

"Dive bomber 160 in a dive!" shouted her radioman.

But the *Princeton* did not even hear the transmission, because the noise from the anti-aircraft was so intense. The forward batteries were firing as rapidly as they could get off the shots.

On the bridge, Captain W. H. Buracker ordered the quartermaster to steer 20 degrees left, in order to miss the bomber. The plane kept boring in, and dropped one 250 kg bomb about 75 feet forward of the after elevator on the port side of the ship. The plane passed over, and was caught by American fighters, which shot it down in short order, after it had passed through the fleet at about 1000 feet and leveled off.

When the bomb hit, Captain Buracker was not particularly worried. It was a small bomb. He thought his damage-control men would be able to slip a patch over the hole in the deck and get back to flight operations in a few minutes. But he was not reckoning with that bomb and the 6 loaded torpedo planes on the hangar deck immediately below. The bomb passed directly through one of those torpedo planes and exploded between the hangar and the second deck. Flames shot down through engineering space aft and then back into the hangar, and spread.

Immediately after the bomb hit, thick black smoke was seen to be issuing from around the edges of the forward elevator, from the hole in the flight deck, and from every access to the hangar deck aft of the island structure. Word was passed on the General Announcing circuit:

"Fire in the hangar deck, fire in the hangar deck."

The Captain immediately called radar plot on the . . . Captain's Command circuit, to reach the Executive Officer, but that officer had already left his battle station to proceed to the scene of the fire.

Below decks, the bomb hit had not been considered very serious either. It was felt as a dull jar, and the First Lieutenant did not receive any immediate report from any station on deck or from any repair party.

The First Lieutenant ordered the conflagration station to turn on the hangar sprinkling system. The order was acknowledged, but there was no positive report that it had been done. Almost immediately the personnel in the station asked permission to abandon the station because of the heat. Was the sprinkling system on? For that was important.

"Aye, aye, sir," came the word to damage control. "We are abandoning."

The bomb had struck very close to that conflagration station, where three men were stationed. The bomb hit so close that fragments were driven up through the deck at the station, and it filled with smoke and heat immediately. The talker at the phone was wounded severely, but kept on. The other two men were driven out of the station and then could not get back in to rescue the third man. A sailor in an asbestos suit came to help, a few minutes later, and tried to get in from the port gallery walkway, but the heat was so intense that the sweat inside his asbestos suit turned to steam.

In a few moments the whole deck was burning furiously; all six TBM's were on fire, and all were loaded with torpedoes and full tanks of gasoline. Aft, a man managed to reach the panel control box and pushed the buttons for the sprinkling system. There was no result. A water hose was brought out, but the pressure failed.

Lieutenant Auclair, Hangar Deck Officer, went to the fire station on the port side and turned on the pressure for two hoses. He ran to turn on the hangar sprinkling amidships, but found the control switches smoking, and telephone talkers there overcome by smoke. He found the Executive Officer and reported. By that time the first talker was dead and the conflagration station had blown up.

On the bridge, Captain Buracker reported to Admiral Sherman that he had taken a bomb and would keep him informed. The ship was making 24 knots. Sherman asked if the *Princeton* wanted to slow down; the Captain asked the Chief Engineer and that officer said it was not necessary. The engineering plant was all right, except it was getting pretty smoky down there.

One of the problems, from the beginning, was the impairment of the fire main pressure, caused when the electrical systems in the hangar sprinklers shorted out.

Commander J. N. Murphy, the Executive Officer, now found it virtually impossible to get into the hangar, and he conferred with Lieutenant Auclair. The Executive Officer tried to get the sprinklers operated manually from the third deck, but there still was no pressure.

The gas tanks on the planes began exploding, and so did the ammunition in the guns and gun belts, and that stored in the hangar. Because of the communications failures, some time elapsed before the Captain knew that the water pressure aft had failed. Then he slowed to 18 knots. He was prepared to stop if necessary. His job now was to get the men out of the spaces below, before they were overcome by heat and smoke.

The repair officers, Lieutenant (jg) Carson and Ensign Christie, kept working to open valves that would divert water into the sprinkling system and hoses going to the log room. They went to the barbershop to find the valves.

In the main engine control room a flash followed the dull jar of the bomb, went into the after engine room through the vent ducts, and burned the Chief of the Watch. Heavy black smoke filled that room, and almost immediately it was cut off from communication with the rest of the ship.

Within one minute after the bomb hit, the forward engine room was filling with smoke "to the point of suffocation and darkness." All hands were ordered to put on their gas masks, even as explosions could be heard from the planes in the hangar.

On deck, the gunnery stations aft to port reported that the heat to port was growing so intense that they must evacuate. Soon the starboard stations reported the same. The Gunnery Officer had them stay awhile, and ordered the gunner's mates to watch the ready service magazines and sprinkle them if the temperature hit 100 degrees.

Aft on the flight deck the heat was becoming so intense that Lieutenant Commander Curtis, the Assistant Air Officer, took shelter under the platform. He and his men tried to work their way forward but could not, and eventually they retreated to the fantail.

At 0941 came a message from Admiral Sherman: "How many planes do you have in the air?"

"Ten," was the answer.

So Sherman began asking the other ships in the task group. The *Lexington* could take 6 planes, the *Essex* 4. They were sent to the other carriers, and that problem was resolved.

There were many incidents of heroism. A carpenter's mate went below into the smoke to try to start fire pumps, but he found the power out in that region of the ship. The Chief Engineer asked the Captain if there was any chance of controlling the fire. Buracker said he thought so. The Chief Engineer said things were getting pretty bad below but they would keep operating. Worst of all, he said, they had lost all contact with the after fire room.

The First Lieutenant continued his work, and was so busy trying to find the extent of the damage that when the Captain asked him for a report he said he was too busy to give one. Captain Buracker had to be content with that for the moment.

Ten minutes after the Japanese bomb struck the deck of the *Princeton*, men were going over the side to escape the intense heat that was building aft. Lieutenant Commander Curtis, who was aft, called the Air Officer and suggested that if the ship could be turned out of the wind it might help keep the heat from building up aft. Captain Buracker agreed and told Admiral Sherman that the *Princeton* was going to change course.

This decision presented a whole new situation, which demanded many changes. The cruiser *Reno* and the destroyers *Gatling, Irwin,* and *Cassin Young* were designated to stay with the burning carrier, while the rest of the task group proceeded into the wind, operating aircraft. There was no other way. The Japanese had been found and the war could not be delayed for the *Princeton.*

The *Princeton* began to move on her new course, coming very close to the *South Dakota* which moved to clear her, and as she moved, the engine room began to clear of smoke. This was reported to the bridge and gave the Captain some satisfaction. It was the first little victory they had attained over the fire.

The men below were in a bad position. At 0955 they reported that the bilges were filling with hot water from the fire fighting, and that this increased the heat so much in the engine room that men were beginning to pass out. The battle dressing stations in the sick bay, below decks, were filling with smoke, and the doctors and corpsmen had to abandon the area. In the wardroom some 20 wounded were being treated, mostly for burns.

At 0956 steering control in the pilot house went out, and steering was immediately shifted to the after station, with the Captain controlling from the bridge. There was no smoke in steering aft, because the vent had been shut off as soon as it started to enter.

By this time, men on the flight deck were pushing the planes overboard; soon 5 fighters slipped into the sea. The gas was drained out of the mains and dropped back into storage without any trouble. Gasoline on deck never did become a problem. But there were plenty of other problems now. Captain Buracker watched from his bridge as they developed.

It was two minutes past ten, to be exact, that the first major explosion occurred and this was from the torpedoes which were mounted in the planes in the hangar. These explosions were severe. The first one was aft and blew out the after elevator. Shortly thereafter there was another one forward in the hangar and about five minutes after ten the forward elevator was knocked up. There was a hole put in the flight deck between the elevators and practically the entire flight deck between the elevators was buckled upward.

Before the forward elevator was knocked out I could see from Ship Control Station in the island structure the smoke and raging fire in the hangar, but the elevator, flush with the flight deck, kept the smoke from coming up in the bridge. When the forward elevator was knocked out it released the smoke and fire to come up the island structure and then I had to take steps to get the personnel out of the island. Those explosions always caused a number of flying fragments. There were some casualties on the bridge. One man, a signalman, was so seriously injured that he died before we could get him off the ship.

Captain Buracker told the people on the bridge to abandon; they moved down over the forward part of the bridge onto the crane, and then down onto the flight deck forward. They could not climb down the ladders and companionways because of the smoke and heat. He also ordered the Chief Engineer to secure below and get all personnel on deck.

"All hands topside," went the call over the general announcing system. The Captain could only hope that every station would hear.

Buracker met Commander Murphy, the Executive Officer, on the forward part of the flight deck and said it was time to execute Salvage Control, Phase One. This meant that most of the crew would abandon ship, and only those necessary to fight the fire would remain, plus a few to man the guns.

As soon as he saw the explosions tearing the *Princeton*, Admiral Sherman detailed the cruiser *Birmingham* to join the standby party. The *Princeton* had moved about 5 miles astern of the task group by this time. And now, the good reason for the heavy screen could be seen. A Japanese air raid began, and as the fighters scrambled, it became apparent that there was a problem. The *Princeton* had been responsible for the Combat Air Patrol that morning. With her out of action, air patrol was diminished, and 2 Japanese fighters got through the air screen and began to approach the *Princeton* with what Admiral Carney referred to as the airman's instinct for a cripple. The *Reno*'s antiaircraft guns began to pound and they shot down the Japanese planes that were moving in.

Captain Thomas B. Inglis was in command of the *Birmingham*, and as senior officer present, he was in command now of the ships that were trying to help the *Princeton*.

When I found myself senior officer present of this group . . . I instructed the destroyers to concentrate on recovering the *Princeton*'s personnel. The *Princeton* had abandoned ship except for the Captain and perhaps forty or fifty men. . . . There were at the time we were approaching *Princeton* something over a thousand men in the water. I also instructed the *Reno* to circle this little group in order to provide anti-aircraft protection and anti-submarine protection to the limit of her ability. . . . The *Reno* was an anti-aircraft cruiser, had an unusually good battery of anti-aircraft weapons, and also was equipped with submarine sound detection gear and depth charges and was therefore quite effective. . . .

Two of the destroyers were alongside the *Princeton* when the *Birmingham* arrived, and it was only with difficulty that the bigger ship managed to "elbow" them aside and come in, hoses laid out and ready.

I got alongside the *Princeton* at about 1100 and immediately thereafter began fighting the fire. I found that it was necessary to run a line to the *Princeton* in order to keep the two ships together since the *Princeton*, with her high sides, made faster leeway than the *Birmingham*. . . . My plan was to start fighting the fires from the forward end of the *Princeton* and as they were extinguished to work aft. . . .

After about half an hour they seemed to make headway and Captain Inglis called for a party of volunteers. About 40 men boarded the carrier and began work there. They continued to work for two and a half hours; by that time they had all the fires under control except one—but that was a bad one, very close to the carrier's after magazine.

The destroyers moved about, picking up men. The *Morrison* picked up a number. The *Irwin* picked up some more, and also took on wounded. By the end of the day, she had some 600 survivors from the *Princeton* and took them to Ulithi. The *Morrison* had come over with the *Birmingham* when Admiral Sherman had decided the *Princeton* needed more help. She moved alongside the *Prince-*

ton, on the lee side, a daring gesture compounded by mis-understanding of instructions from Captain Inglis, to deliver some artificers and engine room men that Captain Buracker asked for when things seemed to be coming under control. But then the *Morrison* became fouled in the overhanging sponsons of the carrier's starboard gun positions, when Commander W. H. Price, the ship's Captain, had to move forward to escape the fire and smoke. He got hoses off his ship and onto the *Princeton*. Lieutenant Bradley, the Assistant First Lieutenant of the *Princeton*, came back aboard from the *Morrison* along with an enlisted man from the hull department.

At about 1300 the *Morrison* was ready to move, but she could not; she was stuck between the No. 2 and No. 3 stacks of the *Princeton*, and in the rolling her topside was taking a fearful mauling from the carrier's stacks and over-hang. Something had to give way, and in her case it was the foremast, the stacks, her searchlight platform, her forward director, and the port side of her bridge. While the *Morrison* was alongside, the *Princeton*'s navigator managed to go back aboard his ship and onto the bridge from the destroyer, and salvage a number of important papers, which he lowered by signal halyard to the men on the destroyer.

The weather, which had been spotty, was definitely worsening as the afternoon came on. This increased the damage to the *Morrison* and she tried to get the *Irwin* to pull her off, but the lines passed to the *Morrison* parted and after almost an hour the *Morrison* was still stuck fast to the carrier.

It was at that time [said Captain Buracker] that we thought there would be no question but that the fire would be put out in a matter of 20 to 30 minutes.

We had received considerable damage by that time but as far as we knew there was no damage below decks, and it was our thought that we would soon have the fire out. Then we would ventilate the spaces below, put the engineers down there, get up steam and bring the ship home. The ship was not very pretty . . . but at least we would bring her back.

The Captain was an optimist, no doubt about it. The Chief Engineer had just been below, wearing rescue breathing apparatus. He found doors hot to the touch, and the smoke so thick a flashlight beam would not penetrate it. The third deck below was hot and full of smoke, and when the Chief Engineer entered the forward engine room he had to hold a battle lantern a foot from the panel to read the gauges. When he was back on deck he advised the Captain that "it might be remotely possible to get the ship underway."

At 1330 the whole salvage project was endangered again by the coming of more Japanese planes. The *Birmingham* pulled away from the crippled carrier, Captain Inglis telling Captain Buracker he must move to fight the Japanese, and avoid a cluster of ships that made a beautiful target for the enemy.

The *Birmingham* recalled her fire-control party, and moved away with the destroyers and the *Reno*. Everyone, with the possible exception of the Chief Engineer of the *Princeton*, was optimistic about the chances for the carrier, and when the *Morrison* cleared away the debris and joined the screen there was something to cheer about. What a beating she had taken! Even a tractor and a jeep from the carrier's flight deck had fallen down on her.

The Japanese air raid flopped, partly because visibility had now gotten so bad at sea that it was possible to see only about 100 yards in all directions from the *Princeton*. The wind was rising, and hit 20 knots. It was raining and the seas were running heavily enough so that the men who had been fished out of the water could be glad they were not still there. The *Princeton* looked much better than one might expect; she was not listing, and she seemed to have about normal draft.

Just after 1400 a single Zero fighter swooped in and the *Reno* opened up with those powerful batteries of 20 and 40 mm guns. The Zero turned and disappeared into the growing cloud cover.

The *Birmingham* now made a report to Admiral Sherman:

"Fires on the *Princeton* now confined to after portion centered about bomb magazines. Prospects very good now. The *Morrison* has lost her foremast. The *Irwin* has one engine out of commission, result of debris in condenser. The *Birmingham* has superficial damage, including two 5-inch mounts out of commission. The *Reno* smashed one 40 mm mount while alongside." A carrier was not a safe ship for others to move about, obviously, with her big overhanging flight deck; but this damage seemed a small price to pay for what had been accomplished in getting the fires under control.

Yet things were not all that they seemed. That one Japanese "snooper" caused more trouble than he could ever have hoped to do.

Captain Buracker was not critical of anyone; he quite understood why the *Birmingham* had not wanted to remain dead in the water alongside the carrier when Japanese planes were overhead. "But the fire, which had been almost put out, started to build again as soon as we stopped fighting it when the ships cast off," he said.

He had signaled at the end of the alert for one of the destroyers to come alongside. The *Morrison* came. The Chief Engineer of the *Princeton* said men could get below; Gunner Grant and Ensign Geney went down to try and open sprinklers that would play on the forward magazines. They opened the valves but nothing happened.

A conference among the officers on the *Princeton* indicated that with the fire now so well under control, it might be feasible to take the ship under tow. The air attack had not developed further, and accordingly, as the *Birmingham* came by on the port side, a semaphore message was sent to her:

"CAN YOU TAKE ME IN TOW?"

"Affirmative," came the answer, and the *Birmingham* prepared to tow.

But now it was seen on the *Princeton* that the fires were gaining headway and that the *Morrison* simply did not have the hose power to put the fire out. So Captain Buracker asked that the *Reno* replace the *Morrison* and fight the fires again. But the *Reno* would take a beating if she came alongside, and the *Reno* could not take the tow either, because she had lost her towing reel on October 14 when a Japanese plane crashed into her fantail. It was decided that the *Birmingham* would come back, fight the fires to extinction, and then take the *Princeton* in tow.

All this took time, and the seas were rising and the wind whistling now. The *Birmingham* began approaching the injured carrier at around 1445 hours, with her bow at an angle to the windward port amidships of the *Princeton*. It was a very difficult approach, and the *Princeton* would drift away, so that the *Birmingham* had to drop off and try again. Consequently the fires burned, and it was not until 1515 that the *Birmingham* came close enough to the *Princeton* for a line to be successfully thrown over to the flight deck of the carrier.

In the meantime [said Captain Buracker], I had sent our air officer, Commander Bruce L. Harwood, with several other officers and men, a total of about 25, aft to the hangar to be there to take the lines and hoses from the *Birmingham* as soon as she could get alongside. I might say that Commander Harwood had been particularly conspicuous all day by his outstanding leadership in directing fire parties and in his constant disregard of personal danger.

There had been no serious explosions on the *Princeton* since 1020 that morning and now it was almost 1530. I had always been concerned about a compartment just aft of the hangar on the starboard side of the ship, which was our ready torpedo stowage and in which we had spare torpedo air flasks and also an overload of bombs which could not be accommodated in the main magazines below decks. I felt concern about this space not only for our own personnel, but also for the ships alongside. There had been fires raging around that space and in that immediate vicinity practically ever since the bomb hit at 0938 in the morning. The place was impossible to get into to attempt to jettison any of these explosive. Also . . . we had none of our own fire fighting pressure aft from practically the time the bomb hit. . . .

. . . I had been led to believe that TNT operates in strange ways at times, so I had hoped, and thought it quite possible, that the explosions that would come from that space had already done so or would not occur. There could have been some low-order detonations which couldn't be told from other explosions we had suffered. However, at 1523, while the *Birmingham* was still in the process of tying up on our port side aft, there was the most terrific explosion of the day in this space.

The explosion was as surprising as it was terrifying. I think it can be well compared to a small volcano. A considerable portion of the after part of the ship above decks was knocked into the air and fell in the water astern. Flying fragments, some huge, some small, burst outward and upward, showering the deck of the *Princeton* from stem to stern. . . .

Practically all of those of us remaining aboard the *Princeton* were injured, those of us who were not killed. Commander Harwood and his party aft in the hangar were all lost. Captain Hoskins, the prospective commanding officer of the *Princeton* (who had just recently come aboard so there had not been time to transfer command), had been standing with me amidships on the port side where we were to receive the lines from the bow of the *Birmingham*. When those of us in that immediate vicinity first hit the deck and then started to run forward to get behind some planes for protection, someone noticed that Captain Hoskins couldn't move. I turned around and saw his right foot was hanging by a shred.

I called for Commander Sala, our senior medical officer, who had been with us just before this explosion, but by some means unknown to him he found himself on the forecastle forward. He was injured. I did not realize this but he proceeded to render first aid treatment to Captain Hoskins. Captain Hoskins had fortunately fallen near a piece of line, which he, with great presence of mind, used to apply a tourniquet to his leg. The doctor made his way to him with some sulfa powder and morphine, using a sheath knife to cut off the part of the leg that was dangling. Shortly thereafter Dr. Sala himself was given treatment for his wounds.

Even with this explosion the *Princeton* was still not listing or going down. All the damage was above the waterline. The Captain wanted a tow and asked the *Birmingham* for it. But the *Birmingham* said she had been hurt by the blast and could not tow. The *Reno* could not tow. The destroyers were too small to tow. So the word went out to Admiral Sherman that the *Princeton* wanted a tow.

Captain Buracker knew that it would be some time before a towing vessel could detach itself from the task group, make its way to the *Princeton*, and get to work. So he decided to take everyone off the ship, temporarily at least, then bring them back when the towing vessel arrived.

In a short time we were able to get alongside some small boats from the destroyers on either side of our bow, forward. Then we proceeded to lower Captain Hoskins by means of a stretcher, then the wounded, and finally the remaining personnel. . . . Before this was done several inspections had been made below decks and throughout the accessible parts of the ship to assure ourselves that there were no living personnel remaining. At 1600 I left the *Princeton*, the last to leave.

Captain Buracker went to the *Birmingham* to receive a shock.

Here is the story of Commander Winston Folk, Executive Officer of the *Birmingham:*

At the time of the explosion on *Princeton* I was on the starboard side of the signal bridge, a few feet from the Captain. We were both struck by debris and knocked to the deck. As soon as I had sufficiently recovered I went to the Captain to see how he was. He had gotten to his feet and said he had been hit but felt that he was all right. At that time he directed me to ascertain the results of the explosion. I set out to do so, completely unprepared for the spectacle that was to greet me. I was still somewhat dazed myself and thought that the principal effects of the explosion had been in the bridge area. I found the main deck, for 140 of our 150 frames, covered with dead, dying, and wounded, and the few unwounded beginning to render first aid. The communication platform was in the same condition. It is impossible, even remotely, to describe the grisly scene of human fragmentation that unfolded before my eyes. I felt as if I were having a horrible nightmare and I remember wishing that I would hurry and wake up. . . .

. . . In the beginning we were still close to the *Princeton* and none knew but what more and greater explosions were in order. Yet not only was there not the slightest tendency toward panic, there was not a single case that came to my attention, directly or reportedly, where anything but praise could be given. And this with men, few of whom had ever come in close contact with violent death before, and none of whom had ever seen decks and waterways erubescent with the blood of comrades.

. . . Men with legs off, with arms off, with gaping wounds in their sides, with the tops of their heads furrowed by fragments, would insist "I'm all right. Take care of Joe over there," or "Don't waste morphine on me, Commander, just hit me over the head!"

What had happened was that 229 officers and men were killed instantly, and 420 were wounded, 219 of these seriously. Four men were missing.

As I made my way about the ship [continued the Executive Officer], I at first attempted to administer first aid myself. As my head cleared, however, and the magnitude of the catastrophe began to penetrate my mind, I felt that I could be of best use by ascertaining as quickly as possible just how badly stricken the ship really was.

It was pretty bad in terms of personnel. The First Lieutenant and the Assistant First Lieutenant had been killed instantly, which deprived the Executive Officer of trusted assistants in damage control. The Exec himself was suffering from deafness and shock and shrapnel wounds.

And the Captain?

When I returned to the bridge to make my report to the Captain I was due for another blow. I found that his first feeling of being all right had been the result of numbness from shock, that actually, because of his many injuries, particularly the bad break of his left arm, he had been forced to turn the command over to the Gunnery Officer, and to put the commander of the *Reno* in command of the unit. The Executive Officer wanted to help the Captain, but Captain Inglis refused. "Never mind me, there are many in worse condition," and gave the command to the Executive Officer.

The way the men turned to help their fellows was remarkable. The *Birmingham* had only one medical officer aboard because the senior doctor had been sent to Santa Fe to perform emergency surgery earlier. The dentist and one chief pharmacist's mate were killed in the explosion, and the junior medical officer had fourteen hospital corpsmen to help him. They directed the ship's company to give first aid, and the doctor found those with perforated abdominal wounds as quickly as possible and began operating. Two groups were formed to splint fractures. When such measures had been taken, the third step consisted of putting patients in sick bay and the ward room. By evening a medical officer came from the *Reno* and the senior medical officer came back aboard.

All this while the *Birmingham* continued to be a ship of war, and much was demanded of her. Said Commander Folk:

Shortly after I assumed command, I was informed that the *Princeton* still wanted to be towed. That seemed almost too much. With over 400 of the ship's company dead or badly wounded, with all the remainder, including some 200 slightly to moderately wounded, who were not actually required on watch working their hearts out with the badly wounded, we were still faced with the prospect of having to continue to rig for towing. Yet when I consulted the Acting First Lieutenant and the Boatswain, the latter painfully wounded himself, their answer was "Yes, if we have to tow we can tow."

Captain Buracker of the *Princeton* went to the *Birmingham* and only then learned of the casualties and that Captain Inglis was hurt. He moved over to the *Reno,* where Captain R. C. Alexander had taken charge of the force.

When I arrived at the *Reno* Captain Alexander informed me that my request for a tow had been sent to the task group and force commanders, but, just as I got aboard, the word came back for the *Princeton* to be destroyed, and for the remaining ships to rejoin the task group.

The decision to destroy the *Princeton* was prompted by the damage which she had already suffered, by the damage suffered by the assisting ships, by the fact that the fire was still not out with night coming on, and by the fact that we were only 125 miles from Manila.

The Japanese had already showed that they had more airplanes up their sleeves than the Americans had previously suspected. Besides this, there was a healthy fear of the Japanese carriers, and during the activities of the day, while the *Princeton* had been fighting for her life, the Ozawa force, including carriers, had been located in the north. Further, it was suspected that the planes that were attacking the task group, and the plane that had dropped the little 250 kg bomb on the *Princeton,* were from those carriers. Nobody in the heat of battle knew all the answers, but the suspicions were enough. A burning carrier at night with the fleet was simply a beacon for the Japanese, who had shown their adeptness at nighthawking before.

The destroyer *Irwin* was supposed to smash the poor *Princeton* with torpedoes, but the *Irwin* had taken such a beating from the *Princeton* in coming alongside that the torpedo gear was smashed. She fired six torpedoes with almost disastrous results to herself—two of them came boomeranging back and very nearly blasted the *Irwin* out of the water; the first torpedo hit the *Princeton* in the bow, doing minor damage, and the rest missed.

So the *Reno* took over the job.

At 1750 the *Reno* launched two torpedoes from a range of about 2800 yards, and I think the first one was all that was required [said Captain Buracker]. The torpedo seemed to hit in the . . . *Princeton's* forward large 80,000 gallon gasoline tank or probably in the after edge of the tank, which is just forward of our forward magazines. There was a terrific explosion. Flames shot high in the air and the ship was under water in less than a minute.

That was the end of the gallant *Princeton* whose Captain had tried so hard to save her. And there was first blood for the Japanese air forces, to avenge the events off Palawan the morning before. It was planes, not ships, that had done this job.

10

BATTLE OF THE SIBUYAN SEA

Early on the morning of October 24 the planes of the American task groups, acting on instructions from Admiral Halsey, were out scouting for the Japanese fleet. They knew it was divided into several forces.

First contact with the Japanese was made by a plane from the *Intrepid* just after 0800. In a few minutes Admiral Bogan had the news, and so did Admiral Halsey. Then the *Cabot*'s planes were on the target in the Sibuyan Sea, complementing and extending the information.

Over the American Channel C came this message from an *Intrepid* plane: "The force consists of 4 BB [battleships], 8 CA [cruisers] 13 DD [destroyers] location is south of southern tip of Mindoro, course 050, speed 10–12 knots. No transports in the group and in all a total of 25 warships."

Immediately the messages began to go out from Halsey's Third Fleet flag plot on the *New Jersey*. First were messages to Admirals Bogan, Sherman, and Davison, to be sure that they had the information; Sherman and Davison were asked specifically to break radio silence to report any information about the enemy. Then Sherman and Davison were asked to concentrate on Bogan's task group, which would pull the carriers together. And then Halsey ordered Admirals Mitscher and Sherman to strike the enemy.

Bogan's task group was the first to be ready to strike, and he so reported. Halsey told him to go ahead and wished him good luck.

This way was not the way that Admiral Raymond

Spruance would have handled the air strikes. Spruance, as Commander of the Fleet, would have entrusted to Admiral Mitscher, the leader of Task Force 38, the carrier groups, the right and responsibility to give the orders for strikes, and all other action. But Spruance was not a carrier admiral, and Halsey was. How could Halsey forget the days early in the war when he had the scrappiest task force afloat? It was patently impossible; Halsey was just not built that way. It was not that Halsey would never listen to reason: he was always listening, right up to the point where he would wag his finger which meant the debate was cut off. But in times when action was needed, Halsey was ready to take active command of a situation.

Naval historians, principally Samuel Eliot Morison, have noted that Halsey "sent orders directly to the task group commanders, by passing Admiral Mitscher, who throughout 24 October was little more than a passenger in his own task force." Halsey said he did not bypass Mitscher any more than was his way.

> I always assigned targets to hit, leaving details to group and task force commanders. I would certainly have been derelict in my duty as Fleet Commander if I did not assign targets for them to strike, and would have been a fifth wheel if I exercised no control or command over the elements of my fleet. I always did this, and in doing it never felt that I was bypassing any junior echelon in the command. . . . I always felt free to assume tactical command, if I thought the conditions warranted it.

This was, of course, a difference in attitude toward his command, a very great difference from Spruance, and one that was to cause future historians to compare Halsey as a strategist most unfavorably with Spruance. Admiral Nimitz used to say that when he sent Spruance out with the fleet he was always sure he would bring it home; when he sent Halsey out, he did not know precisely what was going to happen. By the time of the Philippines operation, Nimitz had made up his mind that he would use Halsey largely to roam the seas in the manner of a buccaneer of old, certain that Halsey would find action if there was any to find, and that Halsey would never shrink from an encounter with the Japanese fleet. Meanwhile, the forthcoming landing operations out of the Central Pacific Command—the major ones—would all be planned so that Spruance, the careful, thoughtful intellectual admiral, would have control of the fleet during those operations.

After the war, comparisons were made by navy men of the two admirals under Nimitz: some said that if Halsey had been at the Marianas in June, he would have sent the carriers out to get the Japanese fleet by day, and would have sent the fast battleships out for a night engagement, that he would have polished off the Japanese fleet right there; or had Spruance been in charge at this operation in Leyte Gulf, he would have behaved entirely differently. Spruance confirmed that, too, even as the battle was going on, and he was waiting and listening at Pearl Harbor.

But at 0800 on October 24 Admiral William F. Halsey was scarcely worrying about what historians of the future would say about him. His next move was to call back Admiral McCain, ordering him to reverse his course from that leading to Ulithi, and then, on the dawning of October 25, to launch a search north and northwest.

This order shows that Halsey was sorting out the picture he had. Here is Admiral Carney's recollection of what was going on in the flag plot on the *New Jersey:*

The reinforced searches were launched in the morning and in view of the fact that we guarded the aircraft search frequencies direct, we picked up the reports as made, and by the forenoon of October 24, had amazingly fine information as to the composition, course, and speed of two enemy groups of surface ships moving to the eastward, one though the Sulu Sea (Nishimura) obviously headed for Surigao and one heading in the direction of the Sibuyan Sea, coming around Mindoro.

At this point it is interesting to note that as far as the Third Fleet was concerned there could be little or no alibi based on lack of information or incorrect information. I don't believe that in the history of any major action at sea has the intelligence information from searches been so good, so thorough, so quickly put through, and so complete.

In flag plot, when the two above-mentioned forces were spotted, it was believed that there must be a missing piece to the puzzle: that was the reason for the order to Admiral Mitscher: find that missing piece. "No operation on such a scale would be undertaken without the use of what the Japs had in the way of a carrier force," said Admiral Carney. "If that carrier force was to be used we felt it would be north and east of the Philippines." There would be other orders later in the day for searches to get that missing piece.

Halsey and his staff were well aware of the "shuttling" technique that had been tried at the First Battle of the Philippine Sea. They called it "beautiful." The carrier planes could make a one-way trip to an airfield via the target, which would be the American force, and by so doing their carriers could be employed from a much farther distance than could the American carriers. The Zeros, for example, and some of the other Japanese planes, were lighter than the American planes; they were not armored properly, if at all, and this gave them greater range. Combine that with shuttling, and one could see how it was possible for the Japanese to launch and carry out a vital strike against the American carriers while the Americans could not possibly reach them. The old adage of carrier warfare was to hit the enemy first, and knock out those carriers. In the Philippines, theoretically at least, the Japanese technique of shuttling represented a terrible danger to the American fleet, and Admiral Ozawa was counting on his greater range to make optimum use of his lesser force.

"If they could employ this very clever tactic they had us on the hip," said Admiral Carney. "We had recognized that from their efforts in the First Battle of the Philippine Sea and had decided that, should this occasion arise, we would make a high-speed run in on them, preferably at night, and prevent them from getting away with any such scheme."

So the messages went out that morning. Soon Admiral Mitscher, who was riding in the *Lexington* not far from the poor *Princeton*, reported that many enemy planes were around them in Task Group 38.3, Sherman's force. Halsey knew then that there was going to be some tough opposition, for Mitscher was never one to overstate the case.

Yet Halsey continued, in spite of all preoccupations, to be concerned with that enemy task force of carriers, and that morning sent Mitscher the following:

TOP SECRET URGENT
FROM COM 3RD FLEET
TO: CTF 38
INFO: CTG 38.2
ENEMY CARRIER STRENGTH NOT LOCATED. KEEP AREA TO NORTH UNDER OBSERVATION.

Then the war heated up.

Admiral Nishimura, with the battleships *Fuso* and *Yamashiro*, the cruiser *Mogami*, and the destroyers *Michishio*, *Yamagumo*, *Asagumo*, and *Shigure*, was steaming in the Sulu Sea, heading for Surigao Strait, when he was spotted just after 0900 on October 24, some 75 miles east of the Cagayen Islands.

The planes from the carrier *Franklin* underestimated the force they saw:

No major units were sighted. Just off Pucio Point, Panay, 2 old-type destroyers and a larger vessel, possibly a *Katori* light cruiser, were sighted. Two of the attack search groups joined to attack. The ships were strafed, hit with rockets, and bombed. The larger vessel was sunk and later 8 fighters and 11 bombers added further to the damage of the remaining ships. However, these were not seen to sink.

The fact was that the damage was confined to one minor hit on the fantail of the battleship *Fuso*, the knockout of a gun crew on the destroyer *Shigure*, and the shooting down of the Nishimura float planes, which left the *Fuso* blind thereafter. This mistake was not uncommon in the battle of the next few hours: the underestimation by the Japanese and the overestimation by the Americans of damage done the enemy.

Admiral Shima's force was sighted by a land-based bomber of the V Army Air Force near the Cagayen Islands that morning:

Confidential. Urgent 7615
From: Fifth Bomber Command
To: All interested CurOps
   This is my second report this force. 2 Fuso class BB (battleships) 1 unidentified heavy cruiser, 4 unidentified (garble) latitude 121-35. Course 60 true. Speed 15 knots. I am returning to base. . . .

One of the troubles with these reports was the garbling of the classification of the last group of ships (destroyers) and another was the misidentification of the ships. Actually they were 2 heavy cruisers, 1 light cruiser, and 4 destroyers in the Shima force. But in this case it turned out to make virtually no difference because of command decisions that were made by Admiral Halsey in the hours to come. The Third Fleet's air arm would concentrate its attacks against the major force of Admiral Kurita during the day.

The first strike of fighters, dive bombers, and torpedo bombers was launched from the carriers *Intrepid* and *Cabot* just after 0900 in response to Admiral Halsey's orders.

Here is the way the strike from the *Cabot* went:

   . . . These planes took off at 0915 and made a running rendezvous with the Strike Commander and his planes from the USS *Intrepid*. The TBMs [torpedo bombers] climbed to 12,000 feet and flew in a loose Vee formation just below the SB2Cs [dive bombers]. One division of Fighting 29 Hellcats [fighters] were at 14,000 feet flying medium cover, and the other was flying high cover at 16,000 feet.
   At 1025 . . . the Jap fleet was sighted in Tablas Strait east of Mindoro Island. . . . At that time the attack formation was 25 miles northeast of this position. The fleet appeared to consist of about 25 ships and was on a heading of 045 degrees True, making an estimated 18 knots. There was a destroyer screen

of about 12 ships surrounding the group, inside of which there were two columns of 4 [cruisers] . . . each. In a single column in the center of the whole group there were 3 or 4 BBs [battleships]. At least 2 of these were of the *Yamato* class. [That was good identification, one was the *Yamato* and one was of the *Kongo* class.]

When the attack formation was 12 miles away, on a course of 265 degrees True, the fleet was at 1400 off the starboard bow.

Instructions for the attack were then received from the Strike Commander. Planes were directed to positions on all sides of the fleet disposition. Torpedo Squadron 29 was directed to attack the leading BB from the starboard side. The Fighting Squadron 29 fighters, which were not carrying bombs, were directed to initiate a strafing attack against units on the starboard side of the Jap formation.

When the attack signal was given, Lieutenant Fecke led his division, which had been providing high cover, in a 70 degree dive from 16,000 feet, going southwest to northeast across the starboard side of the large Japanese formation. Coming through the vicious fire, Lieutenant Fecke strafed a Jap destroyer, firing to a range of 3000 feet, when he pulled out. Lieutenant Thompson, diving immediately after at 430 knots, strafed a Jap heavy cruiser, thought to be of the *Tone* class, across its starboard quarter to its port bow, also firing from 6000 feet to 3000 feet and pulling out at 3000 feet. Lieutenant (jg) Sonner and Ensign Buchanan dove after Lieutenant Fecke and also strafed the enemy destroyer, jinking [sharp turn] on retirement through the thick AA barrage. After making their strafing run these fighters then headed toward the rendezvous twenty miles away.

Lieutenant Fretwell's division which had been acting as intermediate cover at 14,000 feet was directed to make a strafing attack after the bombers went in, with the torpedo attack to be delivered last. Ensign Cozzens took the lead from Lieutenant Fretwell, whose radio was out, and went in immediately after the bombers to make the attack, approaching from south to north. Nosing down through the intense AA fire, Ensign Cozzens picked a *Kongo*-class battleship as a target, dove straight at it, and commenced raking it from the stern forward, firing from 8000 feet through 1500 feet, when he recovered over the bow. Lieutenant Fretwell also strafed the *Kongo*, which was on course 030 degrees T, pulling out at 2000 feet. While jinking in the retirement the Fighting Squadron 29 pilots observed a bomb strike the *Kongo* on its starboard side, aft. A Hellcat which had just completed a strafing run was seen to burst into flames and go into the water ahead. The pilot was not seen to escape from it. Ensign Dunn and Ensign Turner made a strafing attack on a Jap destroyer, raking it across its port bow to its starboard quarter, down to 1500 feet.

While en route to the rendezvous area, Ensign Dunn and Ensign Turner saw Lieutenant Williams of Torpedo Squadron 29 make a water landing about 10 miles south of Marinduque Island. With Lieutenant Fecke who returned they orbited over the spot for 20 minutes, observed Lieutenant Williams and his two crewmen waving from their rubber boat, and finally, being low on fuel, were forced to return to base. The other attacking Fighting Squadron 29 fighters made rendezvous successfully and provided escort for the bombers and torpedo planes on return to base.

The torpedo . . . pilots broke off from the attack formation, went into a slight echelon to the right, and began a glide approach. They took advantage of cloud cover from 10,000 feet on down as far as practicable. From here on they made individual attacks on the ships which were off their starboard bow, still steaming straight ahead, but at about 23 knots and sending up a withering barrage of AA.

Lieutenant McPherson led the attack, which was aimed at the leading BB.

Lieutenant Anderson came in next. Due to his position in relation to the BB, when he emerged from the clouds he was unable to get lined up for a run on it. He therefore selected a cruiser, thought to be a CA [heavy] but otherwise unidentified, that was head of the BBs on the port beam of the formation as his target. . . . His aiming point was the starboard beam, and he led 1½ ship lengths ahead of the bow. While making this run, Lieutenant Anderson's turret gunner strafed as they passed across the bow of the leading BB. During the retirement the gunner saw an explosion amidships on the starboard side of the cruiser.

Lieutenant (jg) Skidmore made his run on the leading BB from the 3 o'clock position. . . . He was not in a position to observe the results of this drop. During the attack his gunner saw two bombs from SB2Cs hit the second BB which was also of the *Yamato* class. One hit between the superstructure and the stack, and the other hit aft of the stack.

The TBM Lieutenant (jg) Skidmore was flying sustained three hits by AA while over the target area. The gasket on the propeller governor was torn out as a result of a hit by a .50 caliber bullet on one of the blades. What was estimated to be a 40 mm shell went completely through the fuselage laterally just back of the radioman's seat, entering from the starboard side. Daniel Joseph McCarthy, ARM2c (CA) V6 USNR suffered shrapnel wounds in his left thigh and heel. The blast from a 5-inch shell bent up the fairing at the port wing hinge.

Lieutenant Ballantine came in at about the same time as Lieutenant (jg) Skidmore. As he had gone down around rather than through the cloud he was in a position to attack the second BB. He dropped his fish from the 2 o'clock position but did not observe the results. During his approach toward the BB his radioman saw an explosion and quantities of black smoke arise from a cruiser in the forward part of the formation on the port side. Although no positive identification is possible, it is thought that this was caused by Lieutenant Anderson's torpedo. Lieutenant Williams' drop was not witnessed by any of the other men of the attack. Following the attack his plane was seen afire 15 miles northeast of the disposition, where he made a water landing. . . .

During the torpedo attack, with the exception of the lead BB which made a slow turn to starboard, the ships did not turn or resort to any evasive maneuvers. One reason for this may have been that the ships at that time may have still been slightly off guard. However, they certainly were not off guard as far as AA was concerned. AA was very intense. . . . The planes retired at 200 to 1500 feet, jinking as they went, until 10 miles out, where they rendezvoused. They then made an uneventful return to base.

So this strike was finished. One man, McCarthy, was hurt. Lieutenant John Wesley Williams had been shot down, along with AOM2c James Eugene Boland and AEMIc Bronislaw Lawrence Raczynski. When last seen, the three were waving vigorously from their rubber boat.

The strikes went on. The *Cabot* made another that afternoon, but this time the Japanese had been mauled by several attacks from carrier-borne planes, and they were behaving quite differently. The fleet had gone into two groups, maneuvering. There were two battleships in each group, each surrounded by cruisers and light cruisers and a screen of destroyers. One of the battleships, *Musashi*, was seen to be smoking heavily.

The planes of Torpedo Squadron 29 started in on the damaged battleship; then she changed course and headed away from them, so they attacked a *Tone* cruiser instead. They could not see the results, but they were sure they secured at least one hit on the cruiser.

Then came the fighters and here is their story:

The two divisions of Fighting Squadron 29 fighters attacking the Jap fleet consisted of:

Lt. Edward Van Vranken, Ensign Francis Collins, Lieutenant (jg) Joseph Chandler, and Ensign Robert Janda; and of Lieutenant Max Barnes, Ensign Robert Murray, Ensign Henry W. Balsiger, and Ensign Emeral B. Cook. These fighters remained as top cover until the bombers and torpedo planes had commenced their attacks. Then they peeled off to drop their bombs on the battleships in the western group of the Jap fleet. One battleship was seen smoking and circling in an apparently damaged condition, and Lieutenant Van Vranken therefore decided to lead his division against the second battleship, identified as one of the *Kongo* class. While the Jap ships fired intense AA and later light and medium AA against the oncoming fighters, Lieutenant Van Vranken led his division in a dive from 13,000 feet at a 70° angle toward the *Kongo* which was then headed east, approaching it from a 7 o'clock position. Lieutenant Van Vranken and his wingman Ensign Collins drove abeam each other and released their bombs at 3000 feet. Pulling out at 1500 feet they passed across the starboard bow of the *Kongo* and executed a 180° turn to port to avoid fire of the units of the Jap fleet ahead. As they made their turn they were able to observe that Lieutenant Van Vranken's bomb had landed 100 feet from the battleship, just abaft the port beam, and that Ensign Collins had scored a near miss with a drop 20 feet off the port side of the ship, about 20 feet forward of the fantail.

Lieutenant (jg) Chandler, in a less steep dive behind Lieutenant Van Vranken, with Ensign Janda on his wing, strafed the *Kongo* from 10,000 feet and continued firing to 4000 feet where he increased his lead and dropped his bomb at an altitude of about 3000 feet.

Making 350 knots Lieutenant (jg) Chandler pulled out at about 2200 feet and followed by Ensign Janda, who had also released at 3000 feet, retired in a northeast direction, jinking over Jap cruisers and destroyers which were firing from below. Lieutenant Van Vranken and Ensign Collins observed Lieutenant (jg) Chandler's bomb strike about thirty feet off the starboard side of the *Kongo*, about 80 feet forward of the fantail. Ensign Janda's bomb dropped about 500 feet from the port side of the Jap warship and slightly aft. All four pilots of this division made rendezvous successfully about 10 miles northeast of the Jap fleet and provided cover for the SB2Cs during the return to base. . . .

When in his dive and at 6000 feet Ensign Balsiger felt his plane jarred by AA fire and saw that more than half of his starboard aileron had been shot away. The impact rolled the F6F around but it still responded to the controls and Ensign Balsiger continued his dive, aimed at the bow of the *Kongo* class BB, and released at 4000 feet with unobserved results. Ensign Balsiger pulled out at 2500 feet and though his plane was hard to turn he was able to make the rendezvous and return to his ship. . . .

Back at the ship, the Flight Commander made reports to air intelligence to confirm and amplify what had been said over the radio during the fighting. The reports of the *Cabot* planes were certainly not exaggerated; on this second strike the fliers made no claims at all except to having attacked.

Nevertheless, in the excitement pilots reported many things, and there were many pilots reporting, because 259 planes attacked the force of Admiral Kurita that day.

Lieutenant L. R. Swanson dived on what is believed to be a *Kongo*-class battleship . . . interrogation indicates that he obtained a direct hit almost amidships and slightly to the starboard side. This hit is verified by personnel of VT-19 squadron. . . .

Lieutenant J. L. Butts, Jr., also dived on the battleship and for an undetermined reason his bomb failed to release whereupon he requested permission from the air group commander to make a second attack, which permission was granted and he made a one-plane attack on a heavy cruiser. . . . [He scored a hit or a near miss.]

Lieutenant P. R. Stradley and Lieutenant (jg) W. P. Wodell are believed to have dived upon a heavy cruiser. . . . The results of Lieutenant Stradley's bomb drop are not known but it is believed that Lieutenant (jg) Wodell obtained a probable hit upon this ship. . . .

Lieutenant (jg) C. H. Bowen dived through the overcast, corkscrewed around a cumulus cloud and dropped upon what he described as either a light cruiser or a destroyer. He dived very low, completely blacked out himself and his crewman, to the extent that his crewman never did see the ship upon which he dropped. It is not known . . . and the question of which ship he dived upon cannot be definitely settled. A. F. Droske, ACRM who was riding with Lieutenant Stradley and who was taking pictures at the time, saw a destroyer explode, break in two and sink almost immediately. The VT squadron in this group did not attack this ship and inosfar as we knew its exploding is unaccounted for unless hit by Lieutenant (jg) Bowen or by planes from another Air Group. We are not attempting to claim the ship, but feel that the important thing is that it was sunk. . . .

Carrier Air Group 16 from the *Essex* made other strikes. Their report was very heartening to their shipmates when they returned.

The VT formation [torpedo planes] was divided into two eight-plane divisions—Lieutenant C. H. Sorenson's division leading Lieutenant Commander Lambert's division. The former went down to the attack before the latter. Since two pilots of Lieutenant Sorenson's division are missing it is not known which targets they chose. . . .

Lieutenant C. H. Sorenson and Lieutenant (jg) L. G. Muskin were the first to drop. When they made their attacks the 2 battleships were almost in column with the *Musashi* in the lead. Of the two pilots Lieutenant (jg) Muskin was the first in. He dropped from 600 to 700 feet at 250 knots at a range of 1300 yards 30° on the starboard bow. His run was made, therefore from SE to NW and his target was the rear BB, the *Kongo*. He states that he had an ideal shot but that the AA was so intense he was unable to see the result. Both crewmen say that the torpedo ran hot, and Lieutenant C. H. Sorenson and Lieutenant (jg) Lightner claim that he made a hit amidships.

Lieutenant Sorenson attacked the *Musashi*. . . . He obtained a direct hit aft on the starboard side, confirmed by Lieutenant (jg) Bleech who saw a large explosion on the *Musashi* on his retirement southward after attacking a CA [cruiser].

Lieutenant Commander Lambert and Ensign A. R. Hodges were next to attack the battleships these men had identified as the *Musashi*. Lambert did not see how he could miss, the two battleships were virtually bow to stern at this point, and he dropped at 650 feet going 240 knots, from 1500 yards out, 80° on the port bow, and was certain he had scored a hit. Ensign Hodges' crewmen said he also scored a hit, and that they heard two explosions as they pulled away over the ships.

Lieutenant (jg) R. L. Bantz came in next, Lieutenants S. M. Holladay and H. A. Goodwin after them, and the others said Bantz made a hit on the battleship. Crewmen said all three of them did, although only two explosions were heard. "In summing up the attack on the *Musashi,* it would appear that at least three hits were obtained, one on the starboard side aft, and two on the port side. . . ."

Three pilots then attacked the *Kongo*. Lieutenant R. D. Cosgrove dropped from only 450 feet, 2000 yards out, and claimed a hit. Lieutenant (jg) R. D. Chaffe claimed a hit on the bow.

"South of the battleships and slightly ahead was a CA, probably of the *Nachi* class. This cruiser was torpedoed by two pilots in Lieutenant Sorenson's division. . . ." Lieutenant William S. Burns said he scored a hit, and the cruiser lost speed as he watched her. Lieutenant (jg) O. R. Bleech dropped from 400 feet at 1200 yards out and thought his torpedo was running true but he was hit by AA fire as he watched and could not tell what happened next to the ship.

But Lieutenant Commander Lambert and other pilots said they saw two different explosions on two different cruisers and another pilot said he saw at least one large explosion on the *Musashi*.

Two pilots, Lieutenants (jg) Paul Southard and W. F. Axtman, failed to join up. Others had seen one plane go down in flames, and the other make a "hard water landing" just outside the Japanese destroyer screen. At the time, no one knew what had happened to that pilot. Later it was learned that Lieutenant Axtman and one of his crewmen had been rescued.

Other *Lexington* pilots that day ran into some very determined opposition by the Japanese air forces, and among them, one of the most successful teams was the division of fighters led by Lieutenant (jg) W. J. Masoner, Jr. Here is Masoner's account:

We took off at 0610. My division escorting four SB2Cs on a 300 mile search from 275° to 285°. We entered a front spreading from about 50 miles from ship to about 20 miles inland. We flew instrument for 25 minutes and on emerging from the front the bombers were out of sight. We finally spotted them circling at 8000 feet over the eastern shore of Lingayen Gulf [Luzon]. As we came up to join them they spotted a group of Bettys [bombers] and I saw them shoot down two. I saw 4 or 5 Bettys scattering in all directions; I picked one and went down on it with my division. I opened with a quartering shot and rode up on his tail. I observed his 20 mm gun firing from his turret. My incendiaries hit his fuselage and right wing root. He burst into flames and hit the water. [The Betty was the bomber that the Japanese commentator earlier had likened to a cigarette lighter because it burned so quickly and then like a Roman candle.]

I pulled up from this attack and saw 8 Dinahs about 100 feet over me. They turned and spread slightly. I came up from below the right-hand plane and put a long burst into his starboard engine. It started to burn—the flames spread and it fell a mass of flames. During this time I saw 4 or 5 flamers and smokers crash on the shore.

By this time no more planes were available so we rendezvoused and continued our search.

About 50 miles out one of the bombers tallyhoed two Nells. We dove down after them and chased them for 5 to 6 miles. I dropped my bomb and then caught up with them. I made a run from above and astern and his right wing burned—exploded and fell off. He dove into the water and burned. I started to make a run on the other Nell but he was burning already and crashed. My wingman [Copeland] got him. These Nells had the new ball turret on their backs and one of these hit my section leader engine. He was able to proceed, however.

We then joined the bombers—flew our cross leg and started home.

As we approached the shore of Luzon we spotted five Nells at about 500 feet. My wingman and I went down on them and he burned one which crashed. His guns then stopped and he pulled up [Lieutenant E. E.] Bennett whose engine was damaged. I made a high quartering run on one Nell and observed hits. I did a wingover and came up under his tail to avoid his ball turret which was firing. I hit him in the fuselage at very close range. He exploded and pieces flew all over. He nosed straight down and hit the water— there was no fire.

I came up from behind and above on the next Nell and hit in the wing root and he exploded, throwing large pieces by me as I pulled up. He burned and crashed.

This left two Nells out of the five. I made two passes on one of them and on the second rode his tail until he burst into flames. This was very low and he hit immediately.

By this time [Lieutenant (jg) W. E. Davis III] my #4 man, had come down from escorting the bombers and we chased the last Nell over the land. We each had one gun firing and though we both got good hits, it wouldn't burn. My guns stopped entirely by this time so we withdrew.

There was no question about these kills—gun cameras from Lieutenant Masoner's plane filmed all 6 of these Japanese airplanes being shot down.

There were other stories from this division that gave the same basic picture:

Lieutenant (jg) W. E. Copeland went after a Betty, it burst into flames and crashed into Lingayen Gulf from 2000 feet after he had made a "stern run" and given it one long burst. Then he caught a Nell low over the water, gave it a long burst, and both engines caught fire. He then found a Lilly at 2000 feet over Lingayen, rode his tail and tried to flame the enemy ship, but it would not burn. The engines died and it crashed into a rice paddy.

Lieutenant Bennett got onto the tail of a Betty and turned

with the other plane "shooting it down from 0400, and then got an unidentified twin engine plane from 0500 which also burned and crashed. I was hit by the turret gunner of a Nell and stayed up high from then on."

Lieutenant Davis got a Betty. "I singled out one . . . and fired several bursts into it. It started into a shallow dive and crashed and burned. Did not see any Bettys get away. . . ."

These were some of the tales the pilots brought home from the strikes against the Japanese that day, and they were obviously very impressive tales. Perhaps it was significant that the pilots of the *Lexington*'s Carrier Air Group 19 were so successful in their attacks, for after all the *Lexington* was in the heart of the fighting fleet, and Vice Admiral Marc Mitscher, commander of Task Force 38, was riding the *Lexington* that day.

The messages of success came steadily. At about noon Admiral Mitscher sent a gleeful message to Halsey:

Morning search reports 2 *Natori* class cruisers, 1 dead in water just off shore northwest tip Mindoro. The other under off west shore Lugang island, I damaged Nachi cruiser in Manila Bay. Enemy has been flying several large groups twin engine planes from Formosa to Luzon. About 100 enemy planes shot down. Now striking enemy fleet east of Mindoro no reports yet of results. We have another large blip heading from the northeast. Launching search 350 to 040 at 1305. The *Princeton* still afloat.

Soon Halsey was reporting to Nimitz in Pearl Harbor of the attacks that were in progress, as he was getting the material from Task Force 38. He reported stopping a destroyer, and then hits by the *Intrepid* planes on a cruiser and a destroyer, bomb hits on two battleships, rocket hits on a cruiser and 2 destroyers, and torpedo hits on battleships and cruisers—so many reports that it seemed obvious the Japanese were taking a serious beating in the Sibuyan Sea. By evening it appeared that the Japanese were thoroughly disorganized. Admiral Mitscher reported them "milling around aimlessly in several groups." That certainly did not sound like a report on a determined enemy force coming through to attack, but rather like a force that had been cut up and did not know what to do. Further, Mitscher now revised his estimate of Japanese planes destroyed to 150 for the day. Yet another slightly sobering note was observed in this same message: Mitscher thought the loss of the *Princeton* force of fighters had hurt them considerably, and he felt the shortage of fighters at that moment.

In Japan on October 23, after the disastrous submarine attacks on Admiral Kurita's force, Admiral Toyoda's combined fleet headquarters assessed the situation as they pieced it together and renewed the orders to the fleet.

It is very probable that the enemy is aware of the fact that we have concentrated our forces. He will probably act in the following manner.

(1) Concentrate submarines in great strength in the San Bernardino and Surigao Straits areas.

(2) Plan attacks on our surface forces, using large type planes and task forces, after tomorrow morning (Oct. 24).

(3) Plan decisive action by concentrating his surface strength in the area east of San Bernardino Strait and Tacloban where he has his transport group. He should be able to dispose himself in this manner by afternoon of 24th.

Our Plans:

(1) Carry through our original plans.

(2) In effecting the operations, the following points are specially emphasized:

    a. Make up for our inferior surface strength by making every effort to direct the enemy to the north toward the Main Body of the Mobile Force [Ozawa, his carriers, and other ships].

    b. Maintain an even stricter alert against submarines and aircraft. Utilize every possible trick to keep enemy submarines under control, particularly while breaking through the narrow strait.

    c. Destroy enemy task force carriers with our shore-based planes, while his carrier-based planes are engaging our surface forces.

This, then, was the plan. The Japanese were far more concerned on the afternoon of October 23 with submarines than with American air power—quite probably because they had just suffered a disastrous encounter with American submarines. But, equally important, combined fleet put the emphasis on the use of the surging Japanese air power in the Philippines for the destruction of the American task force, when it was found, rather than the aerial protection of Admiral Kurita's attack force as it came under the American eyes on its way to San Bernardino Strait. And the emphasis on luring the Third Fleet north was made much greater than it had been before the encounter of the previous day.

The Japanese Second Air Fleet, then, came to Manila from Formosa with its instructions. Commander Mariyoshi Yamaguchi, Operations Officer of Second Air Fleet, said "the first mission [of Second Air Fleet] was to attack the Task Force and wipe out the American landing force in Leyte Gulf. The second mission would be to fight back the Army Landing Force." As for the naval forces steaming in, there was no basic plan for their protection because there were not enough planes to do both jobs. In a way, the Japanese *concept* was not so much different from the concepts of air power enthusiasts everywhere. But it was a far cry from concept to execution, and while the Japanese concept of wiping out the task forces by hitting the carriers was sound enough, it was sound only if the Japanese had the power to do so, and most certainly they did not have it. Whether or not the Japanese planners knew that is still questionable, but it was part of the "one big battle" miasma that they would hypnotize themselves into forgetting what was impossible even when they knew it was impossible.

"More or less," said Commander Yamaguchi, "ten fighters were above fleet movements; ten airplanes was standard to be above a fleet." And it was planned that from Clark Field the Japanese air forces would fan out and provide anti-submarine patrol all the way.

But how it was planned and how it worked were two different matters.

On October 24, the Japanese at Clark Field sent out the planes that Kurita had planned to have above him, but they did not do the job. How could they? The pilots of the *Lexington* reported what happened to those Japanese planes as soon as they headed for an area where the American air strikes were operating.

It had been a great relief for Admiral Kurita to transfer from his perilous perch on the destroyer to the *Yamato* because he had been almost totally out of communication with his fleet during the destroyer period. All they could do was use the blinkers. Yet even on the *Yamato* there were problems; half the communications personnel had been lost in the torpedoing of the *Akagi*, and this was to hamper Kurita in the coming battle.

Early on the morning of October 24, as the force headed through the Sibuyan Sea, Admiral Kurita knew he was likely to be running a steel gauntlet in a few hours, and that he would have to protect himself; the plan was for the planes to attack, not defend. Still Admiral Kurita sent the word to Manila that he wanted fighters. The word was heard loud and clear—throughout the battle communications between Kurita and Japanese headquarters around Manila were very good. The fighter escort did not come, nor did Kurita really expect it. Because he had so few planes, Admiral Ohnishi was thinking desperately of kamikaze attacks, not of an attempt to provide air cover for the fleet. And as for army planes, apparently the liaison between army and navy on the operational level was so incomplete that no naval officer knew how many army planes might be available—if any. Kurita was in no position to make a request directly of the army, at any rate.

Kurita's first warning of what was to come arrived early —when Manila radioed the news of the morning strikes around the Luzon airfields. Kurita knew it would not be long. Then his radar picked up American planes as blips on the screen when they were about 60 to 70 miles out from him.

The Japanese waited.

They waited until after 1000, speeding along as they were through the sea, heading for San Bernardino Strait. From 0839 on, the Japanese ships were at the alert, maneuvering for defense, zigzagging, with their crews at the anti-aircraft guns and the lookouts ready.

The Japanese counted 30 carrier planes in the first wave

that attacked them that morning. Here is Admiral Ugaki's recollection of the attack:

At 1040 this side of the channel [north of Tablas Island] just as we were thinking that the enemy should be putting in an appearance ... about 25 enemy planes came into sight. We shot down 23 enemy planes (SB2C, TBF, and F6F) and thought, well, this isn't too bad, but just the same *Myoko* sustained one direct torpedo hit and fell behind. The flag of Cruiser Division Five was transferred to *Haguro,* and *Myoko,* escorted by one destroyer, headed west. . . .

The Admiral's recollection was faulty, or there was so much buzzing in the air above the fleet that his sources gave him much duplicate information. For the fact was that during the *whole day* the Americans lost only 18 planes of the more than 250 flights made over this fleet. But that was the way of battle. Misinformation was as common as information, and hard to distinguish.

The *Myoko* was a "type" cruiser, over 203 meters long with a displacement just short of 15,000 tons, and capable of a speed of 33.8 knots. She was built at Yokosuka Naval Base in 1929 and later modernized. On this day she was still a tough fighting ship, although not of the class of *Akagi,* for example.

When the American air strike came in the *Yamato's* radar was first to pick up the enemy, and gave the news through the fleet. *Kongo* was first to open fire, and then the others saw and began shooting. The fleet was moving along at 18 knots at this time.

There was some confusion about twenty minutes later when the destroyer *Akishimo* reported a submarine where there was no submarine. Then came a number of strange reports. The *Noshiro* sighted a submarine. The *Naguro* sighted a small aircraft carrier. The *Nagato* really *did* sight American planes in a new wave bearing in on them at 1025. (Japanese and American times differ in these actions. Both are used, in order to give the comparative feelings, even at the expense of historical accuracy.)

The fleet opened fire, sending up a very strong and impressive barrage of anti-aircraft shells. Four minutes later torpedo bombers came in on the *Myoko* from the bow. The Captain saw the wake of a torpedo coming and evaded, but one of the torpedoes struck the starboard side, aft. The engines stopped. The after starboard generator room, the after engine room, the inner and outer shaft rooms to starboard and the electrical system all began to suffer. Soon the rooms were flooded and the electrical system broke down. The ship began to list heavily to starboard.

The crew shifted gear and heavy equipment as rapidly as possible. Port compartments were flooded and fuel oil was shifted. As temporary repairs were undertaken, the divisional flag was shifted and then, at 1138, the *Myoko* was sent on her way, back to Brunei, out of the battle. She could make 18 knots, but she could not be expected to keep up with the fleet or fight with the others now.

The Americans soon came over again, attacking the two Japanese formations with the battleships in the middle, and the ships retorted as best they could, like angry cats, spitting up their hail of steel and fire against the planes. According to Admiral Ugaki:

"There was a visual message from *Musashi* [a battleship] to the effect that she had received a torpedo hit on her starboard side but that her speed was unimpeded." Strange as that sounds it was true at the time. *Musashi* was a huge fighting machine heavily armored, and bombs tended to bounce off her armor plate. *Yamato* took a torpedo, but she too steamed sturdily along.

"If this is the extent of the damage it isn't too bad," wrote Admiral Ugaki, who was keeping a running diary of the fight.

But at 1330 a third wave of planes appeared. Here is Admiral Ugaki's doleful account of the battle and the loss of one of his favorite ships:

From before this, the outer skin of *Musashi's* port bow had become peeled, causing a larger wake. Since the maintenance of high speed became increasingly difficult for *Musashi*, all ships were warned to reduce speed to 22 knots and carry out evasive maneuvers, but *Musashi* still continued to fall behind. Then, *Musashi* was again hit by a torpedo, and *Yamato* sustained one bomb hit and one near-miss on the bow. The other near-misses and evaded torpedoes were too numerous to enumerate.

The small number of enemy planes shot down is regrettable. Since *Musashi* continued to fall behind and there was no hope of her accompanying us, it was decided to have her head for Manila, escorted by [the destroyer] *Kiyoshimo*.

At 1426 a fourth wave of 50 planes, and at 1520, a fifth wave of 80–100 planes attacked. *Nagato* [the battleship] sustained two hits amidships. In the fifth attack, *Musashi*, which was putting up a desperate fight a considerable distance from the main body, started emitting black smoke and listing to port, and became unnavigable. Becoming apprehensive about the situation *Musashi* requested the dispatch of another destroyer. The second section, using its judgment, dispatched *Tone* for us.

The *Musashi* was taking a terrible beating, and although she was a stout battleship no ship could for long sustain power with 10 torpedoes in her, as the *Musashi* had. She had also been hit and suffered near misses by many bombs —and even a near miss is enough to start rivets, loosen seams, and throw structural members of a ship out of line, weakening her in many ways that may not immediately be apparent to the eye. Then, she had 19 torpedoes in her and perhaps 17 actual bomb hits.

The *Yamato* and the *Nagato* had been hit and the battleship *Haruna* was damaged by a series of near misses.

Now, by mid-afternoon, the force of Admiral Kurita had suffered seriously. Whatever would happen to the *Musashi* it was obvious she was not going to go much farther into Philippine waters, with those American planes after her and her situation so grave. Still, Admiral Kurita's force was very strong. He had 4 battleships still going, 6 heavy cruisers, 2 light cruisers, and 10 destroyers [several destroyers had been sent back to escort or help the stricken *Musashi* and *Myoko*].

By this time, the Kurita force was located in the Sibuyan Sea some 20 miles northeast of the north end of Tablas Island.

The ships of the fleet were disposed in two circular formations, about 8 miles apart, with the bigger ships in the middle and the destroyers outside. This formation gave the new anti-aircraft guns the power they needed, and made the Americans very much aware of effective anti-aircraft fire as they dived in. But it was a difficult formation to maintain and take evasive action, and when ships were hit, the whole picture changed.

By noon the force had broken up and reformed, and the *Musashi,* with her plating torn loose at the bow, was literally plowing the sea, as Admiral Ugaki noted in his diary.

Admiral Kurita that afternoon notified combined fleet headquarters: "The First Striking Force is engaged in hard fighting in Sibuyan Sea. Enemy air attacks are expected to increase. Request land-based air forces and Mobile Force [Ozawa] to make prompt attacks on enemy carrier force estimated to be at Lamon Bay."

This was a plea for help, of course, but it was not one that the Japanese could do much about. They had already begun attacking the American carrier force and absolutely all they got out of it was the lucky hit on the *Princeton* that eventually destroyed her that day.

The Japanese plowed on, without the *Musashi,* but at the reduced speed of 18 knots because of the damage to the ships from the air attacks.

At 1530 Admiral Kurita's staff estimated that they would be attacked three more times that afternoon before sundown. They also roused to several submarine scares and the destroyer *Akishimo* carried out a depth-charge attack on a submarine that did not exist.

Combined fleet was preoccupied with the submarine menace and while the ships of the Japanese fleet were licking their wounds and repairing damages between air attacks a message came warning them specifically of submarines that might get them before they approached San Bernardino Strait.

"Be alert," said the message.

"Be alert?" How could Kurita be anything else with this rain of steel pouring down out of the sky, and the buzz of diving planes that scarcely stopped echoing in his ears between air strikes?

"Recklessness alone kept the fleet on its course," said Masanori Ito in his study of the Imperial Japanese Navy. That recklessness, of course, was planned. For Admiral Kurita expected to lose half his ships in this operation. However, he had really expected to lose them in San Bernardino Strait. And now he was becoming aware of the fact that the whole Japanese staff in Tokyo had completely underestimated the American forces they would encounter. When he left Brunei, the best intelligence he could muster gave the Americans some 200 transports, 7 battleships, and an "appropriate number" of cruisers and destroyers in Leyte Gulf. He *never* received another intelligent piece of intelligence. He asked for planes to be sent from San Jose in Mindoro to scout the American force, but he never received the word, except that bad weather had kept the Japanese scout planes from carrying out the mission.

By 1530 then, Admiral Kurita was considering the future course of action, and he decided to turn back—to withdraw outside the sea, past the effective range of American aircraft, and wait for the Japanese air forces in the Philippines to get organized enough (which he really expected they might do) to deliver counterattacks to the Americans. He did not realize that the Japanese land-based air and Ozawa's force were doing all they could and it was like a gnat biting an elephant.

Here is the message Kurita sent to combined fleet:

As a result of five aerial attacks from 0630 to 1530, our damages are not light. The frequency and numerical strength of these enemy attacks is increasing. If we continue our present course our losses will increase incalculably, with little hope of success for our mission.

Therefore have decided to withdraw outside the range of enemy air attack for the time being, and to resume our sortie in coordination with successful attacks on the enemy by our air force.

Now Kurita felt that the plan was already wrecked by the American attacks. The submarine and air attacks together had put him six hours behind time. The plan had called for him to make 22 knots all the way, which would put him into Leyte Gulf at 0600 on October 25, while Nishimura coming from the south would get in about 0500. But now, with six hours' delay, he could no longer even come within an hour of Nishimura, he figured. The 22-knot speed (far below the capability of the fleet) had been established because of the fuel curve. If they went faster the tankers they had could not supply them with enough fuel to get home. Everything had begun very badly. And it continued badly.

One reason Kurita decided to turn back was that he had received, at about 1000, a dispatch from Nishimura stating that things were going sour down south, too. The dispatch was not specific (the *Fuso* was hit but not too seriously) but when accompanied by what Kurita and his staff had seen happening to themselves, they figured that Nishimura was resorting to a little Japanese understatement.

And yet, inexplicably, while turning about himself, Admiral Kurita did nothing to change Nishimura's drive up from the south.

Admiral Toyoda was anything but pleased by the message of Kurita's turnabout, when it was sent at 1600. He did not approve, and there was a suggestion that Kurita was doing less than he should.

But aboard the *Yamato* it was quite a different story. Admiral Ugaki, the diarist, was not party to the decision, but he did not disagree with it.

It is true, if we are attacked by planes as often as this, it will appear that we have expended ourselves before getting to the battle area, but our situation being what it is, we can't retire even if we chose to do so; there is a doctrine that in each and every instance the fastest means of settlement should be elected. My opinion at the time [of sailing] was that the only means available to us was to sortie determined to die. However, I am aware that to reverse course once until evening in order to deceive the enemy will be advantageous for tomorrow.

Ugaki, who was there, knew that Admiral Kurita had no intention of retiring, but was trying to take the heat off his force, hoping for one of those miracles, that the Ozawa force would decoy the American planes away from him as it was supposed to do, or that the Americans would get the idea that he was retiring.

A plane from the *Intrepid* noted the turnabout almost as soon as it occurred and notified his task group, which in turn notified Halsey. By 1620 the message had been received.

Admiral Bogan was cautious in his assessment of the change in course.

He sent this message by TBS circuit:

Flash report 3rd strike enemy force reported at 1600 at 12-42 N 122-39 E. Course 270 speed 17. This force has been 14 miles to the east of this position but reversed course during time attack was over target. 2 BB reported to be of *Kongo* class were damaged and circling. Apparently not controlled, at 12-39 N 122-48 E. The first was listing and afire. The second less damaged. Course to west may be retiring or may be protection for cripples. . . .

Other reports came in from the other carrier groups, and they told of hitting battleships and cruisers and destroyers. The buildup was very strong aboard the *New Jersey*.

By 2000 many things had happened in the Philippines, and they were more or less summed up in the message that Halsey and his staff put together and sent out to Admiral Nimitz, General MacArthur, Admiral Kinkaid, and the task group commanders of the Third Fleet. Here was what Halsey thought he knew.

On 24th launched strong dawn search teams from 3 groups across Luzon and Visayas. At 0745 search planes contacted enemy force 4 BB 8 CA 2 CL 13 DD [Kurita] 15 miles south of Mindoro. 38.2 [Bogan] launched strike immediately and repeated during day.

38.3 and 38.4 [Sherman and Davison] struck same force after initial strikes on their targets. 38.3 reported 1 CA 1 CL 1 DD Manila Bay, all damaged (estimate some damaged by Blue subs). [This was the *Aoba* force which was to take troops to the back of Leyte.] After first strike 38.3 under heavy air attack and shot down about 150 planes. [This was the series of raids that culminated in hitting the *Princeton,* and was the major Japanese air effort of the day.] *Princeton* heavily damaged and *Birmingham* had personnel casualties resulting from explosion on *Princeton* while alongside her. 38.4 first strike enemy force southeast of Negros consisting of 2 *Fuso* class BB 1 CA 4 DD making two bomb hits on each BB, rocket hits on CA and 2 DD, strafed 2 remaining DD. None of these seen to sink. [This was Nishimura's force.] Main body reversed course to 270 about 1400 when 30 miles east of Tablas Island and while again being attacked. Main body: score from incomplete reports; 1 *Yamato* class bombed torpedoed left afire and down at bow. *Kongo* class 2 bomb hits left smoking and apparently badly damaged. Bomb hits on one or both remaining BB. 2 torpedo hits on one of these bombed BB. 1 CL torpedoed and capsized [sheer fantasy]. Torpedo hits on 2 CA and bomb hits on another CA [overemphasis and exaggeration].

And then came the kicker, as far as Halsey was concerned, representing new information that he had been waiting for, the missing piece of the puzzle.

At 1540 [just after he learned that the Japanese fleet in the Sibuyan Sea had turned around] plane from 38.3 [Sherman] sighted enemy force near 18-10 N 125-30 report evaluated as two ISE class 2 CA 1 CL, 6 DD course 210 speed 15. At 1640 another group sighted 18-25 N 125-28 E, 2 *Zuikaku,* 1 CVL, 3 CL, 3 DD, course 270 speed 15. [This was Ozawa. At last Halsey's planes had found him, just when Admiral Kurita hoped they would, to take the pressure off Kurita.] 2 DD 100 miles northeast this group course 240. [Ozawa was still heading for northern Luzon.] Planes from this force may have been attacking 38.3 prior to contact, CTG 38.3 has scuttled *Princeton* and is closing 38.2 and 38.4 which are now concentrated off entrance to San Bernardino Strait. Night air attack by enemy probable. More later.

Before 1700 so much had happened; Halsey had now discovered Ozawa; Kurita was steaming back toward Brunei as far as anyone could see, and no one in an airplane above could read his mind.

What a sad time it was for the officers and men of Kurita's fleet. Admiral Ugaki wrote:

When we reversed course, we passed by *Musashi*, my trusted lieutenant [Ugaki was commander of Battleship Division One, remember], and her damaged appearance was too pitiful for words. All compartments which could be flooded were already flooded. She was listing about 10 degrees to port and though the Imperial Crest was still visible, she was down by the bow. The deck line of the upper deck in front of the turret was barely above the surface of the water. She had sustained 11 torpedo hits and several bomb hits. One of the bombs set fire to the ammunition, damaged the rudder, and blew away the No. 1 bridge, places on a battleship for which precautions are taken in advance. It is said that this bomb, which hit the radar "bedspring," wounded Captain Inoguchi, who was in the AA control station, in the right shoulder and completely destroyed the No. 1 bridge and flag plot.

Make every effort to keep going was my fervent prayer. Further, as commander of Battleship Division One, I suggested that the bow of the ship be beached temporarily in a spot of suitable depth off a nearby island, and emergency repairs effected. No appropriate words of sympathy immediately come to my mind. Thus we passed *Musashi* and when we reversed course once more, we passed by *Musashi* again near sundown, before 1900. . . .

Yes, they had reversed course again. Kurita had done so at about 1715, after the American planes had seen him heading away. If he had planned to change course as he did, switching back as though frightened and running, and then turning around, he could not have taken an action that was more calculated to fall into the plans and thinking of Admiral Halsey. Here was Ozawa, just discovered. Here was Kurita, badly mauled, turned around.

If Kurita had any doubts—and there is no indication he did—that his mission was to get to San Bernardino Strait at all costs, then Admiral Toyoda in Japan straightened it all out with a message that came in from combined fleet at 1815:

WITH CONFIDENCE IN HEAVENLY GUIDANCE THE ENTIRE FORCE WILL ATTACK, said Admiral Toyoda, which was as close to a furious remark as a fleet commander was to receive from headquarters. There was no question to be asked. Timetable off, timetable on, the one big battle was still on.

And that is how Admiral Ugaki saw the *Musashi* again and again that afternoon.

It would appear that all of *Musashi*'s officers and men are remaining at their posts without complaining. I thought that if things remained as they were she might be able to hold out until the following morning. *Tone* [a damaged cruiser] is certainly a problem. She requested that she be allowed to join with the force in its penetration and at 1830 was ordered to rejoin its unit. Excluding some damage-control personnel who remained aboard to help out, all other *Maya* personnel who had been accommodated on *Musashi* were transferred to a destroyer which pulled alongside of her. [Imagine the plight of these Japanese sailors: torpedoed on *Maya*, picked up, sheltered on the big battleship, watched her smashed mortally, and now transferred again to go into further action on a third ship.]

The Japanese fleet of Admiral Kurita steamed on toward San Bernardino Strait and Leyte Gulf, not knowing what to expect; Kurita expecting only the unexpected, ready to do his duty to the death. He had thought he might lose half his ships; now what could he think? He did not even know that the Americans had finally found Admiral Ozawa.

"A little over an hour after sundown," wrote Admiral Ugaki, "a message was received from a destroyer, which had been ordered to stand by the damaged ship, that at 1937, *Musashi* listed sharply . . ." Poor Captain Inoguchi. He had followed Admiral Ugaki's advice and had run for the nearest shore, but he could not change course in the slightest degree as any movement caused the *Musashi* to quiver, and he was afraid that a change in heading would put her over. Three of her four engine rooms were flooded, and on the last one she could barely move. Finally it had happened. At 1850 the bows were completely submerged, Captain Inoguchi gathered his officers, ordered them to abandon ship, and went back to his bridge to be alone.

A minute later, the mighty *Musashi* rolled suddenly to port, and sank—so swiftly that she carried down nearly half her crew of 2400 officers and men.

". . . sunk! . . ." wrote Admiral Ugaki.

This is like losing a part of myself. Nothing I can say will justify this loss. *Musashi*, however, was the substitute victim for *Yamato*. Today it was *Musashi*'s day of misfortune, but tomorrow it will be *Yamato*'s turn.

Sooner or later both of these ships were destined to come under concentrated enemy attack. My sorrow over *Musashi*'s loss knows no end, but when one conducts an unreasonable battle, such losses are inevitable. Should *Yamato* tomorrow meet with the same fate as *Musashi* I will still have *Nagato* but there will no longer be a unit and my existence as division commander will be meaningless. As I had already made up my mind that *Yamato* should be my place of death, I firmly resolve to share the fate of the ship.

This was an indication of the Bushido spirit of courage and resignation that brought the Japanese to the place they had reached this night. Can a non-Oriental understand it? Probably not without years of study of the Japanese spirit. Here was a commander, knowing he and his other brave companions were engaged in a foolhardy venture, yet not complaining, simply determined to live and die by a code of honor. It no longer mattered that they expected to die, or that they could not win, or that their plans had come almost completely unscrewed. What mattered now was honor—and yet Ugaki and Kurita were responsible naval officers, concerned about professional matters as well as Bushido, as the events of the next hours would indicate.

At 1951 [wrote the Admiral], we changed from circular formation to compound column and continued westward. [That was the indication that they were back on the attack and wanted to move fast.] It would appear that the fleet headquarters has received a radio from combined fleet ordering our force to proceed ahead, trusting in divine faith. Today we underwent five or six air attacks, but neither our base air forces nor our own reconnaissance seaplane unit were able to report any definite information on the enemy. The extent of the information was that a task force was present east of Manila, and that the enemy fleet in Leyte Gulf had moved out and there were no large ships in the gulf.

At any event my firm belief has been that once we are able to transit the San Bernardino Strait we should conduct search attack in the area where we are able to approach and contact the enemy. . . .

I have every faith in our ability to engage the enemy successfully. The only other thing which worries me is that the enemy will successively reconnoiter our movements tonight and from after dawn will concentrate his air attacks on this force from a position over 100 miles from shore. Should this be the case, unless there is adequate cooperation from the base air forces, there will be nothing we can do, and our strength will be exhausted. We will have to expect decisive battle and annihilation with AA action alone. . . .

So Admiral Ugaki went to bed as the Kurita fleet steamed ahead toward its rendezvous with who knew what.

11

THE NORTHERN FORCE

It may seem odd, but when Admiral Ozawa set out from Japan with his force of carriers and hermaphrodite battleships and lesser vessels, he hoped to be found even before Admiral Kurita entered the Sibuyan Sea. He wanted to do anything he could, including giving his life and those of his men, to assure Admiral Kurita's success in disrupting the Leyte Gulf landings. But if he were not to give his life, if the Ozawa force were somehow to be saved, then it would need fuel to make the round trip. So Admiral Ozawa sent his supply train out on another route to reach Amami-o-Shima and there to wait for the Ozawa force. Strangely, Ozawa, who wanted to be found, was not found, and the supply force, which wanted to hide, started out and remained in almost constant trouble.

The supply force was made up of two units. The first force consisted of the tanker *Takane Maru*, and 3 escorts. The second force consisted of the tanker *Jinei Maru*, the destroyer *Akikaze*, and 3 escort vessels. The first force left Tokuyama on October 21 at 2100, an escort leading, 2 escorts on the flanks, and the tanker in the middle, zigzagging and making 13 knots. The second supply force would not move until midnight on October 23.

The first force immediately began seeing and hearing things, and in taking evasive action the *Takane Maru* had rudder troubles and lost her torpedo net. She reached the anchorage at Koniya gratefully at 1800 on October 23. But the second supply force was not nearly so lucky: it left Okinoshima around midnight on the 23rd, zigging and zagging, when suddenly at 0400 on the 24th, an enemy submarine torpedoed Escort No. 132. The *Akikaze* was in the lead. Escort 31 was on the port side of the *Jinei Maru*, and Escort 132 was on the starboard, with Escort 43 behind, when poor 132 caught it.

Everyone knew that a submarine was out there; the sonar contacts were definite, and Escort 43 gave chase, pursuing the American ship—for that is what they were sure it was—for 51 miles from the Okinoshima Light, and depth charging. But there was no result, and Escort 43 had a job to do, so it turned over the pursuit of the submarine to the Kure defense squadron and came back to its force, where the *Akikaze* and Escort 31 were disposed on either side of the *Jinei Maru*. But it did not find the force again—so the torpedo attack was doubly fruitful, sinking one escort and successfully diverting a second one from its assignment.

This kind of breakdown of plans and communications was dogging the Sho operation everywhere, it seemed.

What a disappointment it was to Ozawa, who was dispatching dummy messages and faking radio traffic of very heavy volume all the way as he steamed toward the northern tip of Luzon. Poor Ozawa did not know that his *Zuikaku* was having transmitter difficulties and that most of his messages were not getting through.

"Not one of those messages was received by a friendly force. For such a trivial and extremely stupid reason—which too must be attributed to the technical shortcomings of manmade products and man himself—this unfortunate mission, which from the outset was a 'sacrifice hit,' fell short of attaining its objective," Admiral Toyoda wrote.

The Japanese *were* expecting miracles. Radio Tokyo was still boasting, all day long on October 24:

The latest check reveals that since October 12, when the Japanese air force launched their first attack on the enemy in Taiwan [Formosa] waters the Japanese forces have either sunk or damaged 73 warships of the Anglo-American navy . . . 17 carriers . . . 2 battleships . . . 5 cruisers. . . . Early on the morning of October 24 the Japanese air force discovered an enemy fleet and, as the result of our attack during the day, two enemy aircraft carriers, one battleship and two cruisers were all heavily damaged.

Admiral Ozawa's course and speed were taking him toward the island of Luzon in a manner that he hoped would let him arrive about 250 miles off it at dawn on October 24. On the evening of the 23rd he decided that he would draw the Americans toward him and *Zuikaku,* the flagship, broadcast a long message at about 2000. Unfortunately—and infuriatingly for a potential martyr, nobody paid any attention to the message. Either the *Zuikaku*'s transmitter was still performing improperly, or something else was wrong.

He was getting the message about the fate of Kurita's force all this time. He learned at 1400 on October 23 of the *Darter-Dace* torpedoing of 3 of the Kurita cruisers, and followed the changing fortunes of Kurita all that day. By evening, Admiral Ozawa had an estimate of the situation that was not quite correct but was certainly logical: American intelligence already knew of the general fleet disposition, including his force.

Here was Ozawa's estimate as to what the Americans would do:

He will employ his task forces and land-based air strength to attack our first and second striking forces [to the south, the pincer forces] and when the first striking force makes its penetration, he will concentrate his surface strength east of San Bernardino Strait and in the Tacloban area and will seek decisive battle with us.

Ozawa, then heading for the northern tip of Luzon, decided that at 0600 on October 24 he would change course and head southwest, to draw the enemy upward and away from San Bernardino Strait. At 0545 he would launch his search planes and try to find the American carriers. If the planes found them, the one "great" wave of planes would be launched.

"Every effort will be made to recover aircraft aboard carriers in preparation for subsequent interception operations," Ozawa said. Now that was an odd statement for a carrier admiral to make, because in every carrier operation the planes are automatically recovered at the end of the day, maybe not just once but several times. But there was reason for this introspective comment: Ozawa really had very little confidence that the planes could be recovered for a second strike. The pilots were simply not well-enough trained to land again aboard the carriers, and in truth some of the aircraft they were flying were not well suited for carrier operations, for the bottom of the barrel had been scraped to put these planes together on the carriers at all.

If the first search the next day failed to find the Americans, then a second search would be sent out after 1400. Planes would be launched to fight, and the enemy carriers would be diverted to the north. Then, in the event that the carrier planes and the movement of the force did not bring the Americans moving north and stop the pressure on Kurita, a part of the force would be sent farther south into the jaws of the enemy, to lure again.

All this was planned in full realization that the Ozawa force was already low on fuel. Indeed, the Admiral noted that he expected only to have October 24 on which to operate freely, that thereafter he would have to send part of his force back to Formosa to fuel. If the planned operations did not do the job, then Ozawa would move toward Samar and attack again with whatever planes he had left on October 25. The planes would then seek shelter in the Philippines, because if that last event came to pass, it was almost certain that the Ozawa force would be destroyed.

Just after midnight on the morning of the 24th, Ozawa began getting information. He learned that his first supply force arrived at the fueling rendezvous; twenty minutes later one of his cruisers detected a "submarine" and the destroyer *Hatsuzuki* attacked, without results. And at just about this same time came word from the night searchers off the Philippine coast—the shore-based air—that an American task force was sighted.

At 0530, Admiral Ozawa's carriers launched their search planes and at 0830 they had found the Americans—or the Task Force had been found by the land-based air and the

Ozawa fleet knew about it. Ozawa was not content with the base air force findings, and so he ordered one of his own search planes to make contact with the American group, and particularly to observe the weather. Admiral Ozawa, the fighting admiral, knew very well that he really had one strike to make, and he wanted that strike to be as effective as it could be. It was his bad luck that morning to learn from his air search that the weather in the vicinity of the American ships was generally foul, squally. With the pilots of the good old days when Pearl Harbor was attacked, it would not have made much difference. But these youngsters (their average age by this time was 20), with their insufficient flying time, were too green to take the responsibility of tangling with a large American force, the superior American fighters, the superior American pilots, and bad weather to boot. Ozawa waited.

Just after 1000 the *Hyuga* detected on her radar a large air formation, which was apparently the enemy on a bearing of 90 degrees which meant due east of the Ozawa force, out about 170 miles. It could have been a Japanese force coming back from attack on the Americans. More likely, it was a strike from one of the carriers moving toward Luzon. Soon the contact was lost, but the alert was on: Ozawa ordered three planes put up immediately to serve as Combat Air Patrol.

A three-plane CAP was nothing—the Americans put up a dozen to do less work. But it was an indication of Ozawa's nagging problems. It cost him dearly in aviation gas to put up the patrol; it diminished his potential fighting force, already so slim; and putting those pilots up there, he was not too sure that they would get down again safely, at least with their planes. So it was another agonizing decision.

By 1115, Ozawa had more information. No. 9 search plane from the coast reported that an enemy force of more than 10 combat ships had been sighted, although the weather was so bad that the observer could not tell precisely whether any carriers were involved. But a plane from Maktang naval air base had definitely confirmed at least 2 carriers earlier, and of course so had the blips on the *Hyuga*'s screen.

As of 1130 Admiral Ozawa and his staff were thinking this way:

—To launch an all-out air attack against the American task forces as sighted by search plane No. 9.

—Since the weather was so foul around the target, and knowing only too well that his pilots were inferior, it would be most unwise to ask them to fight and try to make it back to the carrier. So the pilots would attack and then, because of the bad weather, they would be told to proceed to Nichols Field in the Manila area, or anywhere else they could put down. Later on, Ozawa would promise, they would be recovered in the waters east of Luzon. That promise was a part of the charade Ozawa was playing for his men and for the Japanese world. He did not for a moment believe that he would ever recover those planes or pilots; he doubted very seriously if the Ozawa force would ever see Japan again, but he was an Imperial Naval Officer and defeat was unthinkable. Only the appurtenances of victory could be enunciated in orders.

—After launching, the force woud proceed westward "to recover planes" said Ozawa to his staff. But it was not really to recover planes that he would proceed west; it was to lure the American fleet north and keep the American planes from striking Admiral Kurita and the American fast battleships from blowing him out of the water.

At 1145 it was all settled and the planes were launched: 40 fighters, 28 carrier bombers, 2 reconnaissance, 6 carrier attack—76 planes to wipe out the American fleet.

As patiently as he could, Admiral Ozawa settled down to await results.

He heard nothing.

Of course, the orders he had delivered, to strike the Americans and then proceed to Philippine air bases, were less than perfect for intelligence purposes. And given the current very threadbare state of Japanese communications in the islands, there were excuses for delays. But not to hear anything at all from anyone. . . !

What he did finally hear was that the American task forces were on a bearing of 210 degrees, about 150 miles away. The direction had changed with his change in course, moving westward. What he also heard was that Kurita had been hit hard early in the morning. So Ozawa knew that the Americans knew Kurita was moving toward San Bernardino Strait and an attack on the ships in Leyte Gulf to stop the landings.

Soon Ozawa had one bit of information: three planes came back to the carriers, landed, and reported that they had been unable to find the enemy. Not very encouraging. Nor was it encouraging to have nothing but silence about the fate of the others.

By 1430 Ozawa was feeling quite low, but with the resiliency of a great commander he began modifying his tactical plan. He knew that the attack must have failed or he would have learned something.

"The Mobile Force Main Body," he said, "so far has been ineffective in its action to divert the enemy. It is imperative, regardless of losses which this force may sustain, that the diversion of the enemy to the north be accomplished in support of the First Striking Force [Kurita]. As a last resort, it is necessary to dispatch the Advance Guard (Cardiv 4 Desdivs 61 and 41) to divert the enemy effectively in conjunction with air attacks and to attack enemy remnants."

The advance group would consist of the hermaphrodite battleships *Hyuga* and *Ise,* and 4 destroyers. They were sent out then, to further the plan. Two more planes were launched to maintain contact with the enemy until dark. Ozawa planned to steam west until 1600 to make sure that the enemy knew he was there, and move east. Actually, Ozawa was under the impression that the Americans knew where he was and had been for hours. He said later that he personally saw the American airplane that sighted his force on the morning of October 24. If so, the American plane never reported the sighting to the Seventh or Third Fleets, because no one knew where Ozawa was until evening.

Ozawa's frustrations continued. He had sent out planes, but by 1725 he had to note that no report had been received from the planes. Had they been shot down? Perhaps, or perhaps they had been forced to land in the Philippines. If they went near the Americans they were probably shot down: the sinking of the *Princeton* had the American combat air patrols buzzing around those carriers like a hive of angry bees. If they did not find the carriers, the weather was bad enough to discourage the most experienced pilots.

As far as the air strike of Ozawa's fleet is concerned, it remains a mystery. The first planes, a flight of 30 fighters, 19 fighter bombers, 4 torpedo planes, and 5 attack planes, were launched from the carriers *Zuiho, Chiyoda,* and *Chitose.* So small a force from so many carriers! The second group, launched a few minutes later, came from the *Zuikaku.* This force, according to Masanori Ito, the Japanese historian, actually did attack the Americans. But if so, what did it accomplish? There were some near misses that day, some damage to LST's and other ships, but no capital ship sinkings except for the *Princeton,* and that ship was damaged very early in the day, obviously by a shore-based plane.

No, the Japanese air forces were not working effectively on October 24, either from land or from sea. Their intelligence reports were fragmentary and inaccurate, probably again reflecting the bad weather and the inadequate training of the pilots who were fighting through the squalls.

What they did note, with some accuracy perhaps, was that the Second Air Fleet on the morning of October 24 consisted of about 200 planes of various types. On the night of the 24th, having been augmented by what was left of Ozawa's force after it "attacked" the enemy, the Second Air Fleet claimed 102 planes left. Considering Ozawa's 70-odd planes, and the fact that the army must have had *some* planes to put in the air that day, the claims of Admiral Halsey's boys for 150 or more planes seem to be understated rather than overstated. But perhaps the Japanese lost a great many to weather that day. Whatever the reason, it could be seen at the end of the day that the way the Japanese were going they would not accomplish anything with their air forces, and even Admiral Fukudome came to the conclusion that Admiral Ohnishi's kamikaze plan was the only way. On the night of October 24 the Japanese air commanders surveyed their slender resources and began discussing the establishment of a single unified naval air command in the Philippines to use the kamikaze tactics.

But just after 1600 the Japanese had one minor satisfaction—if a negative one. Ozawa's force sighted one American Curtiss plane, and knew from listening to the transmission that the report was out that Ozawa existed. At last! Thankful as he was, Ozawa was not chicken-hearted toward the American—he sent up 2 fighters, but the American plane made its way off through the clouds and apparently back to its carrier.

With great satisfaction, Admiral Ozawa sent a message off to combined fleet, to Kurita, and to everyone else who might be interested.

ENEMY CARRIER AIRCRAFT NOW IN CONTACT WITH MO-BILE FORCE MAIN BODY

Everyone knew what Ozawa had now to do.

Just before 1800, the Cruiser *Tama* reported the presence on her screens of more than 20 planes, presumably enemy, on a bearing of 300. Ozawa was not sure what it was (probably this was a late-afternoon strike from Clark Field or an American strike force returning) but he did not want to be hit by carrier planes just there, just then. He knew that the Americans would—or should—follow him north to wipe him out, and so he headed north to escape those planes and lure the American carriers away from their attention to San Bernardino Strait.

Here was his plan:

"Operations will be carried out as scheduled in accor-dance with combined fleet Desopord [order to lure]. Will proceed on 140 degrees course and at 0600 will send off all remaining air strength to renew air action. Every effort will be made to draw off the forces attacking second fleet [Kurita]."

The naval order sounded very impressive, until one stopped to realize that Admiral Ozawa's planes, on all his carriers, could now be counted by two men on the fingers of their hands, give or take a few toes. Some 20 planes left to take on the American fleet! If nothing else, Ozawa's was an exercise in pure courage.

It was not long after this order that Ozawa received information that confused him and caused a change in his plan. Around 2000 came the delayed report that Kurita had turned around, and was retiring from the enemy until he had some information that someone else was doing something to stop the Americans. After all, Kurita knew no planes had helped him that day, and he did not know

what Ozawa was doing. There was something plaintive in
the section of the Kurita message: "resumption of advance should depend on results achieved by friendly air
forces"—even though by the time Ozawa got the message,
Kurita was already moving back into action. There was
something plaintive and shocking about the whole Sho
operation—with its puerile communications network, and
the combination of despair and wild hope with which the
Japanese sought their miracles.

When Ozawa and his staff considered Kurita's action,
they were thoroughly upset.

Despite the order from combined fleet headquarters
directing all forces to advance to the attack, the above
dispatch from Second Fleet [on retirement] indicates
that it had already reversed course at the time and
retired a considerable distance. Since this action
creates great danger of the Mobile Force's Main Body
becoming isolated, the entire force is being ordered to
reverse course temporarily to the north.

So Rear Admiral Chiaki Matsuda and the *Ise* and the
Hyuga were recalled from what was definitely a suicide
mission, and the Ozawa force headed north.

By 2100, however, Admiral Ozawa had had plenty of
time for second thoughts, and he realized that no matter
what Kurita did he still had his own responsibility.
Further, he was made considerably happier to receive combined fleet's direct order to Kurita to get back into action.
So Admiral Ozawa made a new estimate of the situation.

The enemy's action today shows that he is fully
aware of the operational objective of the First Striking Force [Kurita] and has therefore concentrated his
attacks on this force. In view of the threat posed by
First Striking Force's operations, it is very probable
that the enemy on the 25th will again concentrate on
that force. Therefore the Mobile Force Main Body, in
accordance with Mobile Force Main Body Operation
Order No. 1, will risk its own existence and carry
out diversionary operations at all costs. In cooperation with the first striking force's penetration, the

Main Body will advance to the southeast, in preparation for operations tomorrow morning. . . .

And then Ozawa issued a fleet disposition order. Of the force only the *Kiri* was detached—this destroyer was running low on fuel and was sent to Amami-o-Shima to refuel, and then find the fleet again.

The supply force was having its troubles. At about the time that Ozawa was fretting over his course of action, believing that Kurita was abandoning the action, the *Akikaze* and her little contingent were hearing things, specifically transmissions they suspected came from enemy submarines. The transmissions began just after dark and continued long into the night. The *Akikaze* was on the alert and began making sonar contact with what must be submarines. She went out on search patterns, and so did Escort No. 31; they tried evasion patterns but the sonar pings continued, those ominous little noises that sent shivers down the back of a tanker man and tears of frustration to the eyes of destroyer men who could not move within range.

Then, at 0445 on October 25, it came. The little force was heading for Amami-o-Shima and had reached 30°15′ North, 129 degrees 45′ East; the pings grew louder and more insistent.

Wham!

Wham!

Wham!

came three torpedoes that smashed into the side of the *Jinei Maru*. Up she went in a blaze of precious fuel oil, and in a few minutes she sank to the bottom.

In seconds the men of the *Akikaze* were on the alert, searching through the darkness that seemed ever so much blacker than usual in the blinding light of the *Jinei Maru*'s death fire. She and Escort No. 31 began charging across the sea toward the point where the torpedoes must have originated. And there they found—nothing. They set to work to try to find and trap the crew of the American submarine.

Meanwhile, Admiral Matsuda was still moving south against the Americans. He had gone off to the south believing that the Americans had suffered damage to 2 carriers, and that only one carrier and 2 battleships remained in fighting condition. It was supposed that his force could cope with them. Matsuda was no fool. He was doing as he was told, but he had no personal hopes, none at all, that he would emerge alive from this battle.

About 2000 Matsuda and his men observed some flashes of light in the distance. What they might be nobody knew. He thought they might be gunfire from the land fighting, or perhaps even sheet lightning or an electrical storm. He paralleled the course and steamed on, searching for American forces, keyed up with determination to have a night battle.

So great was the tension in this little force that had been sent to spend itself against the Americans, that when Ozawa ordered Admiral Matsuda to turn around and rejoin him—calling off the banzai attack he had ordered—Matsuda did not immediately respond. He kept steaming, kept looking for Americans. If the flashes he had seen were American ships he would close with them around 2100, and he was determined to fight if there was a chance to do so.

But the flashes never materialized as anything identifiable, and before midnight he must either obey Ozawa's orders or decide to disobey them. He chose to obey, and reluctantly turned and sped north to rejoin his chief, meeting the Ozawa force just before sunrise on October 25, and joining up in the prescribed formation.

12
DISCOVERY AND DECISION

If the Japanese conduct of the Sho operation was confused and sorely hurt by the failure in communications facilities, still one must say that the American conduct of the riposte to the Sho operation was equally sorely hurt by human failures in communications, and by assumptions based on the excellence of the American communications network.

There, too, was a failure in the American riposte—certain assumptions made by certain intelligent and brave officers of the American fleet.

If one is to assess the difficulties that began piling up on October 24 in the conduct and riposte of the Sho operation, the two sides—Japanese and American—both suffered from a lack of coordination of their naval forces. Usually, in a battle each side has a commander. But in this battle, as it shaped up, the Japanese had at least four commanders in the field: Admiral Kurita in charge of the pincers movement, with Admiral Nishimura supposedly under his command; Admiral Shima, who was independent of everyone for practical purposes; Admiral Ozawa, who wished he could coordinate with Kurita or someone; and Admiral Fukudome, in charge of the Second Air Fleet, who would take command of all air operations in the Philippines on the following day. Loosely coordinating this as much as anyone was Admiral Toyoda in Japan. At least he coordinated the Japanese effort enough to be sure that Kurita kept moving forward through San Bernardino

171

Strait, and that Ozawa, who was ready to throw in the sponge at one point, knew that Kurita had moved back to the attack. In a way, that was better coordination than anything that happened among the Americans at the command level. Admiral Nimitz was in charge of the strategy of the Third Fleet, and General MacArthur was in charge of the invasion of the Philippines, and neither of these commanders did anything by October 24 that in any way affected the tactical maneuvers of the two important naval units, the Third and Seventh Fleets. If the Seventh and Third Fleets had exchanged high-ranking officers, at the fleet staff level, for this operation, and had the officers been totally familiar with the thinking of their respective admirals, the conduct of the battle might have been considerably different. What was to happen within the next few hours in the Philippines was very much a matter of character and communications. What was to happen otherwise was very much a matter of national character and individual bravery on the part of thousands of men.

In the afternoon, when it was known that the Japanese were moving up through the Sulu Sea and that the forces the reader knows as those of Nishimura and Shima would come through the Surigao Strait and try to strike at the American ships in Leyte Gulf, then Admiral Kinkaid began to put together the pieces of the Japanese plan. He sent a message to all his forces, with copies to Halsey, Nimitz, all the commanders of the task groups of the Third Fleet, Admiral King in Washington, and General MacArthur, warning of fighting to come.

Prepare for night engagement. Enemy force estimated 2 BB [battleships] 4 CA [cruisers] 4 CL [light cruisers] 10 DD [destroyers] reported under attack by our carrier planes in eastern Sulu Sea at 0010/I 24 October [which was about 0900 local time]. Enemy may arrive Leyte Gulf tonight. Make all preparations for night engagement. TG 77.3 assigned to CTG 77.2 as reinforcement [Barkey's battleships to Oldendorf]. CTG 70.1 [PT boats] station maximum number PT's lower Surigao Strait to remain south of 10° N during darkness.

It was obvious since this message came early in the day that Admiral Kinkaid was alert to the dangers, that he was confident of the ability of his battleships, cruisers, and escort carriers to stop the Nishimura and Shima threat.

As for Halsey, he made arrangements in mid-afternoon for the *Independence* of Admiral Bogan's task group to put out night fighters and search planes just before dark to watch the enemy and report on them.

In mid-afternoon, Admiral Halsey directed a message to his fleet commanders, with copies to Admiral King in Washington and Admiral Nimitz at Pearl Harbor.

Battle plan:
Batdiv [battleship division] 7 MIAMI, VINCENNES, BILOXI, Desron 52 less STEVEN POTTER, from TG 38.2 and WASHINGTON, ALABAMA, WICHITA, NEW ORLEANS, Desdiv 100, PATTERSON, BAGLEY from TG 38.4 will be formed as Task Force 34 under V. Admiral Lee, commander Battle Line. TF 34 engage decisively at long ranges. CTG 38.4 conduct carriers of TG 38.2 and TG 38.4 clear of surface fighting. Instructions for TG 38.3 and TG 38.1 later. Halsey, OTC in NEW JERSEY.

As far as Halsey and his staff were concerned, this message simply established the manner in which Admiral Lee and the surface force would operate if it came to a surface engagement. Had Admiral Matsuda continued south that afternoon, and had he succeeded in coming close enough for a night engagement, then Lee would have been detached with Task Force 34, as it was known, and would have taken on Matsuda, his two battleships, and lesser ships for a fight. Or, had Admiral Kurita not turned around and headed back toward Brunei that afternoon in full sight of the carrier planes which reported on the fact, then Admiral Lee would have been standing off San Bernardino Strait ready to fire on the Japanese vessels as they came through.

Meanwhile, all kinds of things were happening. One was that Admiral Kinkaid was an unknown party to this message and he drew some conclusions. Good old Halsey was doing exactly what he should do, establishing the battle line and Lee's command for the future.

"It was . . . a logical, perfect plan," said Kinkaid.

The reason it seemed to be perfect was that Halsey indicated he would keep 2 of the new battleships (*Massachusetts* and *South Dakota*) with the task force, and leave the ones cited with the Lee force, which apparently would be left in the Leyte vicinity.

(But what seemed to escape Admiral Kinkaid's thinking was the fact that the *New Jersey*, Admiral Halsey's flagship, was a part of Battleship Division 7, which had been assigned to Lee. And to think that Halsey would assign himself out of a chase after the Japanese fleet carriers, if he could find them, was to give Halsey a role quite outside his previous character.)

That afternoon, as the information poured in about the forces in the south, Kinkaid and his staff counted noses. They knew that Kurita had 5 battleships with him. They discovered by noon that Nishimura had 2 battleships. So they deduced that if another force was coming down from the north, it would have 2 battleships: the *Ise* and the *Hyuga* were the only battleships left that could be out hunting trouble.

That afternoon in the *New Jersey*'s flag plot Admiral Halsey and his staff pondered the reports as they came in. It was apparent that his boys had been making a lot of hits on the Japanese. He was sure that their fire control and communications had taken serious damage that day. And when he heard that Kurita had turned around and was steaming back westward, he did not attempt to analyze the reason for Kurita's change.

During the day Admiral Davison responded to Halsey's order to close up the task force with the note that he would have to break off from Nishimura in order to do so. But Halsey, Admiral Carney, and the staff of the Third Fleet had considered that.

In reviewing Halsey's thinking of that day, Admiral Carney had this to say:

> To understand his [Halsey's] decision, it is necessary to review the events of the 24th from the standpoint of the Third Fleet. The southern group [Davison] had

located the enemy force coming in through Surigao Strait, accurately reported as two *Fuso* [battleships], apparently a *Mogami* [cruiser] and some small fry. They were damaged by the reinforced searches on contact.

The center force rounding Mindoro and heading through the Sibuyan Sea was formidable, and it was decided to concentrate on the center force with the complete assurance that the piddling force they were risking in the Surigao Strait didn't have a chance against the forces which we knew the Seventh Fleet had to meet them. So, throughout the day of the 24th, the strength of 3 carrier groups was concentrated on the center force and by 2000 a reasonably good analysis of target coordinators' reports and photographs were available to the commander, Third Fleet.

The assessment of Admiral Carney, Halsey's Chief of Staff, was slightly different than that of his chief, made on a different basis. He and the other members of the staff agreed that "the center force . . . kept coming forward, . . . but they had received so much superficial damage that they were not in position to render the best account of themselves nor could they be strong enough to gain a decision even if they pressed through the San Bernardino Strait on toward the objective at Leyte."

In Admiral Mitscher's flag plot aboard the *Lexington*, the thinking was on a slightly different level, as it would be for the Commander of the carrier forces.

The day had started with relatively little information and a general feeling of uneasiness. Of the four task groups, one, McCain's, was off on its way to Ulithi Atoll to replenish planes and supplies. The other three forces —and this was certainly true after the attack on the *Princeton* which immobilized her almost immediately—felt that they were just barely in position to do a job. "We were fighting again on a shoestring," said Commodore Arleigh Burke, Mitscher's Chief of Staff. He referred to the long period at which they had been at it, the attrition suffered since those early October days when the Third Fleet set out to cripple the Japanese so they could not defend the Philippines properly. They had succeeded in that effort, but the cost had been heavy in airplanes and men, and in sleep.

The problem of putting intelligence reports together was quite unlike reading the story of these actions in a book, where the results are known (at least to historians) and it is so very easy to see who did what when, and what he really ought to have done had he known precisely what the enemy was doing. Commodore Arleigh Burke gave a good feeling for the way it looked from the flag plot of the *Lexington.*

They had started out in the morning with reports of Kurita's fleet in the Sibuyan Sea. And then almost immediately they had begun taking heavy air attack. (Sherman's TG 38.3, in which Mitscher's flagship was stationed, took the brunt of the Japanese air attack all day long.) First, in the morning and around noon the attacks came from the west, but in the middle of the afternoon they started coming from the northeast, and Mitscher and Burke concluded it was very likely that these planes were coming from a carrier force off the Philippine coast.

In past weeks Mitscher and Burke had concluded that the Japanese were short on planes, because of the many different types of planes they had encountered around Formosa. But they did not have Japanese production records at hand, or Admiral Ohnishi's reports on the paucity of planes in the Philippines. What they had were their eyes, the sight of the *Princeton* burning, and the sounds of battle as the American Combat Air Patrols and strike forces battled the Japanese planes in the air. "They were well-coordinated attacks," said Arleigh Burke.

In retrospect, the air battle of Task Group 38.3 that day sounds like an easy victory, but nobody thought so at the time. For example, with the *Princeton* burning, Admiral Halsey had asked Sherman to close up on the task group in the mouth of San Bernardino Strait. For another reason, the *Princeton* had sent off a strike, and if she moved that far away her planes might not make it back to her. There were many, many moments of uneasiness that day that do not show in the routine reports.

In the meantime [said Arleigh Burke], enemy air attacks were being repelled. A search to the north and

THE BATTLE OF
LEYTE GULF

DISASTER AND TRIUMPH IN
THE BLOODIEST SEA BATTLE
OF WORLD WAR II

Vice Admiral Thomas Kinkaid talked to everyone, from PT Boat commanders on up (above). Admiral Bull Halsey takes a little ride (left).

It was General MacArthur's show. The purpose of it all was to put President Sergio Osmena back ashore in the Philippines and drive the Japanese toward their homeland (above right). The fleet had to be assembled, and when it was, the sight was enough to impress the most crusty old salt (below).

Rear Admiral C. A. F. Sprague

Rear Admiral R. E. Davison

Vice Admiral T. S. Wilkinson

Rear Admiral T. L. Sprague

The landings begin (above). The Japanese put up what air power they had, but it usually ended up about here (below).

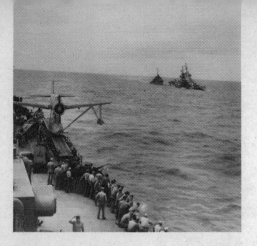

Offshore, the cruiser *Houston* took a torpedo and was in trouble... (above). Those big guns of the *Pennsylvania* could create havoc... (below).

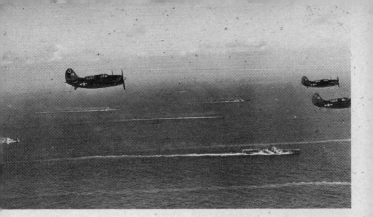

Halsey's plan was to search out and destroy... (above). Flight operations continued to the end of the day (below).

...so it was not long before the troops were ashore. But sometimes a ship got stuck in the mud (above). Admiral Barbey had one landing force, and General Carlos Romulos knew the terrain ... (below right). Commander David McCampbell, this day, became one of the storied heroes of the war... (below left).

Vice Admiral Marc Mitscher was sick, but Commander David McCampbell didn't know it... (left). The planes and the men were ready... (below).

When a Japanese pilot missed —he still had his plane as a bomb (top). And the Japanese even came in at night... (above). The Japanese ships took a beating. This happens to be the *Kumano* (right).

Not long after this, the *Yama-shiro* went down... (top). The Japanese cruiser *Nachi* under fire... (above). Before long, the *St. Lo* was hit, too... (left).

When the *Princeton* was hurt, the *Birmingham* began to help
... (top). Some *Princeton* survivors went off in boats...
(above). The Filipinos helped American survivors, but when
they caught the Japanese it was a different story... (below).

Vice Admiral F. C. Sherman   **Rear Admiral R. L. Connolly**

Rear Admiral G. L. Weyler   **Rear Admiral Gerald Bogan**

The Japanese cruiser *Tone* did not get away ... (above).
Pilots in the Ready Room ... USS *Franklin* (below).

Yamato's turrets look as though she is searching . . . (above).
The *Zuikaku* and *Zuiho* under attack (below).

When the battle was over, there was still some sad work to be done, on other ships as well as *Kalinin Bay*...

northeast with single planes in each subsector. We didn't have many planes in the single task group there. . . . At about 1430 we launched an attack into the Sibuyan Sea, in other words we felt that there were enemy planes to the northeast. We knew that there were enemy planes to the southwest, so we launched every plane that we could get against the fleet that we knew was in the Sibuyan Sea.

In the meantime we sent a very few planes to the northeast in the hopes that they would be able to pick up something. Sure enough, at about 1540 those search planes which we had sent to the northeast did contact an enemy force which was reported as being 3 battleships, half a dozen cruisers, and 6 destroyers, and there was another contact in a different position of 3 carriers, 3 cruisers, and 3 destroyers, on course west, speed 15.

The first of these, of course, was the Matsuda force headed south to undertake the night engagement. The second was the Ozawa force. But of course, the Americans did not know this. Indeed, how were they to know that there was not still another force, or even more? Other Japanese vessels were still at home, including several large carriers. American intelligence did not know that there were no planes for those carriers or that they were not ready for sea. A lot of guesswork was going on, on both sides, and that should not be forgotten in assessing the actions of the admirals.

"At first we thought these reports were of the same group and then we realized that the pilots which we had sent up—got a confirmation from these pilots—and they were positive of what they had sighted and we realized there were actually two groups, one a carrier group and one a surface group."

Admiral Mitscher and his staff set to work planning what they might do. They were too far from the enemy to make an air attack that afternoon. "We made plans to conduct a night attack with the surface forces attached to 38.3 on the enemy carrier task force." Had Mitscher done so, that plan would have meant he sent Admiral Lee with the *Massachusetts, South Dakota, Alabama, Washington,* and perhaps the cruisers *Mobile* and *Reno* up to attack, along with the necessary destroyers. And had he done this, most of the fast battleships would have gone north. "In view of the general tactical situation and the probability that such action would upset the plans of ComThird Fleet, this was not done."

As sunset approached, the plans of the Third Fleet were crystallizing in flag plot on the *New Jersey.*

Halsey's officers were totaling up everything they had learned during the day.

"At this time it was evident that the Japanese Navy was making a major effort, whether for direct attack or transporting troops, or both, was not apparent. If this was to be an all-out attack by the Japanese fleet, there was one piece missing in the puzzle—the carriers."

[This referred to an earlier part of the day, before the carriers were found, but this sentence was most significant in view of Halsey's actions:]

"They were believed to have been in the Empire; there had been sightings and intelligence reports which indicated that replenishment measures might have been taken for some important movement from Empire waters."

In other words, Halsey did not know the status of the carriers; except that previous experience had always indicated the Japanese carriers were extremely dangerous.

"Although our submarines stationed in Empire waters had not reported a carrier force, it was felt that they were sure to be employed in some manner in any operation as great as that revealed on the morning of the 24th."

So then had come the searches and the carriers had been found. "Commander Third Fleet concluded that the Northern Force was disposed in two groups, estimated to contain a total of at least 17 ships and possibly as many as 24 ships."

And there was something extremely odd about the whole operation of the Japanese as it unfolded before Halsey's eyes:

"A curious point was apparent from the contact reports of the three forces: they were all proceeding at deliberate speed and it was inferred that there was a predetermined focus of geographical location and time. The movements indicated that a carefully worked-out coordinated Japanese plan was in motion with 25 October as the earliest date of planned concerted action."

What Halsey and his staff saw, then, was the convergence of Kurita, Nishimura, and Ozawa on Leyte Gulf. He did not know about Shima's little force.

And the Halsey staff, "my brilliant staff" he called them affectionately, had put together impressive figures of the damage done to Kurita. Bogan's force, for example, had flown 146 planes off in sorties, dropped 23 tons of bombs and 23 torpedoes. And look what results Bogan claimed:

1 BB *Yamato:* damaged, 3 torpedo hits
1 BB *Yamato:* damaged, 1 torpedo hit and 2 bombs (possibly same)
1 BB *Nagato:* damaged, 1 torpedo and 1 bomb
1 BB *Kongo:* damaged, 2 torpedoes and 6 bombs
1 CA *Mogami:* damaged, possibly sunk by torpedo
1 CA *Nachi:* damaged, 1 torpedo
1 CA *Tone:* damaged, 1 torpedo

Here were Admiral Sherman's claims:

1 BB: damaged badly
2 BB: damaged
4 CA: damaged
2 CL: damaged

Here were Admiral Davison's claims:

1 BB *Musashi:* damaged by torpedo, down by bow, probably sunk.
1 BB *Yamato:* damaged, 1–3 torpedoes, 2 bombs
1 BB *Kongo:* damaged, 1 bomb
1 CA: damaged
1 CL: sunk
1 DD: sunk
1 DD: probably sunk
4 DD: damaged

"Some details," said Halsey's men, "were not available at dusk, but flash reports indicated beyond doubt tha: the center force had been badly mauled with all of its BB and most of its CA tremendously reduced in fighting power and life."

By the evening Halsey knew that the Kurita force had turned around and was heading once again for San Bernardino Strait. He had now to make a basic decision.

The alternatives as he saw them were these:

1. Divide the forces, leaving Admiral Lee and the battleships of Task Force 34 to block San Bernardino Strait while the carriers with 2 battleships and the cruisers and destroyers attacked the northern force of Ozawa. But the problem here was that the potential strength of the undamaged northern force was too great to leave unmolested ". . . requiring TF 34 to engage the Center Force [Kurita] while at the same time exposed to attack by land-based and possibly carrier-based air attack was not sound. This alternative spread our strength and risked unprofitable damage in detail."

The fact was that Japanese air had shown a remarkable resurgence on October 24, after all that had happened and all that Halsey had been led to expect. He was aware of the Japanese air pipeline technique, of ferrying planes from the home islands to Formosa, and then down to northern Luzon. He did not know how many planes the Japanese had to ferry or how quickly they were ferrying them, or how many planes Ozawa's carriers had left.

2. Maintain the integrity of the striking force of the Third Fleet, and keep the fleet off San Bernardino Strait, waiting to cover the American position. This "permitted the Northern Force to function as planned unmolested, and because destruction of Japan's carrier force would mean much to future operations . . ." Halsey did not like the idea at all. He knew this is what Spruance would have done.

3. Strike the northern force with all of his fleet's strength concentrated, and leave San Bernardino Strait unguarded. Halsey liked this plan. It appealed to the fighting admiral in him, it maintained the integrity of his striking fleet, it offered a chance to hit the Japanese hard and surprise and destroy the enemy carrier force. "It was particularly sound and necessary if the strength of the Northern Force proved to be the maximum reported." And that was a very important matter. HE DID NOT KNOW.

Halsey recognized that the Kurita force might get out of

San Bernardino Strait and do some damage, but he held to the idea that he had hurt its fighting power so much that it could never win against what Admiral Kinkaid had to throw against the Japanese.

And finally, in considering it all, Halsey estimated that the Third Fleet could always return in time to reverse any advantage that Kurita might gain, even if a "temporarily tight situation" were to develop at Leyte.

All this was laid out by the staff as the sun sank and Halsey pondered. It was his way to let his staff have its say, and the staff spoke up.

The Japanese must be making a banzai attack of the kind he had encountered in the South Pacific so often, obeying an Imperial order to do or die.

"From long experience with the Japanese, their blind adherence to plan, and their inability to readjust disturbed plans, the commander Third Fleet had long ago adopted a policy of attacking first." The policy had served him well in building morale in the South Pacific and achieving victory there. Now, he knew the Japanese were dogged—he did not underestimate the courage of his enemy—just the enemy's judgment.

And he decided.

". . . commander Third Fleet was convinced that the Center Force was so heavily damaged that it could not win a decision while the possible maximum strength of the Northern Force . . . constituted a fresh and powerful threat. It was decided that earliest possible attack on the powerful Northern [carrier] Force was essential for breaking up the enemy plan and retaining the initiative. . . ."

"It was a hard decision to make" but Halsey made it.

At 2032 he ordered Admiral Mitscher to take command of the three carrier groups nearby and attack the enemy carrier force. Admiral McCain and his carrier group were racing to join them.

13

IN LEYTE GULF

Before darkness fell on October 24, the various unit commanders were all puzzling over the Japanese intentions and the actions that ought to be taken, but in the face of Admiral Halsey's decision, there was not really much that any of them could do. Halsey was in charge, and he had made a decision.

Admiral Bogan thought it a wrong decision. He suspected, from the change in Japanese course, that Admiral Kurita was coming through San Bernardino Strait. The intelligence from the night carrier *Independence* also indicated this. Halsey had ordered the *Independence* to have planes in the vicinity of the Kurita force just before dark to shadow the enemy and keep him informed of Japanese movements.

That evening the *Independence* reported the Japanese were on course 120, at 12 knots. That meant they were heading southeast, toward San Bernardino Strait, as Bogan feared. At 1935 the *Independence* reported and confirmed it. An hour later the *Independence* reported the Japanese fleet off the middle of the west coast of the little island of Burias, just west of southern Luzon, and then the night carrier planes said the Japanese were moving between Bias and Masbate islands—coming closer.

Admiral Bogan got Captain E. C. Ewen of the *Independence* on the talk between ships, and Ewen said he was sure the Japanese were coming through the Strait. Bogan got a message ready for Halsey. "Recommended from Leo [Task Force 34]," it said. "Leave my group in support and let the other two groups handle the northern force."

He did not send the message just then, although he later said, "I thought that Admiral Halsey was making one hell of a mistake."

In talking with Ewen, Bogan learned one salient fact: although for as long as anyone could remember the Japanese had kept San Bernardino Strait darkened, probably against American submarines, this night navigation lights were all turned on. That certainly meant something to a ship captain. Bogan got the message to the *New Jersey* by telephone, but was cut off.

"Yes, yes," said the voice answering. "We have that information."

And nothing was changed. The risk had been calculated. The information that the Japanese were on course 060, which would lead them to the Strait, meant nothing anymore. Halsey had committed himself.

Bogan did not send his message about Task Force 34.

On the battleship *Washington*, Admiral Lee was working out the plot of the enemy force, and before dark he sent a blinker message to Admiral Halsey suggesting that the northern force was a decoy and that the major Japanese effort would come through San Bernardino Strait. The message was confirmed in receipt, but there was no answer. Lee sent one more message, by TBS, but it did not affect Halsey's decision.

Admiral Kinkaid and his commanders of the Seventh Fleet had been waiting all day, because theirs was the responsibility to continue supplying and protecting the invasion troops who were making their way across the jungles and mountains of Leyte.

Admirals Barbey and Wilkinson were overseeing their sectors. In Barbey's sector the ships went to General Quarters at 0800 on the 24th, because an air raid began. Some 18 Navy fighters were put up by the jeep carriers. A dozen Japanese planes came over, and several of them dropped bombs, two of which hit between the *Blue Ridge* and the LCI stationed nearby, and three more between the *Blue Ridge* and the *Shropshire*. There was no damage, and the Americans watched happily as two of the Japanese were "splashed" off Red Beach.

It was no picnic off Red Beach or anywhere else that day, and the minimal destruction of American ships by the Japanese perhaps tells the story less accurately than Captain Tarbuck's diary, which was put together very shortly after the events:

Enemy dive bombers launch an attack on the starboard bow. All guns open up with a hell of a roar. The *Shropshire* and a destroyer commence firing also and the aircraft are turning away. Fighter pilots can be heard over the radio "tallyhoing" the enemy. Three planes fall burning, one crashes on shore. One LCI bursts into flames from a hit or a suicide plane crash. One Liberty ship is hit by a bomb. There is too much smoke to identify ships now and the burning oil smoke of the LCI rises 5000 feet, flames about 200 feet. Our combat air patrol is being relieved by a new group, arriving on station from the CVE's. The support aircraft circuit announces the splashing of over 20 enemy planes.

The unloading of men and supplies continued through this hail. That morning, the fleet made smoke to screen itself during the air attack, and then let the smoke die when the attack was over. By afternoon the two landing forces had put ashore 144,000 men and 244,000 tons of supplies and equipment since the beginning of the invasion. The Americans were established and had a tremendous stake on shore. A hundred and forty-one ships lay in the Gulf, and the Japanese were coming in harder and harder.

At 1500 there was another alert, another attack. The sky was spotted with flak, and the small craft were making smoke again. A Betty skidded by the side of the *Blue Ridge*, Barbey's flagship, under fire from a destroyer. A Zero came by on the port quarter—both unscathed. "The Japanese are getting bolder and the attacks more frequent," Captain Tarbuck noted. But a Hellcat shot one Val down in his sight, and then another Val went down.

By 1500 the men of the fleet were learning that a battle was brewing, with ships coming in from both the Sulu Sea and Mindoro Strait.

The Japanese air attacks continued, and as the day wore on the smoke over the Gulf became so intense that when explosions were heard, usually on the *Blue Ridge,* no one could guess what they might be. At 1845 the moon began rising, in its first quarter. And then nine Japanese planes came in through the murk, most of them to be shot down by the American fighters.

The word had been passed by Admiral Kinkaid's staff that Admiral Halsey was aware of all their dangers and that the new battleships had been formed into a task force to guard San Bernardino Strait, while Admiral Oldendorf's bombardment battleships of older vintage, and cruisers and destroyers and PT boats, should be available to stop the Japanese in Surigao Strait.

The Americans in the Gulf were not unduly worried. General Krueger, Commander of Sixth Army, went ashore at 1855, to assume command of the Central Philippine Attack Force, and thus to relieve Admiral Kinkaid of the land portion of his responsibility.

Now, all day long on October 24 Admiral Kinkaid had been studying the situation from his flag plot in the *Wasatch.* At 1512 his staff intercepted the dispatch that Halsey sent out with his battle plan for the formation of Task Force 34 under Admiral Lee. Had Halsey known of the eagerness and interest with which this dispatch was read aboard the *Wasatch,* he undoubtedly would have gained an insight into Admiral Kinkaid's thinking that he did not have. Kinkaid and his officers were delighted with the Halsey plan; as much as any commander could ever do under any circumstances, Kinkaid was able to put the danger of the Kurita force out of his mind and concentrate on the problem he faced from the south, where Nishimura and Shima were moving up through the Sulu Sea.

Admiral Kinkaid had a very good idea that the Japanese of the Nishimura force were relatively unhurt, even though the planes of Admiral Halsey's Third Fleet had indicated serious damage. But he had all day to worry about that problem, too. He planned, carefully, and at 1430 ordered Rear Admiral Oldendorf to prepare for a probable night engagement.

Admiral Jesse Oldendorf was already making preparations for a fight, because Kinkaid was a thorough man, and just after noon he had declared the possibilities to his ships —every one of them. When the order came to prepare, it too was done with Kinkaid's usual care. The fighting ships made quite a formidable force. They included the battleships, 6 of them, 8 cruisers, 26 destroyers, and 39 PT boats.

Admiral Oldendorf had been waiting; he, like everyone else, expected a Japanese attack of some kind on the American forces in the Gulf. When the word came, things began to happen. The amphibious flagships closed up on the Liberty ships and lesser vessels in San Pedro Bay. The flagships were marvelous vessels, triumphs of communications genius, but except for anti-aircraft weapons they were unfit to defend themselves. You could not have everything on one ship, and long ago the American Navy had learned that a commander of an amphibious force was better off in a special ship than in a battleship or cruiser with guns belting down the communications every few minutes. The cruiser *Nashville* was also stationed near these ships for it bore precious cargo indeed—General MacArthur. What the Japanese would not give to kill or capture MacArthur. To do so would almost have been worth any price that the Sho operation cost. All concerned were aware of the necessity of keeping a special eye on the *Nashville* and the ships around her. A close screen of destroyers was thrown around these ships to protect them at all costs, and so there would be no mistakes about friends and foes, Admiral Kinkaid said that all ship movements into and out of Leyte Gulf would end at sunset.

Yes, Oldendorf was waiting. He had not been fooled by the apparent ease with which they had landed the forces on the beaches of Leyte. He expected light fast forces of the Japanese to try to interfere with the transports. Indeed, for four nights he had kept his battleships south of the transports, guarding the southern entrance to Leyte Gulf, and his cruisers had been off to port of the battleships; he had not been sleeping at the switch. Rear Admiral R. S.

Berkey's close covering group, originally made up of 4 cruisers and several destroyers, was closer in to the transports. Berkey had been reduced by one cruiser when the *Australia* took that diving plane early in the operation, but was still strong enough in force for the job to be done. So the southern group reported, Oldendorf prepared.

When this group was reported, Admiral Kinkaid directed me to prepare for a night engagement and battle plans were drawn so that a night action could be fought with an enemy coming through Surigao Strait from the south, or attempting to enter Surigao Strait from the Pacific to the east. [One thing to remember in reading about these battles is the huge question mark in the mind of every commander as to the intentions of his enemy. Knowing now what the Japanese were doing and why, a writer can speak glibly, but in study of the materials of war, it is apparent that much more was guessed, sometimes rightly and sometimes wrongly, by commanders on both sides than was ever known to them by observation. Admiral Oldendorf did not know as of the afternoon of October 24 just what the Japanese were going to do. He merely had some very strong suspicions, and acted on them.] As information continued to come in it was manifest that the southern force was actually going to attempt to penetrate the Strait although it was greatly inferior in size and strength to the force under my command.

Admiral Oldendorf prepared his battle plan unhurriedly and sent copies of it over to Rear Admiral G. L. Weyler who was in command of the battleships, and to Rear Admiral R. S. Berkey in the *Phoenix,* who was to command the right-flank forces. Facing Surigao Strait, which runs between Leyte and Dinagat Islands, there were destroyers on the right flank against Leyte, and destroyers on the left flank, off Dinagat. Facing the Strait there were Berkey's cruisers on the right flank, next to Leyte, and Oldendorf's own cruisers on the left flank, next to and behind little Hibuson Island, which juts off Dinagat. Behind were the big battleships, thus protected and able to fire over the lesser ships very easily.

Admiral Weyler was the Commander of the Battle Line; under him was Rear Admiral T. D. Ruddock, who led Battleship Division Four, and Rear Admiral T. E. Chandler, who led Battleship Division Two. Assisting Oldendorf directly, in charge of Cruiser Division 12, was Rear Admiral R. W. Hayler. The Americans had enough admirals involved in the battle so that no matter what happened there could not be a breakdown in command.

The force was ready and in position by darkness on October 24, but since Admiral Kinkaid and his commanders knew that Admiral Halsey was planning to form Task Force 34, the new battleship force, to guard San Bernardino Strait, there was no nervousness when, just before 2030, Kinkaid learned that Halsey was moving north with three task groups to attack the enemy northern force led by Admiral Ozawa.

Kinkaid was much more concerned with his own problems. The battleships were going up and down at the head of the Strait, cruisers and destroyers at bow and stern. And it seemed that everyone was eager: when Kinkaid had sent out the call for PT boats that afternoon, the lamentable report came back that only about 20 of the 50 boats in the fleet were available for action. The others were down with sick engines or something equally serious. But then, when the commanders learned that there was going to be a fight that night—or that there was likely to be a fight—suddenly those engines improved and the number of available boats doubled.

The American admirals of the Oldendorf unit knew exactly what they were going to do. Weyler and Berkey had come aboard the *Louisville* to discuss their problems, the most important of which was that they were heavily laden with explosive ammunition and lightly stacked with armor-piercing shells. Actually the battleships averaged about enough armor-piercing shells for five salvos. These would have to be saved for enemy battleships (nothing less than armor piercing would stop them) so some careful spotting and calculation was in order. Also the admirals agreed to hold fire until the Japanese battleships came within 20,000 yards.

There were a few other little problems: the destroyers were short on torpedoes and no replacements were available, and the destroyers had used up most of their 5-inch ammunition against the beaches, so they had about 20 per-cent left. But the battleships had an automatic position, at the head of the Gulf, that admirals had fought for dozens of times before—the position of "crossing the T."

The idea of crossing the "T" is that one force of ships would steam along faster than its opponent, maybe having the weather gauge in the old days, and then would cut sharply across the bow (well ahead) of the enemy force, so that all the guns on one side of the battle force could bear on each one of the enemy ships in turn as it came along (being the body of the "T," while the crossing ships were the top, or cross).

The American force was arranged across the mouth of Surigao Strait like the cross of the "T," just waiting for the body of the "T" to join.

The poor "body" was in for a frightful time. First, in the Strait even as far away as the Mindanao Sea, the torpedo boats would attack with torpedoes. Second, the destroyers of right and left flanks would rush forward and attack from each side. And third, the cruisers and battleships would take the enemy under fire as each ship steamed forward to help make that "T." Admiral Oldendorf was not crossing the "T"—he was *making* the "T."

"My theory," he was to say later, "was that of the old-time gambler: Never give a sucker an even break. If my opponent is foolish enough to come at me with an inferior force, I'm certainly not going to give him an even break."

So it was a confident American force that waited for the Japanese to come up, and added to it was the force of Destroyer Squadron 54, 7 new destroyers itching to get into the fight, under Captain J. B. Coward. They were detailed to guard the southern force, but Captain Coward asked for permission to join the battle, and Admiral Oldendorf gave it to him.

As for the Japanese on October 24, they were moving into very much of a void, and even among those who were to strike through the Sulu Sea there was much confusion and very little information exchanged.

Take, for example, the case of Japanese Destroyer Division 23, which was detailed as a part of the Shima striking force. While waiting in those days when all the forces were converging on Leyte Gulf, Destroyer Division 23 was ordered to Takao in Formosa to bring base equipment and personnel for the Second Air Fleet, Admiral Fukudome's organization, which was hoping to throw its strength into the balance and secure mastery of the air. This division consisted of the destroyers *Wakaba, Hatsuharu,* and *Hatsushimo,* and what happened to it is among the sad little stories of the Japanese Sho operation.

The destroyers loaded the Second Air Fleet components and set out for Manila, arriving on the afternoon of October 23. They were to unload, refuel, and move out to join up as quickly as they could. But the *Hatsushimo* was delayed in refueling, and so the division was held up in Manila Bay until 2125 on the 23rd.

On the morning of October 24, Admiral Davison's planes found the destroyers on their way and attacked. One plane bombed the *Wakaba,* the flagship, and with one bomb and a near miss by another plane, the *Wakaba* became unnavigable and sank just before 0900. The *Hatsuharu* became the division flagship. She picked up a handful of survivors from the flagship (5 officers and 73 petty officers and men) and moved south on course 160 degrees. Then, at 1152, more enemy planes attacked *Hatsushimo* and one bomb on the port side damaged the ship badly, but she could make full speed. Still more planes came in and there was a bloody battle in which the Japanese claimed to have shot down several American planes. The end result was that the 2 remaining destroyers reversed course, and headed back to Manila Bay, arriving at 0100 on October 25. They had been very definitely driven out of the battle by the carrier planes—and the damage to them, which was included in the overall picture, was part of the confusion, because these ships had never figured in the estimates of the forces sighted. In other words here were 3 Japanese warships that had not been counted in the "sightings," but 2 of them were most definitely countable in the damage count—and the reports simply served to add emphasis to the blow struck the Japanese fleet and to convince Halsey that he had indeed hit hard. After all, counting these ships, the Japanese had no fewer than 5 forces at sea—4 of them coming from the west. It was small wonder that there was confusion.

14

THE BATTLE OF SURIGAO STRAIT— PART I

Following the attack by American planes on the morning of October 24, Admiral Nishimura's 2 battleships, 1 cruiser, and 4 destroyers steamed steadily on toward Surigao Strait. The American attack set fire to the after deck of the battleship *Fuso,* as noted, wrecked an observation plane there, and caused damage below decks. But the damage was not serious enough to stop the *Fuso* or the force, and Nishimura steamed on. Some of his men thought the Americans were specifically diving at their planes—for the *Mogami's* aircraft deck had been strafed before the Americans flew away at about 1000.

Some officers in the Nishimura force were aware of the whole Sho plan, and they believed that Admiral Nishimura and Admiral Shima ought to get together and go into Surigao Strait as a unit. But Japanese naval discipline was such that they said nothing. "Nishimura was older than Shima and had more naval and battle experience; in spite of that, Shima was his superior." This had led to personal bitterness.

And yet the Japanese of this force were confident of victory. They had been told by their superiors that they had a force equal to the Americans, except perhaps in the matter of heavy cruisers, and they fully expected that the balance was evenly matched by the natural superiority of the Japanese fighting man.

The Nishimura force sped on, looking for more air attacks, and a little puzzled because none came. The *Mogami* had sent her search plane out ahead, and for the first time she had a fairly good idea of what they were going to face.

The plane found 4 battleships, 2 cruisers, 4 destroyers, 15 aircraft carriers, 14 PT boats, and 80 transports. Weighed against this, of course, was the fact that there would be a simultaneous attack in the morning, and Kurita's force would be most helpful in diverting part of this enemy. Then, if Ozawa was successful, those carriers would vanish over the horizon. What ships the *Mogami* found was not quite certain; probably they were the escort carriers and the battle line of Admiral Oldendorf, or a part of this force. The weather these days was so bad that no pilot could be faulted for finding only partial forces, but the reports were particularly confusing because the Americans had literally hundreds of ships in the area at this time.

The original plan called for the Nishimura force to reach a point on Dulag at 0430 on the 25th, but during the day, for reasons that are still not known, the Japanese decided to move up the schedule. So they were running ahead, and Kurita was running behind. It did not augur well.

By midday the Japanese of the Nishimura force were completely recovered from the attack of the morning. The fires aboard the *Fuso*, started by the burning of aviation gas on the hangar deck, were extinguished. The destroyer *Shigure* had been hit by a bomb on No. 1 gun house and several of her gunners had been killed by the armor-piercing bomb which exploded right inside. Five men were killed and six wounded, and the *Shigure* had to shift men around in order to get a crew to man the gun. Fortunately for the Japanese, the gun was not hurt.

Such is the difference between the vision of pilots and reality that, sometimes, while the attacking pilots thought they had hurt the force sorely, the Japanese said their speed and fighting efficiency had not been bothered. They moved right along at 18 knots, and as far as battle was concerned, their only encounter was with blips on the radar screens, planes that were busy heading elsewhere not bothering with their force.

After the attack in the morning Admiral Nishimura dutifully reported to Kurita that he had been attacked with light damage and no effect on his navigability or the plan. But the ships did not even know whether the message was received. That day, the Nishimura force did learn that Shima was coming through, having left his anchorage in the morning, but they did not know where he was, they did not sight him (though it would have been relatively easy for these forces to link up), and there was no communication between the fighting units.

Toward evening, the Nishimura force had its moments of apprehension, when Admiral Kurita turned about and sent his message so indicating to combined fleet headquarters. It was some two hours before the confusion was straightened out, and Kurita was back on his course again as far as Nishimura knew. Luckily he had been kept informed, and he had simply kept moving all this time toward his goal: Surigao Strait. It was a mark of Nishimura's fatalistic determination that he did not change course or slow down, even though the message that Kurita had retired would have meant there was no chance of a link-up in Leyte Gulf, and the facts must have indicated that there was no chance of meeting the old timetable of a dawn breakthrough. Nishimura plowed on, giving periodic reports of his position, course, and speed. Whatever Kurita and the others did, Nishimura was following the Sho orders from headquarters and he would do so to the death.

The one difference was that Nishimura was ahead of schedule while the other admiral was behind. One of his subordinates, Captain Nishino of the destroyer *Shigure*, hazarded the guess that the reason for this was Nishimura's long training in the Japanese naval philosophy of fighting night battles against a superior force. That night he increased the speed so that a night engagement became almost certain, and about 2000 he sent the big cruiser *Mogami* and the destroyers *Asagumo, Yamagumo,* and *Michishiyo* out ahead of the main force to reconnoiter and stir up the enemy if he was there. They moved out and Nishimura sent a message to Kurita and Toyoda that he intended to penetrate to a point off Dulag at 0400. The advance group moved northeast, to a point off Panaon Island. The weather was roughening as they neared the Strait, the wind increasing, the waves slapping harder in the wind and throwing spindrift, and the clouds building up jealously to guard the night sky from the water.

Just far enough behind to be of no reasonable use to the Nishimura force stood the Shima force. Shima's whole part in the operation was a badly tattered patchwork, and it was already clearly showing how destructive the combined fleet's heedless plans could be. By dividing the forces, before Kurita was hit so hard, the Japanese had already suffered damage to the cruiser *Aoba,* which kept her out of the fight, and to 3 destroyers which were sent to Manila with troops and supplies, one of them sunk, the other 2 so thoroughly confused that they never did find Shima and join up with him as their orders said.

Here was how Admiral Shima's life had been going since he had moved out of Amami-o-Shima, reached Mako and fueled, was separated from the *Aoba* and his 3 destroyers, went to Coron where he expected to find a tanker but there was none. All this while he had been hearing conflicting reports and ideas on the radio; how the army was, was not and then was going to fight for Leyte, and how the slow Second Battleship Division did not want to get involved with the faster First Battleship Division.

Communications being what they were, when Admiral Shima decided to let everyone know what he thought and what he would do, as he was steaming along on the way to Coron Bay, he sent off one of his seaplanes. The little force was hugging the coast west of Lingayen as he went; the plane soared into the air and headed for Manila to outline the coming Shima operation and radio it to combined fleet in Japan. That way there would be no argument with anyone, and perhaps that was one of the reasons for the independent Shima's action. After all, someone *might* decide that a minor force of cruisers and destroyers should be subject to a major force of battleships.

Shima lost his planes to the Cavite air base. He was in direct radio contact with Kurita, but not with Nishimura, even before he reached the anchorage at Coron Bay. Since there was no tanker, he had to split his fuel from the 3 cruisers with the short-ranged destroyers. The result was fuel to last the force about five days and nights operating at 20 knots, or fighting speed.

Admiral Shima had sailed that morning of October 24 at 0200 with the most sketchy information about the American dispositions. Perhaps the worst thing about the sketchiness was its complete unreliability; the officers had quite lost confidence. Not only were the reports of the air searches conflicting, but the messages were garbled and about all the Japanese knew was that a lot of American ships were in Leyte Gulf. They had no situation report, not even an army report on which to rely as they sailed out to do battle.

The wording of Admiral Shima's orders was so vague that he could do just about as he wished. He and his staff consulted and decided that a localized night action in restricted enemy waters (and waters unknown to this force) could do nothing for anybody. In other words, while Nishimura wanted a night action, Shima did not want a night action at all. He decided that he would penetrate Surigao Strait at 0600 after sunrise, on the heels of whatever the Nishimura force had accomplished. He would steam in a single column with the flagship first. If the American ships were waiting, the cruisers would launch a powerful torpedo attack, and then the destroyers would speed alongside, pass them, torpedo the cripples, and Shima would sweep in victoriously with the cruisers, move around Leyte Gulf in clockwise fashion, knocking off supply ships and perhaps a handful of carriers, with whatever cruisers got in the way. Then, if time permitted and there were any shells left, he would destroy the enemy dumps on the beaches before he steamed victoriously back to Japan.

Admiral Shima steamed along that day, undetected by the Americans. Until dawn they moved at 20 knots. After dawn they slowed to 18 knots.

When Admiral Nishimura let it be known that he was advancing his time of attack, Admiral Shima advanced his time of attack, but not, of course, to coincide with Nishimura—still to come in after Nishimura had paved the way, and retain that important independence of action.

There was more confusion in Shima's force late in the afternoon when the messages about Kurita's turnabout and the subsequent flurry began, and when Nishimura's dispatch was intercepted to the effect that he was steaming on in spite of what Kurita might do. It was regarded aboard the Shima ships as "tragic." They knew, these officers, that Nishimura was heading into a hail of steel, and heading there alone.

And the fantasy continued.

After Kurita debouched from San Bernardino Strait, he radioed the southern force; he wanted them all to meet with him at 1000 off the southern tip of Samar. It was like a sailor making a date with a girl more than anything else; the bravado of it: to come in in full daylight against a force that *must* be formidable and then discuss meeting places as though they were the fronts of soda parlors.

Kurita's message caused Shima to change his plans. He had not wanted to go in in the dark, but if he was to meet the other he would have to do so. He pushed the plans ahead another two hours, and speeded up to 22 knots. That was as fast as he could go. He did not have the fuel to increase the speed by another knot—as it was, he was increasing the consumption curve dangerously, and he would just barely make it home if all went well.

All these decisions were made in an unreal peace and quiet, considering what they knew was happening to the Kurita force, and what had happened even to Nishimura that day. They steamed and saw nothing, until darkness fell and they did see bonfires on the shore of Bohol Island as they passed south. They did not know whether it was native guerrillas giving the sign that they were coming, or what. They simply prepared for action, and as they prepared the weather worsened visibly, and they headed into squalls.

At combined fleet headquarters outside Tokyo, Admiral Toyoda was watching the plot of his forces as they moved along with a good deal of concern. He could see that the heavy damages sustained by Kurita's force endangered the success—whatever chance that might be—of the mission. Actually, Toyoda did not consider the chances of success very great, nor did he seem to realize the full implications of the battles to come. "Actually I did not consider it such a large naval battle." But on the other hand, he was determined to go ahead, no matter what—and that was the reason for his order to Kurita to proceed that afternoon.

. . . This operation from the outset revolved around Kurita's force, and the other forces were merely carrying out coordinated operations. Consequently if the axis were removed the entire operation would collapse. And should this happen, the enemy would land on Leyte unopposed, and using that place as a key position would undoubtedly push step by step his conquest of the entire Philippines. If the Philippines fell into enemy hands, the traffic lanes between the Japanese homeland and the southern areas would be severed and the plan to strengthen conditions for a protracted war by safeguarding the resources of the southern region would be fundamentally upset. Also, at the same time, if the traffic lanes with the homeland were cut, the fighting strength in the front lines would be unable to obtain supplies. Even if the navy were to keep the Kurita force in the southern region, ultimately it would be self-destruction through malnutrition. On the other hand, if it were to pull out and return to the homeland it would be unable to obtain fuel . . . and if communications [with the south] were cut off there would not be a drop of fuel for the ships. . . . In the end even if you had a fleet it would be a white elephant. . . .

So with a sad heart Toyoda had ordered Kurita back, and gave silent approval to the adjustment of the forces heading into Surigao Strait.

The problem—yesterday, today, and perhaps tomorrow —also revolved around the failure of the air force to carry out its part of the Sho task. The battleship and cruisers were without a single plane capable of protecting them. The land-based air forces were insisting on operating on the strike principle, rather than the protection principle, and it has been seen what little they accomplished on the 24th, at such dreadful expense to themselves.

It was planned by the Japanese that a night attack would be carried out in waves between dusk of October 24 and dawn of October 25, using heavy bomber, light bomber, and attack forces. By late afternoon the Japanese forces were so reduced that such a plan was patently impossible. Six bombers took off from Nichols Field at 1600 and raided the forces in Leyte Gulf, and during the night a few snoopers were put up to try to help the Japanese at Surigao Strait, but they were of no help. They could hardly be much help. The Japanese air resources in the Philippines were very slender at that moment. Most of those planes that had been seen over the ships at Leyte Gulf were army planes—the navy planes were attacking the fighting ships of the Americans.

On the naval airfields around Manila, the Japanese pilots were very much upset. They knew that Admiral Kurita had pleaded for aerial cover and had not gotten it. They heard that the *Musashi* had sunk. Here is the way they took it:

Our fliers were frantic. They held themselves responsible for every blow suffered by Kurita, for the sole purpose of the kamikaze corps was to destroy the enemy carriers before they could launch their deadly attacks. So far we had not struck a single carrier—had not even been able to locate the enemy task force.

Near Manila, Admirals Fukudome and Ohnishi were carrying on the argument that had begun several days ago —Fukudome of the Second Air Fleet still holding out for the conventional air attacks, and Ohnishi demanding that Fukudome save the plane strength they had left and make use of every plane as a flying bomb.

The Japanese units moved on against Surigao Strait. Commander Kazuo Tanaka, Captain of the destroyer *Michishio,* considered making one last appeal for the Nishimura force to wait and go in together with the Shima force when it came up, but Commander Nishino was too wise in the ways of the navy to listen to the young man, too knowledgeable about the forces driving Admiral Nishimura.

Admiral Kinkaid had divided his PT boats into 13 three boat sections; they were spread out from the southern part of Surigao Strait as far west as Bohol Island. Their mission was to cut off the ocean entrance to the southern part of Surigao Strait, to report incoming ships, and to attack them—and in that order of importance.

If Admiral Nishimura had wanted to slow down, which he might have in view of a radio message sent by Admiral Kurita to the effect that he would not arrive in Leyte Gulf until 1100 the next day, and that Nishimura was to meet him at 0900 10 miles northeast of Suluan Island—why it was too late for that by the time the message was received and digested.

For at a few minutes after 2230 that night, with its seeping waves and chilling showers, the Americans in PT Boat Section One, operating off Bohol, picked up the Nishimura flagship and protecting destroyers and the other battleship, and came moving bravely in against this formidable enemy, making 24 knots. In fifteen minutes the forces sighted one another, and the Battle of Surigao Strait began. There was now nothing that Admiral Nishimura could do but fight or run for it, and he was certainly not going to do the latter.

The PT's came on, 3 of them; *PT-131*, *PT-130*, and *PT-152*. They had their two tasks, report and attack, and as they came speeding toward the Japanese the radiomen on the little boats were trying to carry out their first task.

The Japanese came after them like a pack of wild dogs. Admiral Nishimura turned his force toward the PT's, and the destroyer *Shigure* began ranging on them. Quickly the little boats were illuminated, and soon the good shots of the *Shigure* were putting 5-inch shells fore and aft of the boats, even though they were zigzagging furiously. The Japanese shooting was good, and the PT boats began making smoke, stepped up the violence of their zigzags, and tried to move in for a torpedo attack. But the Japanese were old hands at fighting in close, and they began scoring hits on the little boats. *PT-152* was hit by an explosive shell which blew up her 37 mm gun, killed one man, and wounded three. Another shell—perhaps armor-piercing—passed right through the plywood hull of *PT-130* but did not explode. The concussion knocked out this PT boat's radio.

Then the Japanese moved on, while *PT-130* rushed along to Section Two's area, to deliver the message of the coming of the Japanese to the safer PT boats. It was some time before the battle force received the word, because it had to be relayed. Meanwhile, the Japanese moved on, jamming the radio circuits, and effectively stopping or at least delaying the report of their coming, but not delaying it enough, because of the fast thinking of the skipper of

PT-130, who was doing by sea what he was being kept from doing by radio: carrying the word.

The Japanese were now disposed in two groups, the battleships and destroyer screen to the south, and the *Mogami* and destroyers to the north. The *Mogami* group was not seen by the radar of PT Section Two, and passed on, Nishimura radioing Kurita and Shima that he was moving right ahead "destroying enemy torpedo boats" as he went. Just before midnight the Japanese reached a point south of Limasawa Island, and there encountered PT Section 3. Two PT boats fired torpedoes at the Japanese but missed. The destroyer *Yamagumo* moved in on them, but the PT's fled, and when one of their number suffered an engine failure, they gave the Japanese a little shock by dropping depth charges to confuse them. Confuse the enemy or not, the Americans escaped, zigzagging and making smoke, and the Japanese moved on, at 18 knots.

The PT boats did their best, but they were not very effective as fighting ships, or even as messengers. There was too much radio trouble, and many torpedoes were fired but not one took effect, in this early stage of the game at least.

On came the Nishimura force. At 0100 Nishimura advised by radio that he would pass Panaon Island in half an hour and then move into Leyte Gulf. All he had seen so far was a handful of torpedo boats, which tried to hit and run in the manner of their kind.

At the time that the Admiral sent off his radio message, the Japanese fleet under his command assumed its battle order. The destroyer *Michishio* led, and after her came the destroyer *Asagumo*, then the battleship *Yamashiro*, the battleship *Fuso*, and the cruiser *Mogami*. The destroyer *Yamagumo* patrolled to the starboard, and destroyer *Shigure* to port. Admiral Nishimura was making ready to charge through the Strait. He had seen torpedo boats. He knew nothing else about the disposition of the American fleet.

As for Admiral Oldendorf, he had known of the coming of the Japanese since shortly after midnight, when the relayed message of *PT-130* reached him. But there was nothing he needed to do; his ships were set to trap the Japanese; as the enemy came crossing up to make the T, all the big ships would be able to fire on the Japanese column ship by ship, and the destroyers might dash in among the Japanese with their torpedoes.

Now the Japanese kept coming, indomitably it seemed. At the narrows where a brief gap separates Panaon and Sumilon islands, PT Section Six darted out to attack just after 0200. Three more boats attacked and fired torpedoes. The Japanese shot back calmly, and the torpedoes missed.

It became a pattern; the Japanese would sight a PT section, trace them with searchlights, and open fire. The PT boats would radio, fire back, and launch torpedoes, zigzag, make smoke, and run. And the Japanese were very pleased with themselves, because they suffered no damage from the PT boats, and had the satisfaction of sinking one of them, hitting nine others, and staying unscathed at the same time. From the standpoint of the PT boats, it was not one of their more glorious hours, although no one complained: they had done their job of getting the information through, and Admiral Oldendorf's quiet assurance, in which he did not even change a bit of his disposition, showed how unnecessary it would have been for the PT's to sacrifice themselves further.

Yet, if the Japanese could claim the honors in the opening phase of the Battle of Surigao Strait, much more was to come, and the PT boats themselves were to have a bigger hand in affairs before the battle was over. Right now, as the Japanese made ready to come through, the PT boys were warned away, because the Americans had something else in mind for Admiral Nishimura and his friends.

Captain Jesse B. Coward, Commander of Destroyer Squadron 54, was a regular Navy officer, and a highly decorated one by the time he set out for Leyte Gulf that fall. He had a triangular face and an odd smile that broadened his cheek lines and crinkled his eyes—but on the afternoon of October 24 the smiling he did was in anticipation of action when Admiral Oldendorf released him from the geographical guardianship his ships had been exercising as submarine pickets.

That had been Destroyer Squadron 54's basic assignment since October 20, and it had been more or less routine. For example, *Remey*, the flagship, had cruised up and down its assigned area looking for submarines or Japanese PT boats for several days. At 1430 on October 21 she had sunk a drifting Japanese mine. At 1523 she picked up a TBF pilot, Ensign E. A. Shaw, and crewmen J. D. Robertson (AOM 2c) and H. J. Hughes (ARM 2c) whose plane had come down in the water; she kept them and transferred them back to their ship on October 24. That day the Japanese air force had caused them a little trouble, but not much. They had fired on one plane without any observable results.

They had learned of the coming of the Japanese at 1800 on October 24, and as Captain Coward made his request, they made ready for their attack.

Captain Coward split his squadron into two parts, taking control of one section himself and giving the other to Commander Richard H. Phillips, Commander of Destroyer Division 108. Actually, Coward split the squadron in three parts, taking the cautious way and leaving destroyers *Mertz* and *McNair* on their dull but essential duty of screening the transports and command ships of the landing force. Coward kept the *Remey*, the *McGowan*, and the *Melvin* on the east, and put Phillips with the *McDermut* and the *Monssen* on the west.

Here, from the action report of USS *Melvin*, was an indication of what it was like that night:

After five straight days of monotonous patrol duty in Leyte Gulf the crew was thoroughly tired of the entire Philippine campaign. However, when word was passed at 1900 on the 24th that a night surface action was expected, everyone quickly regained an interest in the war. When word was passed about an hour later that in event of action we would take a quick trip down the straits for a torpedo attack, all hands immediately acquired a profound interest in life, death, and pursuit of the Nipponese. When we finally received definite word that the Japs were headed up the gulf, it was hard to believe that we were really going in, but everyone understood that there was a job to be done and that he had to do it. . . .

It was the same on all the destroyers. The TBS log (representing ship-to-ship communication) shows how Captain Coward carried out his attack, from the moment that he decided to push his way into the action:

At 7:50 that evening of October 24 Captain Coward called up Admiral Oldendorf.

> In case of surface contact to southward I plan to make immediate attack with torpedoes and then retire to clear you. If you approve this I will submit plan shortly. 19501.

OLDENDORF: Roger. Do you have same boys as last night?

COWARD: Affirmative out.

OLDENDORF: Your 19501 approved. Retire to cover of Dinagat Island and pass between Hibuson and Dinagat. Show IFF. Inform me if enemy is in more than one group and composition if possible.

Captain Coward then gave his plans, in a series of messages; they were approved and the retirement pattern was established (so he would not be shot up on returning by the big ships which would open fire on the Japanese as soon as the destroyer attacks were complete).

The planning and waiting continued.

At 8:20 Coward made this announcement to his squadron: "There are no friendly planes in this area. Anything coming in is enemy aircraft."

Then there was silence for two hours as they waited. Captain Coward set up the rendezvous point for the east and west destroyer groups and announced it over the TBS.

Midnight came and passed. Coffee and sandwiches were served, and the men who could do so tried to catch a few minutes of sleep, or to relax somehow to beat the growing tension.

At 0110 Admiral Oldendorf passed on the report of the PT's sighting 3 star shells or flares 10 miles away, 230 degrees off the southern tip of Panaon Island. He thought they might have been dropped by a plane, and there were Japanese snoopers out that night. Some forty minutes later Admiral Oldendorf gave the first report, relayed at such difficulty by *PT-130* from her farthest station.

Captain Coward began forming up his group for the attack. "Go to condition 1 (ready). Cut in all 4 boilers. (Ready for high speed without warning.)

He put his destroyers on station.

Another message came from Oldendorf: "Target being attacked by PT is trying to drive them off with gunfire."

At 0225 Coward gave the word to Oldendorf: "I am going to start down in a few minutes."

The TBS log then became filled with technical messages, setting courses, speeds, and methods of attack. The chronological account kept by *Melvin* gives an indication of what it was like:

0152 (1:52 in the morning): Received report of enemy force bearing 140° distance 18 miles from Taancan point.

0155: This ship was directed to report to the vicinity of patrol station No. 4 preparatory to forming for attack. [These patrol stations were marked on the charts of the ships.] All boilers were cut in and the ship went to General Quarters. [That meant she was ready for action, and every man at his battle station.]

0220: Eastern Attack Group formed column in order of *Remey, McGowan,* and *Melvin.* Distance 500 yards [between ships] standard speed 20 knots, course 180°.

0242: Enemy formation picked up on . . . radar bearing 184° True, distance 33,400 yards. Only two large pips were visible on the screen at this time.

0250: Changed speed to 25 knots.

0251: Column changed course to 150° True to obtain good attack position. Instructed by ComDesRon-54 that we would fire fish only. [No shooting.]

0253: Enemy force became very distinct on radar screen and was made out as a seven ship formation. Two heavy ships in column were made out [*Yamashiro* and *Fuso*] with [the cruiser *Mogami*] a smaller one behind, and a group of four ahead [the destroyers].

0257: Changed course to 135° True.

0258: Enemy searchlight made a 10–15 sec. sweep over our group, and was then turned off.

The American destroyers began firing. The *Remey* fired on the first target, the *Melvin* and *McGowan* on the second. From *Melvin's* account again:

0300: Directed by [Coward] to fire torpedoes on second target. Course changed to 090° *Remey* swung to course 090°T and then back to about 120°T. *McGowan* attempted to follow, and this enabled *Melvin*, which had been about 800 yards astern, to close to about 500 yards on starboard quarter of *McGowan*.

0301: Our group was again illuminated by enemy searchlight which remained on. It was evident that enemy had discovered us and as it was felt that in a short time we would be subjected to heavy fire from a superior force, orders were given to fire torpedoes before ship might be prevented from doing so.

0301.20: Fired full salvo of nine torpedoes to starboard with target bearing 212° T distance 11,480 yards. Target was estimated to be on course 000° T speed 17 knots. Base torpedo course. . . .

0301.50: All torpedoes away.

0302: Came left with full rudder and headed north, commenced retirement. Came left immediately as it was not considered wise to turn in same waters as ships ahead; to have done so would have put us in a knuckle, and subjected *Melvin* to enfilade fire. Commenced making funnel smoke. Star shells commenced bursting over our group and 6- or 8-inch salvos were landing close by. The enemy formation appeared to change course to about 345° T when we fired and increased speed two knots.

0304: Steadied on course of 018° T. At this time *McGowan* was about 800 yards on starboard quarter of *Remey* and *Melvin* about 1000 yards on her port quarter. *Melvin* stayed on port quarter to avoid enfilade fire and because it appeared that our smoke was helping to screen *Remey*.

0305: Began zigzagging sharply to lay smoke across track. Enemy salvos continued to land close.

0308: We made a radical change of course to port and then back again to starboard, endeavoring to screen ourselves with our own smoke.

0309: Approximate time that our torpedoes crossed enemy track, two large and separate explosions seen.

0310: Enemy changed course to 015° T as though attempting to dodge torpedoes. The left wing enemy destroyer disappeared from the radar screen. Changed speed to 29 knots.

0311: Star shells and salvos commenced dropping short. Changed speed to 25 knots.

0313: Enemy ceased firing. Changed speed to 20 knots.

0316: The speed of enemy formation dropped to 10 knots.

0319: Ceased making smoke.

0320: Changed speed to 20 knots. *McGowan* and *Melvin* formed column astern of *Remey*.

0322: Enemy formation appeared to break up. From 0322 until 0334 the enemy force seemed to be disorganized and no clear plot could be made.

0324: Changed course to 030° T.

0326: Changed speed to 15 knots.

0328: Commenced steaming on various courses standing into patrol station #3 between Hibuson and Dinagat islands.

0340: Formed column with *Remey* and *McGowan* on patrol station #3.

0345: Secured two boilers.

0619: Resumed normal patrol duties.

The *Melvin*'s laconic chronological account, so typical of naval action reports, does give a sense of what happened and how—in those brief minutes, less than half an hour, between the time that the Japanese column was first picked up on the radar screens and the torpedoes began to hit. In a way, however, a better feeling for the action is given in accounts by men aboard the *Monssen*, who were de-tailed by Commander C. K. Bergin, the skipper, to report what they observed as the second group of destroyers went in from the other side.

Here is part of Lieutenant (jg) B. F. Goldsworthy's report of the action:

Upon the sounding of the General Quarters alarm at 0207 I took my battle station as O.O.D. relieving Ensign Begle. The captain had the conn and was stationed on the open bridge forward of the pilot house. I remained in the pilot house. . . .

When I arrived at my battle station we were proceeding in a general southerly direction. A group of five destroyers in column . . . [Desron 56] were four miles southeast of us. A turn to the left was executed taking us outside and to the east of these destroyers. Standard speed was changed to 20 knots and we were ordered to steam at standard speed. Shortly we were ordered to steam at 25 knots.

The captain ordered me to go to the open bridge forward of the pilot house and to watch things for a moment. He went to the public address system and spoke to the crew and the officers substantially as follows: "To all hands. This is the captain. We are going into battle. I know each one of you will do his duty. I promise you that I will do my duty to you and for our country. Good luck to you and may God be with us." The captain then returned immediately to the open bridge.

. . . we turned slightly to the west. The captain gave orders to the steersman Smith, A.R. QMC 2c, through the open ports. Those orders were repeated by the chief quartermaster who remained on the bridge with the captain. Smith was fatigued from long periods on his feet at the wheel during General Quarters. Occasionally he got the order to the helm reversed, but since he loudly repeated back what he heard as the order, the error was quickly detected by the captain and rectified. Continuous transmissions over the three radio circuits in the pilot house made it very difficult for Smith to hear the captain's orders. . . .

The pips from the enemy ships to the southeast were now clearly and constantly visible at distance of about 12 to 15 miles. . . .

When the range to the enemy closed to about 10 miles, I observed a light to port and upon going to the port wing of the bridge I saw two star shells. . . .

We were ordered by ComDesDiv 108 by TBS to

"stand by your fish." This word I passed to the captain. . . .

While we were going in for our attack, perhaps during the last three minutes, I had the distinct impression that we were being fired upon by the enemy. The basis for this impression is hazy in my mind but I seem to recall hearing gunfire and shells whistling overhead and of feeling the ship slightly jarred. I saw sharp flashes of light although this could have been the result of fresh star-shell illumination to the southeast. The greater part of my time my eyes were on the scope.

CDS 54 [Coward] reported via TBS that "we had been straddled." Shortly after that the order was given by the captain to "fire your fish." This was repeated to Mr. Lawton at the port torpedo director. Almost immediately Mr. Lawton gave the order to "fire five" etc. The torpedoes were fired in rapid succession following Mr. Lawton's loud and clear orders. Everything took place similar to the exercises I had seen him conduct many times before, during dry runs. The last torpedo to be fired gave off a scraping noise as if it were scraping against something.

After firing the fish we made rapid turns principally to the right. Order was given by the captain to "make all the speed you can. . . ."

. . . We were illuminated by searchlights which seemed to stay directly on us for only a short time and then to sweep back and forth. I asked the captain if we could not open fire on the ship which was illuminating us. He refused . . . as the enemy did not apparently see us as he did not train continuously on us. . . .

. . . After this we maneuvered closer to the beach, following the *McDermut*. By the scope we seemed to come within 1500 yards of the beach. By now it did not appear that we were being fired upon. We clung to the beach for several minutes, making high speed. . . .

And here is an unusual worm's eye view, the report of Ezra L. Karn, seaman 2nd class, who was also asked to observe and put down what he saw for the Captain:

. . . everything went along fine until about four minutes before we fired the torpedoes when the enemy must have sighted us and began throwing star shells up. All of the stars were way short.

During this time Mr. Chester was on the starboard director with phones and was setting the director up while Hickman TM1c and Giambra TM2c were setting the director on the port side. Before I forget it just as we started out the captain told us over the PA system what was going to take place after which he gave a short prayer, which I think helped a lot. Now to continue, in a couple of minutes the torpedomen had the director set up, and they called for Mr. Lawton who was in the pilot house. He came running out and started to sight through the scope. In about half a minute he yelled up to the pilot house that the fish were ready to fire.

. . . We were illuminated by the searchlight of the enemy. Previous to this time the light had not hit us but was illuminating the beach in front of us. We were now turning hard to starboard and the light was still on us. At this time the captain ordered the engine room to make smoke. We began to smoke heavily which cut down the light. At the completion of the turn the searchlight went off, and I heard a shell go over the ship. About half a minute later we were being illuminated from the beach by some kind of a greenflare which made a lot of light. Just at that time I was standing alongside Hickman and he said if we are going to hit something it should be about now. He had no sooner said this when we felt two good explosions. We continued to steam up alongside the beach. The captain again talked over the PA system and said "we got them" and also that we all had done a grand job. About this time the battleships opened fire . . . and they sure put out the salvos.

Around 1630 we were back at our old screening station of number six with a great relief to me. . . . Oh, yes, prior to making the run we had a casualty in the after fire room by having a gasket blown on one of the strainers. . . .

But that was just about the only casualty on the ships of Destroyer Squadron 54 in what was to go down as one of the gallant gestures of the war, and one of the most effective.

For Captain Coward's attack was enormously successful. Here is what the Japanese saw, beginning in the evening as they headed toward the battle scene.

At 2315, west of Panaon Island, the *Mogami* and the scouting force had engaged a succession of PT boats until it joined the main force at midnight. At 0100 there was an attack by several torpedo boats at the southern entrance to Surigao Strait, and these were brought under fire. The enemy fired perhaps ten torpedoes at the *Mogami*, the Japanese said, but not one hit, and neither did any torpedoes hit the battleships or the destroyers. The Japanese knew they had damaged one torpedo boat; they were not sure about others.

Then things began to happen.

At 0200 (Japanese report) they sighted 2 enemy destroyers at 6500 meters and opened fire on them without shining their searchlights. The enemy craft withdrew under smoke, said the Japanese. (For some reason the Japanese admiral did not seem to consider that the enemy might also have launched torpedoes before withdrawing. He did not change course.)

Ten minutes after the first destroyers, a second pair was sighted behind the smoke, and then torpedo boats were also seen underneath a parachute flare. The Japanese saw torpedo wakes, and began to take evasive action. But it was late, very late.

Here is *Mogami*'s account:

Direct torpedo hit on starboard side of *Fuso* amidships, causing ship to list to starboard and lose speed. *Fuso* fell back and *Mogami* moved on behind *Yamashiro* [the second battleship]. Thereafter several torpedo attacks received. . . . Because of the torpedo attacks it was almost completely impossible to fire on the enemy ships and it became difficult to distinguish our own ships from those of the enemy as a result of evasive action. *Asagumo* was seen with her bow severed and pouring forth smoke. . . . Direct torpedo hit observed on *Michishio*, and bow severed. Direct torpedo hit observed on *Yamashiro* [apparently near the bow]. . . .

The American attack was so surprising to the Japanese, with their feeling of superiority in night action, that Commander Nishino of the *Shigure* would have sworn that the American destroyers did not fire a shot or release a torpedo, but came, saw the Japanese, and turned tail. To be sure the weather was squally, but the Japanese were seeing what they wanted to see.

Commander Nishino's description was quite different from that of the survivors of *Mogami*.

. . . Torpedo attack was received from both port and starboard sides. Hits were registered on the first three destroyers, the third destroyer *Yamagumo* sank, the *Michishio* and *Asagumo* were hit and though they did not sink were unnavigable and fell out of the disposition. The hits that sank *Yamagumo* came from port. The *Shigure* took evasive action and avoided all torpedoes. This was comparatively easy for *Shigure* since at the moment of attack we were still heading northeast in the transition from approach to battle disposition. I think the torpedoes which passed close to us came from the west but I am not sure. I did not see the hit which registered on *Yamashiro* but those who did told me she received a torpedo hit amidships, which side is not known, evidently it hit the magazine and the ship exploded and broke in half. No damage was inflicted on *Fuso* and *Mogami*.

So, some said the *Fuso* was hit by a torpedo, some said not. One thing was certain: Nishimura knew he had been attacked.

"We have received a torpedo attack," he said on the TBS to the *Shigure*. "You are to proceed and attack all ships."

Nishimura was busy for a few moments sending messages from *Yamashiro*, the flagship, but the one just quoted was also his last. Just after he sent it, the magazines of the *Yamashiro* blew up and that was the end.

Here is Commander Nishino's account of what he did next in the destroyer *Shigure:*

> . . . I increased speed to 26 knots after the torpedo attack at which speed *Shigure* maintained a northerly course for a time without any sightings and without knowing my exact position. I then made a complete turn, proceeded south for a very short distance, as I was concerned about the whereabouts of *Yamashiro.* I went back to find out what had happened to *Yamashiro* and to get orders if possible, then made a second turn and proceeded north again. *Mogami* and *Fuso* were still continuing north at this time, and . . . I gave up the search for the *Yamashiro* which had been for the possibility of finding out what had happened to the flagship and also of the possibility of transferring the flag to my ship. . . . [I] decided to go to the van of the force; we were unable to make telephone communication with *Yamashiro.* While searching . . . the lookout informed me he had sighted what he thought was the *Yamashiro* sinking. I did not attempt to pick up survivors but shortly after this information proceeded to continue the battle. I was able to maintain communication with the *Fuso.*

Rear Admiral Masami Ban took charge of the Japanese force then, since it was pretty clear that the *Yamashiro* was gone and so was Admiral Nishimura. Or that is what Commander Nishino thought. He did not actually get in touch with Admiral Ban at any time.

The confusion was very nearly complete, and the Japanese ended the battle with so little in the way of survivors or information that the true story is hard to piece together. Here, from Admiral Morison's version, is the American story of how the battle went, pieced together by detective work long after the fact.

When Captain Coward's destroyers attacked from the right and from the left and then turned quickly and sped out of the Japanese range at 35 knots, the surprise was complete. The Japanese had not expected the Americans to be able to mount that kind of night attack that had so long been a Japanese specialty. The Emperor's admirals and captains had quite underestimated the American skill.

The *Fuso*, it seems, *was* hit by a torpedo from the *Melvin*, and dropped back. And then along came the second division, and the *McDermut* let go with some really accurate torpedoes: it was decided later that she had hit 3 Japanese destroyers: *Yamagumo, Achishio,* and *Asagumo*. The first blew up and sank. Scratch one destroyer crew. The second began to sink. The third had her bow blown off but was able to limp away.

Then the *Monssen* made one hit on the *Yamashiro,* which jolted but did not stop the Japanese flagship. And, said the Americans, Admiral Nishimura then sent off his last message by radio to Admiral Kurita and Admiral Shima, telling part of the awful truth:

"Enemy torpedo boats and destroyers present on both sides of northern entrance to Surigao Strait. Two of our destroyers torpedoed and drifting. *Yamashiro* sustained one torpedo hit but no impediment to battle cruising."

Did the *Yamashiro* know that the *Fuso* was out of it?

Who knew what the Japanese knew—except that their force was thrown into confusion.

What the Japanese did not know, for a few moments, was what awaited them on the other side of those torpedoes they had not expected. More torpedoes!

They came from the destroyers of Destroyer Squadron 24 under Captain K. M. McManes.

McManes was on the right flank of the American force, just waiting. He saw Coward's group go in, and come out.

At 0300 I was directed by Commander Task Group 77.3 "Proceed to attack. Follow down shore line. After attack retire to north. Make smoke going down."

At 0305 . . . I directed Attack Group 22 . . . *Arunta, Killen, Beale* to follow the east group down and that I would follow the west group down.

At 0310 I directed Attack Group 22 to break off and commence their approach. Meanwhile, with Attack Group 12 [*Hutchins, Daly, Bache*] I proceeded south at speed 20 with the idea that if the enemy turned south to make his escape I would place myself to the southward of him and be in position to attack if he came down. This I accomplished and as it later developed the enemy did turn south and I started to chase but evidently his southerly turn was made to avoid torpedoes, for he continued right around and headed north again.

[He moved in.]

During the attack by Attack Group 22 the enemy appeared unaware of our presence to the west of him and we received no attention from his guns. At 0330 Attack Group 12 fired its torpedoes. The torpedo runs to target took about seven minutes at the end of which flashes were seen and the sound men reported loud underwater noises. . . .

Immediately after torpedoes were fired gunfire was opened with five-inch. To this the enemy responded vigorously. We were taken under fire by five-inch (small splashes), six-inch (middle-size splashes), and eight-inch or larger (big splashes). He fired star shells which were 1000 or more yards short with only an occasional over. His gunfire was sporadically short and over. At one time, however, he walked down a ladder on the *Hutchins,* the last of the three salvos being 50 yards over and detected by *Hutchins* in time to make a 20° change of course and to observe that the fourth salvo fell in the wake where *Hutchins* had been. *Daly* reports having sighted at least two torpedo wakes close astern of *Hutchins* and ahead of *Daly.* By 0345 our destroyers were hitting him hard with five-inch and the enemy gunfire on us had practically ceased. Fires had been started on two or more of his ships and one large ship (battleship or cruiser) was dead in the water and a fine torpedo target for *Hutchins.* I, therefore, directed *Hutchins* to let him have it. *Hutchins* reports two hits out of five torpedoes. . . .

But it was time for the destroyers to leave.

The Japanese confusion was terrible to see, if one had been an impartial observer. "I made radar searches but was unable to locate the enemy force," said Commander Nishino. . . . "I heard and saw vague flashes of fire in Leyte Gulf but we got no reaction on the radar screen and made no location . . . being unsuccessful in finding the enemy and determining that the rest of our force had been annihilated, I decided to withdraw without receiving orders from anyone. . . ."

Of the seven-ship force, here is how it stood as Captain McManes finished his run:

The *Fuso* had been hit by a torpedo from the *Melvin* and had fallen out of column. One battleship hurt.

The *Yamagumo* had been hit by a torpedo or torpedoes and had blown up and sunk. Scratch one destroyer, to the *McDermut*.

The *Michishio* had been hit by another torpedo from the *McDermut,* and was in bad shape, taking water heavily. An injured destroyer.

The *Asagumo* had her bow blown off. Another injured destroyer, credit to the *McDermut.*

In this new attack by 6 destroyers under Captain Mc-Manes, the destroyer *Killen* put one torpedo into the *Yamashiro* (which the Japanese on the *Shigure* thought was already sunk, so great was their confusion). She slowed.

There were 3 Japanese ships still very much in action —the *Yamashiro,* the *Shigure,* and the cruiser *Mogami,* but they were no longer functioning as a unit. They were 3 fighting ships, struggling for survival.

Admiral Berkey, second in command to Admiral Oldendorf, ordered Captain McManes to come back and get out of the way of the battleships which were eager to begin firing. So McManes left, but as he did so the torpedoes of the *Hutchins* overtook the poor *Asagumo,* the destroyer whose bow had already been blown off by *McDermut*— and the *Asagumo* blew up with a tremendous flare and blast, and sank.

As the Americans retired, the Japanese on the battleship *Yamashiro* straddled the destroyers with salvos, but did not manage any hits.

Now Admiral Oldendorf sent in the last of his destroyer squadrons, DesRon 56, which was on the left flank of the American line. Only five of the Japanese ships were still afloat (if the *Fuso* had not yet blown up—which it would do any moment, leaving four). And of these ships, only three were still moving toward the American line—for the *Shigure* at this moment was still in the fighting.

Nine more destroyers were ready to go into action. First came the *Bryant, Halford,* and *Robinson,* which dashed in, fired torpedoes that missed, and retired near Hibuson Island. Then came the *Bennion, Leutze,* and *Heywood L. Edwards,* which fired on the *Shigure* and the *Yamashiro*—and missed. The Japanese were now taking evasive action and firing back, and came very close although they were not scoring hits on the fast little ships.

Then came the destroyers *Albert W. Grant, Richard P. Leary,* and *Newcomb,* which came threshing down the center of the Strait, just as the *Yamashiro* turned west from north. The American destroyers turned with the battleship and began launching torpedoes. The *Leary* fired three, the *Newcomb* fired five, and the *Grant* fired five.

Meanwhile, Admiral Oldendorf had been observing and directing the battle from his flagship. Here is his recollection from his narrative:

> . . . Everything worked according to plan. DesRon 54 reported the approach of the enemy which had previously been picked up by radar and was being plotted. The enemy approached in two groups, which on the radar screen appeared to be an echelon formation. Upon reporting the enemy, DesRon 54 attacked and retired, followed closely by DesRon 24.
>
> One interesting feature of this attack was that when the destroyers attacked they attacked fairly close together and the enemy radar evidently was not very discriminating as to bearing, so that the two destroyers appeared as one blip on the enemy screen and they fired at the center of the blip which made their shells fall exactly between the attacking destroyers so that none of the destroyers in this attack were hit. Upon receiving the report that DesRon 24 had attacked, DesRon 56, which was with the left flank forces and inside the cruisers, between the cruisers and battle lines, were directed to attack. . . . As the DesRon 56 moved out for the attack, I asked the captain of my flagship what the range was. His reply was "17,000 yards." I asked him if he had a good setup, and [he] replied, "Yes." I gave the order to open fire.

Previous to this I had closed the battle line in to the flank forces so that the battle line was only about two or three thousand yards to the northward of the cruisers. Upon giving the order "Open Fire" it seemed as if every ship in the flank forces and the battle line, opened at once, and there was a semi-circle of fire which landed squarely on one point, which was the leading battleship [*Yamashiro*]. Explosions and fires were immediately noticed. The *West Virginia*, leading the battle line, opened fire and fired directly over the *Louisville* [Oldendorf's flagship], the leading ship of the left flank of the forces, so that I had a good bird's eye view of exactly what a salvo of 16-inch shells look like when they go overhead and hit a ship. It was beautiful to see.

The semi-circle of fire evidently so confused the Japanese that they did not seem to know what target to shoot at. I remember seeing one or two salvos start in the direction of my flagship, but in the excitement of the occasion I forgot to look to see where they landed and have no idea. The two light cruisers on the left flank and the light cruisers on the right flank were firing very rapidly and made a continuous light. This seemed to be the point for which the enemy later directed his fire, as most of the straddles and fire from the Japanese battle line were directed at these ships.

. . . the flagship, the *Louisville*, was so anxious to open fire that they fired the first salvo without giving a preliminary buzz on the buzzer and I was so blinded by the first flash that I couldn't see anything at all and decided that I had better go in to the flag plot and observe the action from the PPI. Upon going onto flag plot I noticed the screen and counted 16 different blips on this screen but the noise of the loud speakers was so distracting in there that I decided to go out on the flag bridge and observe the action from there. . . .

The timing of opening fire and the attack of DesRon 56 was to be so that the fire from the guns would cover the approach of DesRon 56. This was effective except that the head of the Japanese line turned left about the time that the center division was to fire their torpedoes and the center division turned right or west to cover this maneuver. When they did so they were taken under heavy fire by the leading Japanese battleship. . . .

As the torpedoes swished through the water, Captain Roland Smoot saw the skies of the American sector begin to light up, ordered a quick retreat under the plan laid down earlier. The *Newcomb* and the *Leary* sped away, shells falling all around them from Japanese and American guns, but the *Albert W. Grant* was not so lucky. Here is her story.

The *Albert W. Grant* had been a busy ship on this invasion, and even the greenest of her crew was an old hand at war after these last few days. On October 20 she had seen the *Honolulu* take that Japanese torpedo and she had gone alongside and screened her while the *Richard P. Leary* and a tug took off wounded. She had come under fire that day by Japanese planes and had fired back, and thought she got one Japanese plane. She had laid down harassing fire on the beach the next day, October 21, and had been straddled by two bombs dropped by a Japanese plane. Her AA hit the Japanese plane and knocked a piece out of its tail, but the plane flew away. She was attacked again that day by a bomber that missed, 25 yards off the port quarter. She helped splash another one of those flaming Bettys later in the day. Indeed, her log was not a bad indication of the heavy attack from the air that the Japanese were levying on the transports and other ships of Leyte Gulf during the invasion—without, however, accomplishing very much. The problem, as seen from the *Albert W. Grant,* was that the Japanese plainly missed many good opportunities, and she had suffered several near misses in the fighting. It was the story the Japanese admirals of the air knew so well: the pilots were not experienced enough to do their jobs properly, and it showed on the Leyte beaches. Another problem for the Japanese seemed to be the size of the ordnance: the *Albert W. Grant*'s men said the bombs that nearly hit her were 25- and 50-pound bombs, scarcely big enough to do much damage to a ship, probably bombs from army planes designed for work against personnel on the beaches, not against warships.

Anyhow, every day of the invasion, the *Albert W. Grant* had been involved in Japanese air raids, firing and being fired upon, and she was "blooded" and ready for a fight by the early morning hours of October 25.

The *Albert W. Grant*'s ordeal began at 0402.5 (the ship's log) when a Japanese torpedo missed astern by 20 feet. "This was a torpedo wake, hence torpedo should have been a hit. Miss probably due to deep submergence of torpedo."

At 0403 came an explosion in the Japanese ships, just as the *Albert W. Grant* launched her torpedoes. A minute and a half later the ship began to be straddled by gunfire. The first hit came at 0407, a shell that landed among empty powder cases stacked across the fantail. The blow knocked 5-inch gun No. 5 out of commission.

By 0408 the *Albert W. Grant* had launched all her torpedoes, and had suffered several shell hits amidships. Steam was pouring out of No. 1 stack and the forward fireroom and forward engine room were out of commission. The after fireroom had been abandoned because of excessive heat caused by steam escaping from two shell holes in the forward engine room.

The *Albert W. Grant* was still following her division leader in column, last in line.

Then came trouble in spades:

0408.5: Additional shell hits began to riddle ship. Hit forward at waterline flooded forward storeroom . . . and forward crew's berthing compartment. Hit in 40 mm gun #1 exploded 40 mm ammunition and started fire. Hit through starboard boat davit exploded, killing medical officer, five radiomen, and almost entire amidships repair party. Other hits in forward stack, one hit on port motor whale boat, one hit and low order explosion in galley. One hit in sculler room, one hit in after crew's berthing compartment, and one additional hit in forward engine room. All lights, telephone communications, radars, and radios out of commission. Steering control shifted aft.

Two and a half minutes later the ship was losing speed, steam pressure was dropping, and the officers were beginning to investigate. The acts of heroism began as the ship started to go dead in the water. Her captain, Commander T. A. Nisewaner, was far from being last in these actions —before they were finished, he went below and hauled injured and blackened men out of the steaming engine room.

When it became apparent that there was trouble in the engine rooms, Lieutenant B. B. V. Lyon, Jr., who had the conn, was relieved by the Captain and started below. He could not see to enter the forward spaces; the steam was pouring out, hot and blinding. He moved aft, and secured the boilers there, and found that one boiler could still be operated. He rounded up a scratch crew and tried to reenter and light off the boiler. A man could not stand more than three or four minutes in the fireroom because of the heat of the escaping steam, and so they entered in relays. The lights were out, so they used battle lamps and "feel" to do the work. After a time they got the boiler going, which gave the ship steam power again.

Lieutenant W. J. E. Crissy was stationed forward with Repair Unit No. 1 when the first shell hit the ship. He sent Seaman Edwards below and he and Chief Brown checked the ship for water power.

"He turned to on aid to the wounded being brought to the forecastle. He got four men together who didn't know how to give syrettes, showed them how, and got them started. . . ."

The wounded were coming down. Altogether there would be 34 officers and men killed and 94 wounded— most of them by shells fired from American ships. Lieutenant Crissy and the crew turned to, to save ship and men. He led crews to plug holes in the hull, and got emergency pumps working.

Ensign J. P. Marsh got permission to leave his battle station in the director, and went below to the ammunition handling room where he found temperatures rising to 130 degrees. He organized a crew and began moving ammunition, moving the hoist by hand, because the power was out. He toured the magazines, and found those under guns No. 1 and No. 2 in danger of flooding, so he dogged the spaces, and then went forward to the fireroom to help get out the dead and wounded and moved them to the fantail, where he organized a treatment party.

Ensign F. D. Case was hit by shrapnel when one of those first shells came in. Severely wounded and weak from loss of blood, he refused help and set about aiding others. He helped carry two wounded men to the battle dressing station in the wardroom and was manning one end of a stretcher when he collapsed. He could not move but lay against the deckhouse, directing others. He could not walk, so gave his shoes to a man whose shoes had been burned off his feet.

The officers were not the only heroes, by far.

MM1c R. H. Parker heard the safety valves of the forward engine plant blow and ran through intense shellfire to shut off the steam valves forward, thus saving the lives of a dozen men trapped by steam in the forward fireroom and engine room. He then ran and shut off fuel supply to the engines involved, and went into the steam-filled compartment and began bringing out the wounded.

RM1c W. M. Selleck had both legs blown off and was taken to the wardroom. He refused treatment. "There's nothing you can do for me, fellows," he said. "Go ahead and do something for those others." Then he died.

PM1c W. H. Swain, Jr., was the only surviving man with any medical training. He took care of the wounded on the ship, and instructed others while he ran the station in the crew's head aft.

RT1c J. M. Flaherty was wounded by shrapnel; after giving himself morphine, he went around the ship giving aid to others. He would not stop for treatment until the more serious cases had been handled.

GM2c C. S. Canada rushed down into the bilges of the steam and engine spaces and removed unexploded shells there. He helped with the removal of the ammunition, although the temperature rose above 146 degrees in the magazines. He watched the rising temperatures and kept the Captain informed, and when the ammunition was out of the way, he moved to the emergency pumps.

MM3c R. W. Brown was with Canada, feeling around trying to get those unexploded shells out of the bilges in the dark. GM3c J. R. Howard was put out of action by a shell that knocked his gun out, and then went below to rescue wounded. WT3c W. G. Hertel, wounded so that he could not move his legs, sat on the deck and made others bring men to him and then treated them. MM2c D. W. Barnes beat out flames on men with his bare hands, and TM3c W. W. Nagel stuck to his post in the forward torpedo tube mount, after his companion was wounded, and singlehandedly got away the torpedoes by hand, with shrapnel flying around him, firing by percussion when the automatic machinery failed.

There were a dozen others. Coxswain Al L. Kelly was stationed aft on 40 mm gun No. 1 when a shell plowed in and set the ammunition afire. He grabbed a mattress and rushed into the blaze and extinguished it before the shells began blowing up. And that was about par for the men that day. At 1620 the *Albert W. Grant* was dead in the water, operating her guns on manual but still fighting. By 1640 she was in touch with others by blinker, asking for a tow. At 1700 the *Newcomb*'s boat came alongside with a doctor; 43 minutes later the *Newcomb* was alongside and the wounded were being transferred. By 1840 the *Newcomb* began to tow her back to safer waters.

As soon as Admiral Oldendorf learned that the destroyers were under fire, he ordered the battle line and cruisers to cease fire, and the pressure on the *Albert W. Grant* was removed. It was the cruisers that had been hitting her (luckily for the *Grant*) mistaking her for a Japanese destroyer, and not the battleships with their big guns.

The destroyers had done a pretty good job of wrecking the Japanese move through the Strait; and what they did not do, the cruisers and battleships undertook.

They had begun firing at 0351 and continued for 14 minutes, the *Yamashiro* and the *Mogami* heading bravely into this fire, along with little *Shigure*. Although Admiral Nishimura sent one message to the *Fuso* at 0352, that was the last one, and soon Nishimura was either too stunned or too busy to send any more—or his communications were knocked out by an early shot.

The firing was heavy. The *West Virginia*, for example, fired 93 rounds of armor-piercing 16-inch shells in those 14 minutes. The *Tennessee* fired 69 rounds of 14-inch ammunition; the *California,* 63 rounds. And there was the *Maryland,* which fired 48 rounds, and all those cruisers shooting so fast that they were lit up like Broadway shops. The *Mississippi* fired only one salvo and the *Pennsylvania* did not fire at all, but there was a huge rain of steel on the two major ships coming up the Strait, while the Japanese hit only the unfortunate *Grant* and made a near miss on the *Claxton* from a heavy gun. The Japanese were so busy taking fire that they could hardly shoot: the cruisers fired literally thousands of rounds of ammunition (the *Columbia* alone fired 1100 rounds), and many of these hit—so many that the Japanese were stunned.

About ten minutes after this punishment began, even little *Shigure* was feeling it. "I was receiving a terrific bombardment," said Commander Nishino. "There were so many near misses that the gyro compass was out, the ship was constantly trembling from force of near misses, and the wireless was out."

If that was the condition on the *Shigure,* which was squirming like a baby all this time, and took only one shell aboard, imagine what it was like on the main targets, the big ships, where the hits were numbered in the dozens and scores. Destroyer Captain Smoot, who was watching, called the gunfire "devastating," "accurate," and "beautiful."

But then Admiral Oldendorf learned of the *Albert W. Grant's* plight, caught in the fire of the American cruisers, and he ordered the firing ceased. It saved the *Grant,* and it gave the Japanese a respite. The *Yamashiro* had been burning so brightly that she was lit up from end to end. She increased her speed to 15 knots and turned and headed south. (Soon she capsized and sank, taking down all but a handful of her crew.) The *Mogami,* the cruiser, had been taking a great deal of punishment, with shells falling even on her bridge and killing the Executive Officer, Commanding Officer, and all others there. But it was shells in the engine room that began to bring her down, and she slowed. Still she was fighting. It was her torpedoes that came close to the *Richard P. Leary* in that last torpedo attack.

For ten minutes the firing stopped, and the *Mogami* and the *Yamashiro* moved away, along with *Shigure.*

Here Admiral Oldendorf recalls how it seemed to him that night:

When the situation as to DesRon 56 had been clarified the order was given then to resume fire, but most of the enemy ships had disappeared from the screen. Destroyer Squadron X was then ordered to report to the officer in tactical command and upon reporting was directed to proceed down the strait and attack the enemy. As soon as it was thought that DesRon X was on its way the left flank forces were then taken into the straits to pursue the enemy.

On proceeding down the straits I noticed two ships on fire, one of them burning very heavily. The other had been burning but the fires were getting under control. As we approached I noted destroyers at the sides of the straits firing, and not knowing whether those destroyers were our own or the enemy's I could not take them under fire. If they were enemy destroyers I was proceeding into torpedo waters, so having gotten the right-hand ship of the two enemy ships proceeding down the straits within range, I turned across the straits on course 250° and when the five cruisers were around the turns (*Louisville, Portland, Minneapolis, Denver* and *Columbia*), I gave the order to open fire on the right-hand ship, which was making about 11 knots.

The heavy cruisers opened fire immediately and started hitting the right-hand ship, which again burst into flame. The *Columbia* and *Denver* opened fire on two destroyers, one was standing by the right-hand ship and another standing by the left-hand ship. A few salvos and those destroyers disappeared. When it was evident that the right-hand ship had been hit badly and would not escape the cruisers then turned and retired up the strait . . . to try to find DesRon X. . . .

As soon as daylight arrived the cruiser divisions were again turned south down the straits and a large destroyer of the *Terutsaki* class was seen on the eastern side of the strait. . . . The bow of the ship had been blown off about down to turret two by a torpedo and a single stack made it look like a tanker with a stack aft. The *Denver* and the *Columbia* took the *Terutsaki* class destroyer under fire and it shortly disappeared from the scene.

At this time there were eight columns of smoke arising from the surface of the ocean but very little if any of the upper works of any ships could be seen. A plane was fired from the *Louisville* to investigate and to attempt to ascertain if there were any ships to the southward of this group of burning ships, which were about in the middle of Surigao Strait. . . .

The plane's report was negative—and just about this time Admiral Kinkaid sent a message to Admiral Oldendorf reporting that the escort carriers east of Leyte Gulf were under heavy fire. Oldendorf was to move to that scene as quickly as he could. Oldendorf had just sent down two destroyers to pick up Japanese survivors, but now he recalled them, and as a result of this and the unfriendly natives on the Philippines shores, there were very few survivors of the sunken Japanese ships. As Admiral Oldendorf turned, the *Mogami,* burning and smoking, was moving south, with the *Shigure* moving along too. They were all that remained of Admiral Nishimura's force— they and the hulks in the water (half of the *Fuso* was still floating) and the survivors swimming, trying to make up their minds whether to face the Filipinos with their guns and bolos (they used them, too, that day) or the sharks and other dangers of the sea.

15

THE BATTLE OF SURIGAO STRAIT—
PART II

As far as Admiral Nishimura was concerned, all that had
happened had occurred between 0300 and 0419, the time
at which the *Yamashiro* capsized and sank, taking down
the Admiral and all but a handful of his crew. And if he
did not send any messages to Admiral Shima, coming up
behind him, there was less reason to believe this was a
matter of jealousy or pique than a question of communications. If *Shigure*'s communications were out—and
she was not even hit—then what must have been the state
of the *Yamashiro* when she had thousands of shells
thrown at her?

As Admiral Shima's little force of cruisers and destroyers steamed up toward Surigao Strait behind Nishimura, Shima had brave notions of rushing through the
Strait and torpedoing any ships that moved. In fact, he
was thinking in terms of doing what the Americans did to
Admiral Nishimura.

The weather for Shima continued to worsen as it had
for Nishimura, and from 2200 the Shima force had the
feeling that it was being tracked by American torpedo
boats. (What they probably heard on the radio were reports on Nishimura's force.)

About midnight Shima's communications men heard
over the voice radio that Nishimura was engaged. The
weather was now so bad in Shima's position that from
his flagship the destroyers and even their wakes were
sometimes lost from sight, and the formation had to be
kept together by frequent corrections on the TBS system.

Then, about 0100 Shima had his first indication of action: he saw gun flashes ahead when the squalls let up enough for him to see anything.

The voice radio was fragmentary and most unsatisfactory this night, and the fragments were tantalizing and frightening: ". . . hit by one torpedo" came a report frcm the commander of Battleship Division Two. And then, infuriatingly there was nothing else. Dead silence. And then came another transmission from Nishimura, ordering a turn—obviously a battle maneuver. Then silence again.

Admiral Shima's ships were having their communications problems too. The destroyer *Ushio* lost her TBS transmitter sometime during the night, and in the squally weather this made formation-keeping a serious problem. How serious? Here is a report from one of Shima's staff officers:

Suddenly sighted mountains on the port bow through break in the clouds. Shortly thereafter was able to make out the coastline. "Turn 4.5." At this time issued orders so that destroyers would fall in astern (up to this time we were unable to confirm their positions and they were becoming separated to the north). It was at this time that the commander of the left flank screening ship *(Ushio)*, the voice telephone of which was inoperable, on his own judgment swung radically around to the left and thus saved the ship from running aground. The ship then fell in astern. (From about this time the squall ceased but visibility was still extremely unfavorable.)

At midnight Shima was about 40 miles behind Nishimura, and it was about 0315 when things began to happen to convince Admiral Shima that all was not going as it ought to.

The column had just changed into attack formation, with the flagship in the van, and then changed course at 0315 to 010 degrees. Out from the Panaon coast at this moment came an American torpedo boat *(PT-134* in fact) which came skimming in, launched torpedoes, and strafed. The attack alerted the Japanese, but did not sink any ships. The torpedo missed.

Then, 0325, the cruiser *Abukuma* and the other ships were swinging left, when suddenly out of the darkness came another PT attack, and the *Abukuma* was hit on the port side beneath the bridge by a torpedo. She began taking water very quickly, and soon was going down by the bow it seemed. Her speed fell to 10 knots, and she dropped out of the formation, as the other ships turned north and swept on. Shima had no extras in his formation to leave a destroyer as guard for the *Abukuma*. The cruiser would have to fight her own battle and make her own way home. Shima's task was to storm the Strait and get at the ships in Leyte Gulf as Kurita came down from the north.

On the bridge of the *Abukuma* they assessed the damage. The explosion had come on the side of the forward radio room and had killed nearly all the personnel handling radio and TBS. Communications again. But the *Abukuma* had to fight her own battle now, with the torpedo boats and the deadly sea.

Shima, in the flagship *Nachi*, increased speed to 26 knots and moved on. On the *Abukuma* the Japanese did not know they had been the victims of an ironic fate. *PT-137*, which had fired the torpedo that put the cruiser out of action this morning, had not been firing at her at all, but at one of the destroyers steaming south to take place in the new battle formation that Shima had just ordered. The torpedo had missed the destroyer, and hit the cruiser beyond it.

Shima now moved on in single battle formation: the *Nachi* ahead, bearing the Admiral himself, then the cruiser *Ashigara*, and then 4 destroyers in a line. He headed into storms, squalls, and the confusion of battle that is only later separated by intelligence men and historians.

We sighted a large fire and a burning fireball a considerable distance ahead [said Commander Kokichi Mori, one of Shima's staff officers, recalling the battle later], and as we approached we saw two large ships afire. We concluded that they must be the two battleships of Battleship Division Two [*Yamashiro* and *Fuso*. Actually they were the two halves of the *Fuso*] which were completely afire and burning furiously, silhouetting their hulls. Also at this time, sighted ahead near the limit of visibility flashes . . . from friendly and enemy gunfire and were able to conclude that *Mogami* and the destroyers of the Third Section had penetrated and were now engaged in furious combat.

Moving past the burning pyres of steel and wood, Shima's little fleet went on at 26 knots. By 0400 they still had not found the Americans, deterred by the heavy smoke laid down by the destroyers and from the battle that had been fought in the Strait, and was still being fought at that time by the cruisers and battleships laying down their rain of fire. The smoke was so dense to the north that the Japanese could see nothing, and their radar showed nothing either.

Shima was reduced to guessing conditions from what he saw and heard. Here is what he assumed:

"The enemy has concentrated his strength and is lying in wait in the narrow sector of the northern entrance of Surigao Strait. He is laying smoke to cut off our visibility, and will carry out radar-directed fire from behind the smoke or launch a simultaneous attack immediately after we have penetrated."

Admiral Shima's decision:

"When we sight or detect by radar the enemy, the cruisers will execute a torpedo attack, and then the destroyers . . . will penetrate and attack. Then, while the cruisers give support to the destroyers, battle disposition will be formed with the destroyers in the van, and the assault will be launched."

A brave plan. The Japanese did not know, of course, that the Americans had three squadrons of destroyers immediately available, plus those battleships and cruisers, and that only one American destroyer had so far been put out of action. In fact, the Japanese of the Shima force knew nothing at all beyond what they saw—and they saw incorrectly the result of the *Fuso*'s explosion.

By 0415, when Admiral Oldendorf had ordered the cease fire to protect the *Albert W. Grant* from further destruction by the American cruisers, Admiral Shima was still confused.

Shima was becoming concerned. A few moments later, when he sighted a ship completely afire and dead in the water, he did not know if it was friend or foe, but he did not like it. In his nervousness he ordered an attack on two pips that came up on the *Nachi*'s radar.

It was determined later, by American naval authorities, that what Admiral Shima saw on the radar scope that day was not an American ship or ships, or any ship or ships at all, but the two Hibuson islands, which were about 15 miles away, and at that distance might have looked to excited men like ships about half that distance away.

So the Japanese attack by torpedoes damaged nothing visible, but it did bring about further Japanese tragedy.

While the attack was in progress, officers on the bridge were watching the flaming ship that seemed to be dead in the water. They ascertained that it was the *Mogami*, not dead, but moving very slowly southward. And as the attack proceeded, and the cruisers changed course to launch the torpedoes, the Admiral ordered right rudder, not knowing that the ship ahead was moving.

Right rudder it was, and the new course took them directly toward the stricken ship. Later it was learned that the *Mogami* had been so sorely hurt that all the officers on her bridge had been killed, steering had been knocked out from the bridge and moved to manual steering aft, and it was all that could be done to keep her on a straight course moving south. She could not get out of the way, and the cruisers were bearing down on her.

On came the Shima cruisers, at 26 knots, and on limped the *Mogami*, directly into their line of approach.

"We turned rudder full to starboard," said Commander Mori. But it was too late.

The *Mogami*'s bow crashed into the *Nachi*'s port quarter at an angle of about 10 degrees. The *Ashigara* was luckier; she managed to evade by swinging to the outside, but the *Nachi* caught it squarely. The knifing bow of the *Mogami* sliced through the shell and into the anchor windlass room which flooded, and then into the steering room which began to flood. Bells rang and sirens screamed, and the *Nachi*'s speed fell immediately to 18 knots.

The Captain turned her south, then, and ordered his officers to report on the damage, to see if the ships could still go into battle. For ten minutes it was in balance, then the reports came that she was still battle worthy, and Admiral Shima ordered the ship to head north once again.

But hardly had that decision been made than Admiral Shima had some cautious second thoughts. He did not know the situation up ahead; the smoke, and what he had seen of burning ships, was upsetting. Equally upsetting was the damage done to the *Nachi*, which certainly cut her down as a fighting ship. He decided that discretion was the course to follow, and that he would not valorously plunge into the fray—as had Nishimura—but would live to fight another day. He would withdraw from the battle area, "temporarily." "Then, after regrouping his force and determining the [Kurita] movements he would plan the future course of action and a second attempt in coordination with the main body."

Now whether by "main body" he meant Kurita or Admiral Nishimura is interesting but not very important. For Admiral Shima was backing off to try to find out what was happening to the other Japanese forces. During the period of his approach the tremendous gunfire ahead had suddenly stopped. He had seen burning ships—all Japanese—and he had not seen any non-burning Japanese ships from the Nishimura force. All the information Shima had about the advance of Kurita to the north was negative— the bombings of that day, the reports that Kurita had turned back, and then the firm order from Admiral Toyoda that all would go ahead—no matter what the cost was certainly inherent in that message.

Having made his decision, Admiral Shima sent a radio dispatch to Admiral Mikawa, Commander of the Southwest area in Manila, under whose command he had been placed in the confusion of making the Sho plan go, and to the other commands that were supposed to have such information. At the same time he ordered his ships to reverse course, and headed back south, whence he had come.

About half an hour after the turn back, Admiral Shima sighted the destroyer *Shigure* and asked her to join up. At about 0630 the little force arrived at the southern entrance to Surigao Strait, and there encountered some more of those bumblebee PT boats, which promptly attacked. The American boats fired torpedoes and their machine guns, but no serious damage seems to have been done to either side; *PT-321* was hit, but not sunk as Shima thought it was.

Here, apparently, Admiral Shima had some second thoughts about retirement, or wanted to see if he was being chased. He ordered the destroyers to turn around and make full speed north, which they did for half an hour. Admiral Shima ordered the ships back again. By dawn, he had picked up the *Abukuma,* which had made emergency repairs and was limping south. The battle of Surigao Strait was over. The Japanese had not forced their way through, but had lost the battleship *Fuso,* the battleship *Yamashiro,* the destroyers *Yamagumo* and *Michishio,* and the cruiser *Mogami,* destroyer *Asagumo,* and cruiser *Abukuma* had been sorely hurt. The *Nachi* was also in trouble from the collision with the *Mogami.*

Dodging torpedo boats, and coming into fights with several (*PT-194* was hit and several men were hurt), the Japanese stood in toward the Mindanao shore, making 16 knots, and retiring in as good order as was possible under the circumstances. The *Mogami,* screened by one destroyer, moved along more slowly, at 12 to 14 knots.

The Americans were chasing, but the smoke, the confusion of battle, and the inability to find an enemy that was moving determinedly away militated against renewal of the battle in these night hours. It had been relatively simple when the Japanese were trying to force the Strait, and the Americans were lined across it, determined that they would not pass. But even with radar, tracking down the survivors was something else again, and there was nothing easy about it.

The cruisers and 6 destroyers of Division X went south hunting, but not carelessly. The Japanese still had sharp teeth, and the Americans knew it.

Here is the report from *Claxton,* divisional command ship:

The orders came at 0432 in the morning. ". . . ComDes-Div XRay with three ships in the van and three in the rear of the battle line ordered his ships to clear the battleship formation and form column natural order astern of the *Claxton.* The *Claxton* went to 20 knots. . . . It was intended to go to 30 knots when second section was closed to 4000 yards. Radar contact on the retiring enemy unit was regained at 0513 at a range of 31,000 yards [about 17 miles]." It was only one ship, moving at about 13 or 14 knots—probably *Mogami*.

By 0515 we realized that it was going to be a long chase and that daylight would soon arrive with its complications in connection with a surprise torpedo attack. Course of 160°, speed 25 knots was held and plans were made to change course to the south at about 0540 after clearing our cruiser formation, thus placing us in the middle of the strait. Two additional contacts were established at 0525 and their plot appeared to be very erratic. The tendency showed slow movement on the part of these targets in a southwesterly direction, but by 0538 the contacts disappeared from the screen, presumably having sunk.

As the division was about to clear the cruiser formation, and pursue the single contact we had on the screen at the time, orders were received . . . to cease the torpedo attack and join the screen of the left flank cruisers. At 0550 the *Claxton* took station . . . in the formation. As daylight came at about 0552, the *Claxton* sighted numerous Japanese survivors in the water very close aboard, and upon orders from [Oldendorf] maneuvered independently to pick them up as prisoners. It is estimated that there were a minimum of 150 men within a radius of 2000 yards. . . .

But among those men was an officer. They had come upon the survivors, or most of them, of the *Yamashiro*, and the officer was determined that the survivors should not be captured by the Americans, but instead should go to a watery grave that would be fitting for Japanese naval heroes. "Three prisoners finally decided to come aboard. . . ."

Meanwhile, Rear Admiral Hayler had found the destroyer *Asagumo*, with her bow shot off, and was taking her under fire with the cruisers. The *Claxton* joined. "By 0715, one fleeing badly damaged destroyer, presumably of the *Shigure* class, came within gun range and we opened fire." The cruisers and two other destroyers were shooting at the poor *Asagumo* too. "At 0718 the destroyer exploded and sank, after which our course was reversed and the formation proceeded north at 20 knots."

Something was brewing in the northeast, something very dangerous. Admiral Kurita had broken through San Bernardino Strait, and was already engaging the very vulnerable escort carriers with his battleships, cruisers, and destroyers. All the American forces were needed up north.

As for the Japanese, their defeat here was exemplified by the three prisoners taken from the *Yamashiro*. Imagine the thousands of men who had been thrown into the water by the sinking of the *Yamashiro*, the *Fuso*, and the lesser ships. Literally thousands of men died in the water in the darkness, mostly because no one stopped to help them, partly because they would accept no help from the enemy. And if there is any need to emphasize the breakup of the Japanese here, the story of the destroyer *Shigure* tells the tale. On her way back from the battle, the *Shigure* was so shaken by near misses and the one hit that she lost steering control, and for about half an hour was dead in the water, victim of any American ship that might find her. As the crew was making emergency repairs, Admiral Shima's force came by, said Nishino, and he identified himself, but did not offer any information about the battle.

As with everything about the Japanese side of this battle, there is confusion about the chronology of the report. It is not very likely, however, that Commander Nishino would tell such a story on himself, long after the fact, if it were not true.

So great had been the shock of the battle, so complete the American surprise of the Japanese, that Nishino must have lost any taste for strategy. All he knew was that he was not responsible to Admiral Shima, and he was desperately loyal to Admiral Nishimura.

And as for poor Nishimura, he had gone down with the *Yamashiro*, the first of the fleet leaders of this engagement to meet his death.

16

THE BATTLE OF
SAN BERNARDINO STRAIT—
PART I

Admiral Kurita was a worried man. Since the morning of October 24, when he heard from Admiral Nishimura that he had been attacked by American bombers, Kurita had been concerned about the ability of the Japanese forces to link up in Leyte Gulf. As the day wore on, and Kurita surveyed the power of the American planes and the damage they did to his force, he built up in his mind the same kind of damage for Nishimura. That mental image was to have its effect on his thinking.

As can be seen throughout this account, the basic problem of the Japanese in this whole complex operation was an almost total failure in communications. Admiral Kurita should have known, hour by hour, what was happening to the Nishimura, Shima, and Ozawa forces, and also what Admirals Mikawa, Fukudome, and Ohnishi were up to in Manila and the rest of the Philippines to support his desperate drive for the Leyte beaches. Instead, he received virtually no information. The same must be said about the reports he received about American dispositions. As of the afternoon of October 24 he placed the American task forces 80 to 100 miles off the coast of Samar, northeast of Leyte Gulf. That was the picture he had fixed in his mind; it, too, was to be vitally important in his later thinking.

The damage to Kurita's force troubled him greatly; such things as the partial destruction of the *Nagato*'s communications system made his task that much harder. But the task was set, and if there had been any hesitation in Admiral Kurita's mind about the importance that Imperial

Naval Headquarters placed on the pursuit of this mission to its end, it had been removed by the strong tone of that last message from Admiral Toyoda.

Toyoda's message to combined fleet headquarters that evening reflected a confidence that Admiral Kurita did not necessarily feel. "This fleet intends to charge into Leyte Gulf at 1100 on the 25th without regard for any damage we may suffer," he said, and in the log of the force, the words "chancing annihilation" were used. But at this time, about 2200, Admiral Kurita was still hoping for a better performance the next day from the land-based air forces of Admirals Fukudome and Ohnishi.

Of the 32 ships that had set out from Brunei Bay, 22 were now left to form a single column at 2330 that night and begin moving through the narrow Strait. The Japanese accounts say there were no lights—some say it was pi'.h dark—but Admiral Kurita said it was good light weather and the moon was very bright, so that he could navigate visually to bring his force through. It seemed easy, easier still when they emerged on the far side of the Strait safely at 0035. Admiral Kurita had been bracing himself for the flash of guns; he knew only too well how easy it would be for the Americans to do to him what in a short time they would be doing to Admiral Nishimura farther south.

Admiral Kurita was as suspicious as a wolf approaching a cabin. He formed his force on a broad 13-mile front, and ran eastward until 0300, and then moved southeast down the coast of Samar toward the target area. An hour before sunrise the force proposed to move into the circular pattern (destroyers outside, battleships in the center) that had been used the day before and had enabled the Japanese to throw up a strong anti-aircraft fire.

Kurita was in the dark, literally and figuratively. At 0230 there had been one message from Nishimura, saying he was entering Surigao Strait, and that he had seen nothing except some American torpedo boats. It seemed odd. At 0335 Nishimura had reported that he had sighted three enemy ships. Then came long and ominous silence, and at 0532 a message from Shima saying that Nishimura's force had been *destroyed.* Just like that, two battleships snuffed out, and the *Mogami* seriously afire. And then nothing.

Actually, flying boats conducting night radar searches had been out that night, working well. They had found four enemy ship concentrations, and had reported on them thoroughly by 0400. The information had been passed along to the land-based air headquarters and used as their basis for attack formations for the coming day's operations. But nobody thought to inform Admiral Kurita until long after the battle off Samar was over.

Here is the way it looked this night to Admiral Ugaki:

. . . We safely navigated the San Bernardino Strait, taking advantage of the light clouds which filmed the brightness of the moon (phase of the moon). Turning east, we formed No. 19 Alert cruising disposition. At 0400 we changed course to 150° and proceeded south ten miles off the coast of Samar. We expected the penetration into Leyte Gulf at 1100, after first rendezvousing with the Third Section [Nishimura] at 0900 at a point 10 miles east of Suluan Island.

Communications operations of the reconnaissance airplanes which had deployed to land bases on the 24th were not smoothly effected, and we were unable to obtain their reconnaissance reports. . . .

The reason, guessed by Admiral Ugaki: change of flagship and the inferior communications setup of the *Yamato*, jamming by the Americans, and inferior base communications facilities in the Philippines.

It is the rainy season in this area [wrote Admiral Ugaki], and the weather on the east coast is particularly unfavorable. It is almost impossible to determine when day breaks, and scattered dark clouds accompanied by squalls hang low, making visibility poor. At 0644, just before the order to form circular formation was issued, four masts, apparently destroyers, were suddenly spotted bearing 060 to port—37 kilometers from *Yamato*. . . . This was followed by the sighting of three carriers, three cruisers, and two destroyers. . . .

Confusion, confusion! The Japanese were ready to go into their circular defense formation; instead Admiral Kurita ordered the attack. The result was that "no heed was taken of order or coordination," said his Chief of Staff later. Admiral Ugaki was a bit less harsh, recalling it on the same day:

It was a surprise encounter since no situation reports had been received since the previous night, and although we had long considered various measures for such an event, the ships, I thought, were extremely slow in reacting because of their lack of enemy information. Measures taken by the fleet headquarters, too, occasionally seemed lacking in promptness. At any rate at 0658 Battleship Division 1 opened fire with its forward guns at a range of 31 kilometers. . . .

The Battle of Samar was joined.

The Japanese were coming down. The left, or outside, was a destroyer screen led by a cruiser. Then came the heavy cruisers *Suzuya, Kumano, Chikuma,* and *Tone.* Next grouping was the heavy cruisers *Haguro* and *Chokai.* And inshore of them was another destroyer squadron, led by a cruiser.

Three miles behind this force steamed the battleships *Yamato* and *Nagato,* and alongside, *Kongo* and *Haruna.*

What happens in battle is nowhere better indicated than what happened this morning. Admiral Kurita's lookouts saw planes overhead fourteen minutes before they saw the American ships. When they spotted the Americans they misidentified the ships, in part because the lookouts were not familiar with the profiles of the escort carriers (mostly on converted tanker hulls) and did not know what they were. So one report had it that the area was full of cruisers and heavy fleet carriers. Admiral Kurita's Chief of Staff thought they were up against fleet carriers; so, obviously, did the Admiral.

If the shock was great for the Japanese, who were after all on the offensive, imagine what it must have been for the Americans in the ships ahead, for they rested secure in the belief that no Japanese force was going to debouch from San Bernardino Strait with the pride of America's fleets—the new fast battleships—lying across that body. Admiral Oldendorf was extremely proud of the fact that his battleships at Surigao Strait had performed so well. Actually, as it had turned out, the *Pennsylvania*'s fire-control system was so ancient that she never did get into action, *Mississippi* trained her guns first on the stops, and finally got away one salvo, and old *Maryland* only managed six salvos. The work was done by the *West Virginia, California, Tennessee,* and by the cruisers. Given the new battleships and the larger force of Admiral Kurita with the *Yamato*'s 18-inch guns (largest in the world), it still would scarcely have been a fair fight for the Japanese.

In his flag plot on *Wasatch* Admiral Kinkaid had spent a busy, and until now, a relatively satisfactory night. He was conscious of things that did not go right: the destroyer *Albert W. Grant* got into line of fire by turning the wrong way, one battleship nearly caused a collision when she misunderstood a signal, and the fire-control problems of *Pennsylvania* were nothing short of disgraceful. This was an admiral's concern—let the men under him have the credit for the valor and the victory, let him not have too many problems with ships and men! He had planned as carefully as he could for every contingency. Knowing the ammunition difficulties of his force because of the need to bombard those beaches, he had taken two ammunition ships and put them up off the coast of Samar, safely away from nearly everybody else, so that in case somebody got them they would go up alone and not take the fleet with them into oblivion. (He was very lucky so far; the Japanese had not bothered those ammunition ships at all although they had bothered just about everybody else.) Here is Admiral Kinkaid's recollection of that night:

The night before [24th] I had directed [Admiral] Sprague to have attack groups ready on deck [of the jeep carriers], looking forward to what might be the morning situation. I'd directed him to send one attack group down into Mindanao to get any stragglers or escapees from the night action, which he did. I'd also directed him at daylight to send a search to northward along the San Bernardino Strait. I did that mostly out of curiosity to know what had gone on up there, because I thought that [Admiral] Lee was there with Task Force 34, and I didn't expect to find anything that we had not planned. I was quite wrong in that.

Unfortunately that search did not get off. Sprague got off his anti-submarine patrols, and he got off an attack group against stragglers from the night action. . . .

The order to fly these searches was given by Admiral Sprague to Admiral Stump in the escort carrier group known as *Taffy* II: 6 escort carriers and 7 destroyers and escorts. Admiral Stump passed the order to the escort carrier *Ommaney Bay*. And *Ommaney Bay*, which did not get the order until just after 0500, had difficulty in getting the planes ready on the wet, careening decks, and did not get the strike launched until 0658, the moment at which the Japanese ships appeared out of the squalls and began firing.

Also, Admiral Kinkaid had made other plans for search: "I had directed the PBY's to make a night flight and they had trouble and got no results. . . ."

Part of the trouble came with the five planes (Black Cats), or special patrol bombers equipped for night flying. They were anchored in Hunangen Bay, Leyte, where they had barely arrived. Only three could take off that night, and only one of these headed toward Kurita's force. He flew to San Bernardino Strait, arrived before Admiral Kurita entered it, and missed him completely.

The Black Cats were wary—not of the Japanese, but of the American ships. "Every time they'd get near one of our ships they'd be fired at, and I think they spent most of their time trying to avoid our ships, rather than advancing to see what they could find around San Bernardino Strait," said Admiral Kinkaid. One could hardly blame either the Black Cats or the American ships for that; no matter how badly the Japanese air performed in the daytime, a constant succession of Japanese "snoopers" could be heard at night, and they did not sound unlike the PBY's, particularly in the noises men heard at sea.

So the circumstances built up. As far as Kinkaid was concerned: "Had Lee been in the straits with Task Force

34, he would, if he had made any contacts, have reported them immediately to everyone. The mere fact that in the morning there was no report from him seemed to indicate that everything was all right."

Yet there were little signs of concern, even when all the avenues seemed covered. "In the middle of the night or early in the morning of the 25th I called a meeting in my cabin of the staff and everyone connected with operations to see if there was anything they had forgotten to do, or anything doing that was wrong, to see if anything needed change or to be added to. All went over the situation."

The meeting ended at 0400 and as Commander Dick Cruzen, the Operations Officer, was leaving he turned and said:

"Admiral, I can think of only one thing. We've never asked Halsey directly if Task Force 34 is guarding San Bernardino Strait."

"All right," said Admiral Kinkaid. "Send it."

The message went out, but Halsey did not receive it for two and a half hours. All this time, Admiral Kurita was steaming in watchful curiosity, wondering why the Americans had left the back door unguarded. Another communications failure!

At this time the American escort carriers were moving inshore from their night operating areas off the coast, and were heading into the northeast wind to launch planes to carry out their various missions. "At about 0200 Admiral Kinkaid instructed me to prepare to pursue the damaged vessels [of the Surigao Strait battle], the ones that had escaped, so we got busy about three hours before daylight and loaded torpedoes and the heavy bombs in order to catch the ones that were undamaged and were escaping, and to dispense those who were damaged and who couldn't move very fast."

Rear Admiral T. F. Sprague was in the south, east of Dinagat Island, so he would send the planes farthest west. Rear Admiral Felix Stump, in *Taffy* II, was operating off Homonohon Island, and he would take care of the check on San Bernardino and put up an air patrol over the Leyte ships. So would Rear Admiral Clifford Sprague in the north. It was "Cliff" Sprague's ships that came into sight when Admiral Kurita saw those American masts that morning.

Here was the vaunted American task force, said Kurita's men, and about time, too. Planes could be seen taking off from the decks of the American ship.

"By heaven-sent opportunity we are dashing to attack the enemy carriers," radioed Admiral Kurita to combined fleet headquarters. "Our first objective is to destroy the flight decks, then the Task Force."

What Kurita thought was obvious—this was the southern of the three groups of the American task force. What a chance to hit the enemy—smashing those important carriers. For Kurita, like Admiral Yamamoto, under whom he had trained, had absorbed the carrier admiral's philosophy: get the carriers first, then get the fleet.

At Kurita's order, "the battleships opened fire (range 31 kilometers, or 18.6 miles) and damaged one ship with two or three salvos, then changed to another target. The enemy reversed course and began retiring eastward under cover of smoke and rain squalls."

"For some reason," wrote Admiral Ugaki, who was on his bridge on the *Yamato*, "fleet headquarters ordered the battleships and cruisers to attack and the destroyer squadrons to follow in the rear. The attack course of the entire fleet was now divided, making one doubt the intensity of the spirit for close-quarter combat."

So Ugaki suggested to Kurita's Chief of Staff that he be given control of the battleships, and that was done.

At about 0700 it was said that there were six carriers. From 0706 we advanced generally on an easterly course and employed our secondary guns at the enemy who appeared from behind the smoke. It was generally about this time that one carrier was sunk, one carrier was heavily damaged, one cruiser was sunk, etc. We were now rapidly approaching the enemy— the range by radar was 2200 meters and visibility was gradually improving from the east. We hoped to destroy the enemy at one blow if he came out from behind the smoke. In the meantime we were attacked by enemy aircraft. Several salvos from medium-

caliber enemy guns fell near *Yamato,* and two shells
hit the starboard after gallery and outer boat shed. . . .

Admiral Ugaki's observations represented the desperate
American counterattack as the little jeep carriers—whose
flank speed was 17.5 knots as compared to the Japanese
speed of almost twice that—tried desperately to escape,
yet could not move south into Leyte Gulf because they
would endanger the entire Seventh Fleet, being restricted
in such narrow waters. In other words, when Admiral
Sprague asked Admiral Kinkaid if he could move, the
answer was "no." If the carriers had to be sacrificed to
save the fleet, so it would be.

There were three lines of defense for the Americans: to
run for it, which would at least keep the Japanese from
ramming them; to put the destroyers to work screening and
fighting; or to use those escort carrier planes for all they
were worth. The Americans chose all three.

"Ziggy" Sprague, the admiral in charge of *Taffy* III,
began to act. He ordered his ships to flank speed; he
ordered the destroyers into action; he ordered every fly-
able plane into the air. Three minutes after the attack
began, he broadcast a plain English report and call for
assistance from anyone. This report, and the reply, were
picked up by the Japanese, and they were to have profound influence on the battle later.

The destroyer screen of *Taffy* III consisted of the *Hoel,*
the command ship, *Heermann,* and the *Johnston,* and they
swung into action. The *Johnston* was first. Here is the way
it went:

This ship had secured from morning alert, the first
carrier's plane strike, ASP [anti-submarine patrol] and
CAP [Combat Air Patrol] patrols had been launched.
At about 0650 word was received by TBS: "We are
being pursued by a large portion of the Jap fleet."
General Quarters was sounded and this task unit
headed in an easterly direction to launch planes. At
this time the enemy fleet was about 34,000 yards distant bearing approximately 345° from us. The Japanese force was closing the range rapidly, their speed
being 22–25 knots. The captain [Commander Ernest E.

Evans] immediately gave orders to the engine room to light off all boilers and make maximum speed. The captain also ordered the engine room to commence making funnel smoke and ordered the smoke screen generator detail to make . . . smoke. [Later the ship's crew proudly claimed that they had started smoke ten minutes before the order came from the flagship.] This ship then commenced zigzagging back and forth between the enemy and our own formation, laying a heavy smoke screen. By 0700 the carriers had launched all available planes and the formation turned to a southwesterly course. Ships were informed by TBS at this time for destroyers to make smoke. This unit had been under fire by the Japanese fleet since 0650. [*Johnston's* time was eight minutes off.]

At 0710 the range to the nearest cruiser had closed to 18,000 yards and fire was opened with the 5-inch battery on this cruiser. The planes were at this time striking the Japanese force, completing their strike at about 0715. As soon as this ship commenced firing on the enemy we in turn were taken under heavy fire from more than one Jap unit. This ship was straddled during this period. As a result of the heavy gunfire, the captain gave the order to stand by for torpedo attack at starboard and turned and headed for the enemy. Torpedoes were set on low speed because of heavy fire to insure the firing of our torpedoes. This decision was made by the captain to insure being within torpedo range and to insure being able to fire our torpedoes even if this heavy fire should put the ships out of action. [Everything Commander Evans did that day was to the end of smashing the enemy—he was a single-minded, purposeful man, part Cherokee, heavy-set, and determined. He was meeting the moment for which he seemed to be created.]

The ship closed to within 10,000 yards of the enemy before the torpedoes were fired. The point of aim was the leading cruiser. . . . The torpedoes were fired . . . at a depth of six feet . . . and a spread of one degree was used. . . . All ten torpedoes were fired at three-second intervals and were observed to run hot, straight and normal. During the run in, the 5-inch guns fired in rapid salvo fire with the leading cruiser as the point of aim. Over 200 rounds were fired at this cruiser . . . and numerous hits were visually observed. . . . It is believed that this heavy cruiser was severely damaged by at least 40 five-inch shells.

The men of the *Johnston* were disappointed not to see the results of their torpedoes, but they were retiring behind a heavy smoke screen at the time the torpedoes should hit. The cruiser they were aiming at, it was determined later, was the *Kumano*, and she and the other cruisers were firing on the *Johnston* all this time, using dye shells of various colors—mustard, purple, yellow—by which the observers could track their aim.

Results of the torpedo attack were not observed visually . . . it can be positively stated, however, that two and possibly three underwater explosions were heard by two officers and many enlisted men in the repair parties at the time our torpedoes were scheduled to hit. Upon emerging a minute later from the smoke screen, the leading enemy cruiser was observed to be burning furiously astern.

Then the *Johnston* began to catch it—partly because her angle of attack was such that all the Japanese cruisers within range could fire on her, and they did.

At this time, 0730, this ship was hit for the first time. It is believed we were hit by three 14-inch projectiles [those were battleship shells] followed thirty seconds later by three 6-inch projectiles [from the cruisers]. These hits knocked out the after fireroom and engine room, all power to the steering engine, all power to the after three 5-inch guns and rendered the gyro compass useless. . . .

The ship was slowed to 17 knots, about half its regular top speed. Steering had to be moved aft, and done manually. The radar went out for five minutes, and the radar antenna was snapped off by a shell, but the fire direction radar was still operable. The guns had to be controlled either manually or partially so, instead of automatically by computer.

Luckily, after having taken this smashing, the *Johnston* managed to find a rain squall and hid in it for ten minutes while the officers found the damage and began controlling it. Then the *Johnston* went back into the fight, first taking on a Japanese destroyer, then bulldogging after the cruisers again. All this was done in the storm, by radar, and 100 rounds were fired. "At 0750 [*Johnston*'s time was still not that of the others] received orders by TBS for small boys [destroyers] to make torpedo attack." Here is the TBS report of what happened in the next few minutes. It was all done in code, using code names for the ships, and code designations for the maneuvers, but the sense of urgency certainly lies in these signals made between ships.

THE ORDER CAME FROM THE FLAGSHIP AT 0745:
SMALL BOYS FORM UP FOR SECOND ATTACK, OVER.
THEN THE TRANSMISSIONS HURRIED UP:

This is Taffy 3	All Great Danes stand by to open
This is Georgia	up
Overture from	Wilco out
Taffy 3	Are your torpedoes ready over
	Affirmative
This is	Affirmative
Dreadnaught	
This is Taffy 3	All small boys go out and launch
	torpedo attack
This is Overture	Wilco
This is Taffy 3	All carriers make smoke over
	Torpedoes are heading toward
	carrier group
Mercury 3 from	Execute upon receipt signal turn
Taffy 3	shackle George Xray Unshackle
Fido from	Are you hit over
Taffy 3	
This is Fido	Negative
Taffy Three from	Fish headed for Great Danes out
Juggernaut	

0802 Mercury 3 from Taffy 3	Signal execute upon receipt Turn shackle Nan Peter King Unshackle out [These were maneuvering instructions to the fleet from Admiral "Ziggy" Sprague.]
Fatima 4 This is Fatima	Do you have planes coming in on 290
0414 Mercury 3 from Taffy 3	Negative but they show light Signal execute shackle george king roger Unshackle out
0820 Taffy 3 from Catnip	The forward engine room is flooded Say again
Fido from Taffy 3 This is Fido	Have you been hit Negative Good going
0821 Taffy 3 from Catnip	I have been hit hard I have lost one engine over
0824 This is Taffy 3	Roger out
0825 This is Taffy 3	Small boys on my starboard quarter intercept enemy cruiser coming on my port quarter
Small boys from Taffy 3	Intercept enemy heavy cruiser coming in on Bendix port quarter I have him . . . closing in now . . .
0826 Taffy 3 from Mongrel	We have no fish left
Mongrel from Taffy 3	Stay on station and continue smoking
This is Figleaf	We have no fish left
This is Taffy 3	Roger out
Small boys from Taffy 3	On starboard quarter interpose with smoke between me and enemy heavy cruiser
This is Mongrel	Wilco out
This is Overture	Wilco out
This is Figleaf	Wilco out

When the order had come for "small boys" to make torpedo attack, the destroyers formed a formation, with the *Johnston,* which had already fired, furnishing fire support for the *Hoel, Heermann,* and *Roberts,* which were going in.

As we turned to retire after the other destroyers had fired their torpedoes, range closed to 6000 yards on the leading Japanese cruiser and many hits were obtained on it at this time. Retirement was commenced with the aid of a heavy smokescreen. At approximately 0810 the *Johnston* emerged from a heavy smoke screen only to find the USS *Heermann* on our starboard bow on a collision course with us at a distance of about 200 yards. The captain backed full on the one remaining engine and the *Heermann* was observed to back on all engines. A collision was thus avoided by the narrowest possible margin. . . .

. . . At about 0820 there suddenly appeared out of the smoke a battleship of the *Kongo* class 7000 yards distant on our port beam. . . . By this time the captain had given the order not to fire on any target unless we could see it, the reason being that enemy and friendly ships were now in the melee. Approximately forty rounds were fired at the Jap battleship, at our necessarily reduced rate of fire, before retiring behind our own smoke screen and before being taken under fire by this battleship. Several hits were observed on the pagoda superstructure. . . .

[A carrier, the *Gambier Bay,* was hit.]

This ship attempted to draw fire away from the *Gambier Bay* by taking the cruiser under fire at this time. The range was closed to 6000 yards and maximum fire was brought to bear on this heavy cruiser. This attempt, as was to be expected, was unsuccessful, despite numerous hits being observed. . . .

At about 0840 fire was checked when it became obvious that the Japanese destroyers on our port hand were closing rapidly on the carriers. Upon receiving this information from combat, the captain directed our course toward the enemy destroyers, who were deployed in a column with the apparent leader in the van, followed by two divisions consisting of three destroyers apiece.

The Japanese destroyers were sighted at a range of about 10,000 yards and fire was immediately opened on the destroyer leader. Our fire appeared to be extremely effective and the range continued to close to about 7000 yards. This ship was hit several times during this one encounter by 5-inch shells. Approximately 12 hits were obtained on the leading Japanese destroyer before a most amazing thing happened. The destroyer leader proceeded to turn 90° to the right and break off the action. Fire was immediately shifted to the second destroyer and hits were observed at initial range of around 8000 yards. During firing on this second destroyer, the captain [what a doughty man he was] attempted to cross the T on the Jap column. However, before this was accomplished, amazingly enough, all remaining six Japanese destroyers turned 90° to the right and the range began to open rapidly.

The TBS transmission (as noted earlier in the TBS report) had been received just prior to our opening fire on these Jap destroyers, directing the small boys to interpose between the carriers and Japanese cruiser on their port quarter. We checked fire as the Jap destroyers retired, turned to the left and proceeded to close the range on the Jap cruisers. For the next half hour this ship proceeded to engage, first the cruisers on our port hand and then the destroyers on our starboard hand, alternating between the two groups in a somewhat desperate attempt to keep them all from closing the carrier formation. The ship was getting hit with disconcerting frequency during this period. . . .

The *Johnston* could very well have retired at any time after the initial torpedo attack in which one of her engines was shot out and she was so sorely injured. But Captain Evans chose to fight, and thus must be credited very heavily with the salvation of the American escort carriers that day. He fought for two hours.

During this rather hectic time [reported Lieutenant Robert C. Hagen, who was to be the senior officer surviving the battle], we were engaging many ships at only medium ranges. There were several occasions where the ship still could have crept away and escaped further damage which she was continuing to receive. At this time we had taken 12 to 14 hits. We had two guns that were fully in operation, two others that could have fired only in manual. Our maximum speed was still 15 knots. Killed and wounded littered our decks.

Despite all this it is interesting to note that the captain still refused to leave the area and fought the Japanese force, continually turning them back until the ship was finally snowed under with an avalanche of shells. . . .

The Captain had been injured very early in the game. When the radar was snapped off the mast, three officers were killed by or on the bridge and all Captain Evans' clothes above the waist were blown off. Lieutenant Hagen reported:

. . . He was . . . injured rather severely at 0730— two and a half hours before we abandoned ship—to the extent of a couple of fingers blown off, an unknown number of shrapnel holes in his back and superficial wounds about his face and neck, all of which were drawing considerable blood. Despite these things the captain fought that ship as no other man has ever fought a ship.

The shells that came hurtling in knocked out the *Johnston*'s remaining engine room and fireroom. The director and plot lost power. All communications failed. All the five guns failed except No. 4 where the crew continued to the last, firing manually. It was about 0945. The Captain gave the order to abandon ship, an order every man had been expecting at almost any time. Ten minutes later the survivors were off the ship, and she rolled over and sank 15 minutes after that. Just to make sure, one Japanese destroyer closed to within 1000 yards and fired at point blank range even as she went down.

Then came an ordeal that no one aboard the *Johnston*

had really expected: the survivors stayed in the water for many hours.

No one knows how many survivors there were in the beginning. The Captain was alive when they went into the water, and so was the Executive Officer. Also in the water were perhaps 200 other officers and enlisted men, in various conditions from badly wounded to totally unhurt. They had three life rafts and two floater nets to keep them alive. They thought it would be a matter of a couple of hours if they could only stay afloat.

The sharks came, attracted by the blood. They took some men, and spat out one particularly sour old salt, who would carry the marks of the shark's teeth with him. Within two hours, the men's hopes were raised by the appearance of several planes, which zoomed and apparently went on to report their presence in the water to friendly forces. But no one came. The hours went by, and still no one came. Men died, and no one came. Men slipped off the ropes from exhaustion, and no one came. The Captain disappeared, and no one came.

It was cold and lonely in the sea, even if the weather was hot and humid. The planes did not come back. They did not bring life rafts or survival gear or anything. The heroes of the *Johnston* were left alone to face the rigors of the cruel sea.

Believe it or not, *two days and two nights* went by before anyone thought to save the men of the *Johnston*. During that period at least 45 officers and men, including the gallant Captain, succumbed to wounds or died of exposure or shark bite. One more day, said Lieutenant Hagen, and no one would have survived. But, after 50 hours, help finally came, and 141 officers and men were saved.

Part of the reason for abandonment of the men of the *Johnston* was the thorough confusion into which Admiral Sprague's escort carrier force was thrown by the Japanese attack. And there were plenty of other casualties.

The next ship to get it from the Japanese was the destroyer *Hoel*, a part of the same screening force. The *Hoel* was the lead ship, with Commander W. D. Thomas aboard as the man in charge of the screen. Her captain was Commander L. S. Kintberger.

Like the rest of the task group, the men of the *Hoel* were shocked when the word came that the Japanese were firing on an American plane. "How a large Japanese task force like this could sneak up on our escort carriers is something that I will never be able to understand," said Lieutenant Maurice F. Green of the *Hoel*.

Here is the story of her attack and adventure, as told by Lieutenant Green:

We decided to fire a half salvo at the leading battleship and save the other half for the leading cruiser because it was definite that we would have to turn at least two columns of ships in order to be of any assistance in screening the CVE's . . . all the Japs turned and fled. There is no explanation why. They could have rubbed out every ship in our formation. . . .

At 0725 we received the first hit on the bridge which destroyed all of our voice radio communications and also the remote Radar PPI on the bridge. This shell also killed several personnel . . . helmsman . . . captain's talker. . . .

It was less than five minutes later that we received a hit on the main battery director putting it out of action and also killing our anti-aircraft officer, making it necessary for the anti-aircraft guns to go into local control. We had an officer at each 40 mm mount . . . there was nothing within range of the 40 mms to fire at. . . .

The ship launched its torpedoes. The first torpedoes had been aimed at the battleship *Kongo*, and she avoided them. The second torpedoes were aimed at the *Haguro*, leading the cruiser column of the Japanese.

The *Hoel* was being hit. Her port engine was knocked out. Her rudder jammed and she headed directly for a Japanese battleship, hardly a healthy maneuver. Her after guns would not fire. She kept getting hit.

It was 0735 when that second group of torpedoes were fired, under extremely difficult circumstances. They were on one engine and hand steering from aft. The torpedo officer, Lieutenant (jg) Glen W. Coleman, was on No. 2 torpedo mount, and had no communication with the others.

He rushed down to the mount from the bridge in 30 seconds after communication failed, and discovered the situation. (The hits were coming fast.) His chief torpedoman had been killed. Five forward torpedoes had been fired. So he went to the after mount, and found it had been trained out according to instructions he had given earlier, and he had a setup on the leading cruiser *(Haguro)*: 5000 yards at an angle of 50 degrees. He fired five torpedoes. They ran hot straight and true, and large columns of water arose at the side of the *Haguro* at the time that the torpedoes should have hit. The Japanese, however, claimed the *Haguro* was not torpedoed. There again—the discrepancies of battle stories—came through the confusion.

"With our ten fish fired we decided it was time to get the hell out of there," said Lieutenant Green.

It was nearly impossible. They were now boxed in by Japanese ships, and it was estimated that, in all, some 300 two- and three-gun salvos were fired at the *Hoel*.

They tried to go southwest, chasing salvos, on the theory they might thus escape the next one. "This proved impossible because we were boxed in on all sides by enemy capital ships. We fishtailed and chased salvos and made all possible speed on one engine which enabled us to continue to remain afloat. . . ."

The Jap battleships were 8000 yards on the port beam. We had heavy cruisers 7000 yards on the starboard quarter and we had only two guns left to fire. They were forward which made it difficult to continue firing while attempting a retirement. These two forward guns must have expended 250 or 300 rounds each. . . .

At 0830 we lost power on the starboard engine due to several more hits in engineering spaces and throughout the hull. These hits must have been armor-piercing ammunition because very few of them detonated. Some of them, which I believe to have been 16-inch shells, came through one side of the ship and went out the other side without detonating. The smaller shells, the 5-inch shells or smaller, which appeared to be anti-personnel shells, did detonate and they are the ones that caused us to have such heavy casualties.

. . . When our power was lost in the starboard engine, leaving us with no engine power at all, all of our engine spaces were flooding and our number one magazine was on fire. Five minutes later word was passed to prepare to abandon ship. All this time we were losing way . . . practically dead in the water. At 0840 with the ship dead in the water and a 20° list, word was passed to abandon ship. . . .

Then they had to send back forward for the gun crews of the two 5-inch guns, who kept on firing until the list was so bad it was obvious she was settling by the stern.

The enemy continued to fire on the *Hoel* until 0850. Some of these shells did drop short, those that hit killed many men attempting to abandon ship, those that fell short killed men in the water. At 0855 the ship rolled over on her port side and sank, stern first.

I was about 50 yards away from the fantail at this time. I was alone in the water but did manage to swim to a life raft. Later we joined the captain and the commodore [Commander Thomas], who was pretty badly hurt, and we managed to tie three life rafts together.

Now came a repetition of what happened to the *Johnston*. The task group simply abandoned the men of the *Hoel*.

We spent 48 hours in the water with no visible attempt being made to find us, which we questioned later and found that no attempt had been made. No planes were sent out, no destroyers were sent out. When we were picked up by an LCI, a very small one, No. 341, 48 hours later, we found that they had been sent to the wrong location to pick us up. Somebody certainly fouled up here because we had been operating in the same water every day in the same area. . . .

So they waited. There were no underwater explosions, luckily, and all they worried about were sharks and rescue. Two men managed to float to Samar Island, and were picked up by guerrillas, after four days in the water. Only 19 were formally listed as dead at the end of the battle, but 252 were listed as missing or dead, and only 82 came home.

There were two other casualties in the screening group. One was the *Heermann*. She went into battle gladly under her captain, Commander Amos T. Hathaway.

"Buck," he said to Lieutenant Robert F. Newsome, his officer of the deck and navigator, "what we need is a bugler to sound the charge."

The *Heermann* followed the *Hoel* in on the torpedo attack, without certain results. But the results to the *Heermann* were not long in coming. Said Commander Hathaway:

After we fired our last three torpedoes at the enemy battleship, I went inside the pilot house, called the admiral on the TBS and told him my exercise was completed. I don't know quite why I used those words. I remember having an idea in my head that the Japs might be listening in on the circuit and I didn't want them to know that I didn't have any more torpedoes. I don't believe the admiral understood me either, as a little while later they asked me if I had any torpedoes left.

While Hathaway was inside making this report, his crew said they saw one of the *Heermann*'s torpedoes hit "the enemy battleship" in an after gun turret. It was marked by a huge geyser of water—the depth setting on the torpedo had been only 6 feet, which was much too shallow for battleship torpedoing, but they had identified the battleship very late.

Captain Hathaway decided to get out of the area, and closed on a destroyer, which he thought was the *Hoel*. It turned out to be the *Johnston*. He went with her for a bit, and then left because the *Johnston* was obviously unable to keep up speed (she was mortally injured then). Her radar was hanging down on her yardarm and she sent the mournful message: "Only one engine, no radar, and no gyros." That was only part of what was wrong, of course.

The *Heermann* was trying to make 35 knots to get out of the area, and suddenly out of the gloom the *Fanshaw Bay* appeared, one of the escort carriers, and it was only by backing suddenly that Hathaway managed to avoid a collision. He had no sooner avoided this ship than the *Johnston* came at him. "This time it was too close for comfort. We missed the *Johnston* by a mere matter of about 3 inches. People could have touched as our bows missed each other. Everyone thought we would hit." They passed safely as men on both ships cheered in relief.

The Japanese were firing on the escort carriers, and as the *Heermann* came rushing back from her attack, she neared the *Gambier Bay,* one of the escorts under fire, and the Japanese cruiser which was shooting took the destroyer under fire for a time. *Heermann* started shooting back.

"It was 0841 when we started firing at the *Tone*-class cruiser. There were three other heavy vessels identified as heavy cruisers astern of her and two other vessels, possibly these were destroyers, I zigzagged and chased splashes for about 20 minutes."

Four minutes after the action began, the *Heermann* took her first punishment, a shell on the bridge, which killed three men and wounded the steersman mortally. It also brought a touch of tragic irony.

On the day before, the *Heermann* had picked an aviator named Lieutenant (jg) Dahlan out of the water and Hathaway said he never saw a man more grateful for rescue. This morning, Lieutenant Dahlan came up on the bridge and asked to help in the fight. The Captain told him to go help the gunnery officer on the director in spotting planes that might come in on them, and off went the pilot. But after awhile, when there were no Japanese planes, he went back to the bridge to find the Captain and get another assignment. Just then the shell came in and killed the Lieutenant who had gotten his second lease on life the day before.

The Captain probably would have been killed by that shell too, but a few moments before the shell came in, he had decided the bridge was a bad place for fighting the ship because the shell splashes of straddle shots were sending water so high that he had difficulty seeing. So he had climbed up to the fire-control structure, and thus saved his life.

When the steersman was killed, Chief Quartermaster John P. Milley was thrown to the deck, too. He got up on his knees, reached over the wounded steersman, and took the wheel, carrying out an unexecuted order from the Captain with the coolness of a man on an exercise. The talker repeated the order with the same coolness, just to be sure Milley had it, and when the voice tube was damaged by shrapnel, the talker moved closer to the Captain so he could hear. QM2c Jack Woolworth, another survivor on the bridge, had been badly wounded in the buttocks, but he never whimpered and took over the jobs of the engine order telegraph man and the bridge radioman after they were killed.

The battle seemed almost unreal, as it apparently did to everyone.

We were under fire from four of the enemy ships at this time. I realized that it was four ships by the fact that there were several colors of splashes. There were red, yellow, green, and no color splashes around us. It looked like a rainbow. There was more red than anything else, in fact it looked kind of rosy, looking through it, although I guess it was probably rosier for the Japs than it was for us at this particular moment. . . . All they hit us was—they had one 8-inch hit in the uptakes and one down on the keel, one about the waterline forward of gun mount No. 1 and one hit our sound dome.

Then the *Heermann* was hit by a salvo, which caused considerable damage. The damage control parties got busy.

At 0905 I turned the *Heermann* and started across the rear of the carrier formation to lay another smoke-screen. We couldn't see any targets that were within our gun range at the time and it looked to me as if the screen was getting a little thin back there and I decided to lay another. . . . About 0907 a *Maya*-class cruiser closed us from astern. We squared off with her and started to shoot it out. She engaged us for three minutes and then retired and opened the range further than we could shoot.

One of the interesting facts about the action this day, when the Japanese came swooping down on this little force of destroyers that was all that stood between the slow, lumbering escort carriers and total destruction, was the fierceness with which the Americans fought. It translated itself into misrepresentation on the part of the Japanese. The escort force was made up of destroyers and destroyer escorts. But because the destroyers did not fear to engage 6- and 8-inch cruisers in gun battle, the Japanese got the mistaken impression that they were engaging cruisers and destroyers, and it made them that much more cautious about coming up and polishing off the fleet as they certainly could have done.

It was 0910 when we quit [said Commodore Hathaway]. We finished laying the smokescreen across the rear of the carriers. A very few minutes later the admiral [Sprague] told the small boys . . . on the starboard quarter to go out to the port quarter and get there fast as they could. I had seen that both the *Hoel* and the *Johnston* were damaged and realized that the *Heermann*, even though she was damaged, was probably the most effective destroyer left. I started to try to get out there. Being flooded forward it was very difficult for us to make much speed, we were asking the engine room for full power and they were giving it to us, but with all the flooded condition by the bow we actually were not making but about 25 knots, I believe. We were down so far that our anchors were plowing a furrow through the water even though it was a particularly calm day. By 0930 the admiral had ordered formation 5 Roger, our normal cruising formation . . . and I realized that the enemy must all of them have retired. . . .

How fiercely the Americans fought, and under what conditions (destroyers and escorts and airplanes against a 22-ship enemy fleet including the biggest battleship in the world), is very well illustrated by the behavior of the little destroyer escorts. These ships had not been nearly so heavily used in the Pacific as in the Atlantic, but their purpose in both oceans was the same: to work against submarines and to serve as rescue ships for downed aviators. They were much smaller than destroyers, and their major weapons were torpedoes, but they had been so slightly used as attack ships that the group of DE's in the Leyte area this day were totally untrained in attack tactics.

Thus, when the "pros" of the destroyer force—the *Johnston*, *Hoel*, and *Heermann*—went in to attack the Japanese one of the "little wolves," DE *Samuel B. Roberts*, tagged along behind, her captain, Lieutenant R. W. Copeland USNR, going in even though the regular Navy officers of the destroyers had more or less indicated that he ought to go off and play by himself where he would not get hurt.

Here is the story of *Samuel B. Roberts*.

When Copeland asked if he might come along, the screen commander [in *Hoel*] gave him a quick no, but told the DE's to form up for an attack of their own. Apparently none of the other DE's heard the order.

After waiting about five minutes for some indication that other DE's were forming for an attack, and finding none, the commanding officer, finding his ship in an advantageous position from which to make a torpedo attack, called upon CIC for a torpedo attack course and followed in about 3000 yards astern of *Hoel* and *Johnston*.

One might suspect that the Skipper of the *Samuel B. Roberts* waited just long enough so that he would not be accused of getting in the way before he made his own charge on the Japanese fleet.

The *Samuel B. Roberts* "snuck up" on the enemy, through smoke made by the bigger destroyers ahead of her, and she was not seen. She did not fire her 5-inch gun forward, although the Captain itched to do so. "The *Roberts* was able to approach to 4000 yards without being detected"—which meant she and the Japanese cruiser column were coming at each other at a speed of nearly 50 knots.

Now the *Roberts* began to take it. As they moved in

close, the speed of the torpedoes should have been changed to compensate, but while passing the retiring *Johnston,* the *Roberts* caught a stray shell, aimed at the larger ship, which hit the radio antenna and knocked it down. The antenna fell on the torpedo tubes and dislodged the speed-setting wrench. So they had to go with what they had, at intermediate speed. They fired. "Flame smoke and a column of water were observed near the waterline below the secondary control of the *Aoba*-class heavy cruiser leading this column. . . ."

At 0805 the little DE began firing on a *Tone*-class cruiser, starting at 10,000 yards, and working down to 5300 yards just to be sure she was close enough. She fishtailed and sped and slowed and turned, and tried to stay out of the way of the Japanese fire, and she fought, fought, fought with unbelievable vigor.

What confusion existed among these little ships fighting for the lives of their big sisters! Here is an indication from the *Roberts'* action report:

At about 0840 the *Roberts* got clear of a near collision between the *Johnston* and the *Heermann* [all ships were laying smoke and firing at Japanese to port] and changed course to left to interpose between Japanese cruisers and our carriers as directed about five minutes previously by Task Unit Commander. By 0851 she received her first hit, a salvo, which put a hole below the waterline in No. 1 lower handling room, and ruptured main steamline in No. 1 fireroom, putting No. 1 fireroom out of commission, and reducing maximum available speed to 17 knots. As the range closed to 4000 yards at about 0900, hits were coming in rapid succession. No. 1 engine room was hit and knocked out, and a heavy shell, either 8- or 14-inch, hit the superstructure deck house aft, and exploded, completely obliterating the after twin 40 mm mount and after 40 mm Mark 51 director. No further trace of the mount, gun, shield or director was ever seen.

About 0900 a tremendous explosion took place, believed to be hits from two or three 14-inch high-capacity shells, which tore a hole some thirty feet or forty feet long and about seven to ten feet high in the port at the waterline. This salvo wiped out No. 2 engine room, ruptured the after fuel tanks, and started fires on the fantail. All power was lost at this time, and the ship, aft of the stack, was left an inert mass of battered metal. The ship was now incapable of motion and without offensive or defensive measure left to her.

After all power, air and communications had been lost, and before the word to abandon ship was passed, the crew of No. 2 gun, who as a crew distinguished themselves throughout the entire action, loaded, rammed, and fired six charges entirely by hand, and with the certain knowledge of the hazards involved due to the failure of the gas ejection system caused by the air supply having entirely been lost. While attempting to get off the seventh charge in this manner, there was an internal explosion in the gun, killing all but three members of the gun crew, two of whom subsequently died on rafts.

"No underwater explosions were noted . . ." as the ship's crew abandoned at about 0910, and those left—nearly half the crew—moved off the ship, first placing the wounded on rafts. The *Samuel B. Roberts* listed, lay over on her beam ends, and then gave a twist and sank by the stern.

With the men in the water it was the same story as for the others. "After retiring, three of the Japanese ships, a *Katori*-class light cruiser, and two *Asashio* destroyers, passed close aboard survivors of this vessel who were in the water clinging to nets and rafts, and took motion pictures, but did not fire on any of the survivors in the water. . . ."

Then they waited. The men were in the water for 50 hours. They were in two major groups, one raft and one floater net and a group of two rafts and a floater net. But some were adrift, hanging onto 5-inch powder cans, or shoring or staging.

Those men, sadly enough, were not rescued. ". . . During the afternoon of the action we were sighted by friendly aircraft, one of which had buzzed us from low altitude to let us know we had been sighted. We were amazed and our morale reduced by seeing no activity indicating a search for us on the following day. . . ."

And men died, who need not have died, until the searchers came for them.

Other destroyer escorts fared better. They were the *Dennis*, the *John C. Butler*, and the *Raymond*.

The *Raymond* took on an enemy cruiser that was moving in on the formation. Between 0735 and 0740 a torpedo wake was observed to be approaching and passed the ship 20 yards to port. Then, at 0743, Admiral Sprague ordered the escorts to attack with torpedoes and the *Raymond* headed toward the enemy. The Japanese, meanwhile, were launching a torpedo attack of their own against the escort carriers, using eight or nine destroyers.

The *Raymond* fired her torpedoes, three of them at 0756 from 10,000 yards. Some men thought they hit the cruiser they were aiming at—possibly it was the same cruiser that the *Samuel B. Roberts* fired at. Then she turned, and returned to the formation without being hurt. The *Roberts* was taking the punishment.

At 0828 the *Raymond* was ordered off to port to intercept the Japanese cruisers that were moving in. She started shooting. She was straddled once, but not hit, and meanwhile she expended 414 rounds of 5-inch ammunition herself in firing at the enemy. No wonder the Japanese thought they were fighting cruisers and destroyers!

The *Dennis* went after a cruiser, too, and fired her full salvo of three torpedoes at once. She began firing and hit a Japanese cruiser with her 5-inch gun; then, at about 0845, she was closed by eight Japanese destroyers and began taking hits. One hit on the port side three feet above the first platform deck, and went out the starboard side three feet above the waterline. A man in a repair unit was killed. Shell fragments damaged the hull. Another hit on the 40 mm after director killed two men, and other hits came near the No. 1 gun. There was some flooding and the men threw overboard, in weighted sacks, some registered publications, just in case. Then came Sprague's order to resume formation—and suddenly, no one knew quite how, the

Japanese were gone. Six men were killed or died of their wounds and were later buried at sea.

The *John C. Butler*'s story was much the same, except that she did not manage to get into position to fire her torpedoes. One of the cruisers took after her with salvos, four of which landed close aboard, but that fifth one never came, luckily, and she was soon dispatched to make smoke to protect the escort carriers again. She got off free—the luckiest of the bunch of "wolves and little wolves" as they were so rightly called in this particular battle.

17

THE BATTLE OF SAN BERNARDINO STRAIT— PART II

If the battle occurred off Samar, and not actually in the San Bernardino Strait, still, at the end of it, was one phase that stuck in the memory of all concerned. It concerned the Strait through which the Japanese had debouched to make their surprise attack upon the Americans.

The Japanese were deliberate rather than aggressive in this action. "They made very little effort to close the range except in certain cases. . . . They stood off and continued to fire with 8-inch guns . . . and 6-inch guns for about two hours and a half. . . ."

The object of this shellfire was only incidentally the destroyers and the escorts, although they were worrying the Japanese fleet like the wolves and little wolves they claimed to be. What the Japanese wanted to knock out were the six escort carriers of *Taffy* III they had swooped down on so suddenly.

Admiral "Ziggy" Sprague was truly beleaguered. His ships were much slower than the fast fighting ships of the enemy. He was being attacked on the two flanks by a column of destroyers and a column of cruisers, and coming up behind, capable of blowing him out of the water easily, were the battleships. He could not head into Leyte Gulf and hide; he could not overrun *Taffy* II (Admiral Stump's command) and bring destruction to him. He had to zig and zag and hope for help.

Sending the destroyers out to fight a holding action, he turned east, then the cruisers came up on the left and he turned southwest again. The destroyers threatened (they ran a fruitless torpedo attack) and he zigged again. The Japanese cruisers were close enough so that the 5-inch guns of the escort carriers were firing on them. That was what they had: 5-inch guns, one each of those, the ability to make smoke to conceal themselves, and their airplanes, if they could get clear enough to move into the wind to launch and recover. Otherwise, launch and recovery was very dangerous.

The *Kalinin Bay* was the first escort carrier to get into trouble. The formation was roughly two lines of three ships each, with the center ship in the forward line slightly ahead, the center ship in the second line slightly behind the others. The *Kalinin Bay* was in the center position in that second line, and was thus the last ship of the formation.

She had been having trouble that morning. At 0415, long before anyone suspected the coming of the Japanese through San Bernardino Strait, she had trouble with her port engine and emergency repairs were made so she could keep up and launch her aircraft when the time came. Actually, she had no responsibility that morning and no planes were launched at dawn. But not for long. Her action report gives a feeling for the urgency of the manner in which the Japanese presence was discovered that morning:

A plane on anti-submarine patrol from USS *Kitkun Bay* reported to the OTC [Officer in Tactical Command] a task force composed of 4 enemy battleships, 6 cruisers, and numerous destroyers bearing 270° T. distance 20 miles from this formation at 0654. The pilot of the plane definitely identified the task force as enemy. This information was conveyed to this ship over the Interfighter Director Net (37.6 mcs). Immediately after this report, excited Japanese voices were heard over the IFD net. A frequency test was made and it was found that the Japanese were directly on 37.6 mcs. On orders from the OTC General Quarters was sounded at 0658 and speed increased to flank. . . .

Scheduled or not for the morning, launching began on the *Kitkun Bay*. All available planes were made ready and the pilots were instructed to attack the Japanese and then shuttle to Tacloban airstrip, which, although an army installation, could be presumed to be friendly. As it turn.d out it was not very friendly; the army was awaiting the coming of army planes, not navy planes, and it took the army men some time to recognize the emergency aboard the ships for what it was. But that is not properly a part of the story of the fleet.

By 0725, while shells from the Japanese cruisers were falling all around the carrier, she had launched what she had to launch. The force included 3 TBM's loaded with 500-pound bombs (one each) and 8 5-inch rockets each; 6 TBM's loaded with 10 100-pound bombs each and 8 5-inch rockets each; a TBM loaded only with ammunition; and 10 FM-2's (fighters) with ammunition. There were also 2 TBM's on the hangar deck which were temporarily out of commission. These were loaded with torpedoes in anticipation of repair. And finally, later on, 3 more fighters were launched.

By this time the crew of the *Kalinin Bay* was talking ruefully of their ship as "tail-end Charlie," and betting that they were taking more fire than anybody else in the formation—an honor they would gladly have given up to anyone in sight.

The escort carriers ran, making smoke and firing, and the Japanese cruisers chased at a very leisurely pace.

The *Kalinin Bay* took her first hit at 0750, and took 14 more shells before the Japanese broke off the action. All the shells were 8-inch shells from cruisers. Here is the damage they did, as the ship twisted its way behind its smoke:

—The first shell entered the port side about two feet above the deck in the bosn's stores and went out directly opposite one foot lower, without exploding. That meant the shell was armor piercing. (This was a very definite Japanese error in shooting at the unarmored escort carriers, for high-explosive shells would really have wreaked havoc with these hits.)

—The next two shells entered the port side almost together at the platform deck, and caused flooding to a depth of five feet.

—Shell No. 4 hit the carpenter shop, six feet above the

hangar deck, passed the elevator pit, and went out the starboard side. No explosion.

—Shell No. 5 was a near miss. Maybe from a battleship.

—Shell No. 6 entered an officer's stateroom, passed through a storeroom, and exploded in the port aviation lubrication oil tank. This did some real damage, flooding the forward engine room temporarily.

—Shell No. 7 came in across the port, hit in the aviation armory, went through a bulkhead into the ship's armory, down through the platform deck, and through the machine shop before it exploded. The machine shop was a mess, all motors flooded and doused with oil, and the compartment was flooded to a depth of ten feet before it was pumped out and controlled. The shell started a fire in the aviation armory and the upper part of the machine shop, a fire that lasted for two hours and was put out three times before it subsided finally.

—Shell No. 8 exploded under the counter of the fantail and did some serious structural damage to the ship, smashing part of the sprinkling system too.

—Shell No. 9 exploded five yards off the fantail and the nose smashed through the mess attendants' compartment, severing cables, too.

—Shell No. 10 went through the flight deck, and then broke up, sending dangerous splinters through one officers' room, and out the starboard side, rupturing the forward chain of the elevator.

—Shell No. 11 was a bad one. It came through the flight deck wrecking the I-beams that supported the elevator, exploded, and wrecked the forward elevator platform control box and twisted the platform. Radio room II was smashed partially, and the radar control room too. One fragment hit an acetylene bottle near the carpenter shop and started an intense fire in the hangar deck. Another fragment ruptured fire lines and flooded the deck.

—Shell No. 12 came through the flight deck, too, damaging the radar equipment very greatly and starting a serious fire.

—Shell No. 13 passed through the forward starboard stack just outboard of the catwalk.

—Shell No. 14 came through the flight deck, raised riot in the flight crew lockers amidships, and tore holes in the crews' bunkroom bulkheads, another fragment damaged four I-beams in flight deck.

—Shell No. 15—the last—went through the flight deck and tore a hole in the stack starboard and went out through the starboard side, wrecking three I-beams in the flight deck.

Surprisingly, perhaps because so much of the fire was armor-piercing, all day the ship suffered only 5 men killed and 55 wounded. Meanwhile, she was giving back a good account of herself with the 5-inch gun. Here are the *Kalinin Bay*'s claims for the day:

When the enemy cruisers closed the range to 18,000 yards at about 0800, the 5-inch .38 caliber gun of this ship was ordered to open fire. . . . The cruisers closed to 17,300 yards. Fire was continued. . . . At about 0825 at a range of approximately 16,000 yards a direct hit was scored on the No. 2 turret of the *Nachi*-class heavy cruiser by this vessel. The 5-inch gun commenced rapid fire after observing this hit and another hit was made on the same cruiser just below the previous one. After the first hit the No. 2 turret was observed to be slowly enveloping in flames and the second hit caused a quiet burst of flames which completely obscured the turret. The cruiser then turned hard to port and withdrew from the formation temporarily.

It was a tough, frightening fight, and from the carrier point of view is not better described than as seen from the decks of old "tail-end Charlie":

At about 0830 5 destroyers were sighted on the starboard quarter "head on view" approaching in column formation. Their identity was not known, and at first they were thought to be friendly units coming to assist. It was not until they opened fire on our formation from a range of approximately 14,500 yards that they were known to be hostile. At this time the heavy cruisers attacking from the port quarter were obscured by the smokescreen laid down by friendly escorts.

The men of the *Kalinin Bay* kept on firing at the Japanese, but shifted to the destroyers. On came those destroyers, closing in, until they reached a point 10,500 yards away, and then they were recognizable with high bows and two gun mounts forward and heavy tripod masts. The Japanese destroyer salvos came close—many passed overhead—but they were not shooting like the cruisers.

The smoke faded, and the cruisers started shooting too, which made it futile to try to take evasive action by zigzagging. The ship might zig to miss a Japanese destroyer salvo, and then zag right into a cruiser salvo. This was the period when the hits by the cruiser became most severe. According to the ship's action report:

At about 0930 a direct hit amidships was scored on one of the Japanese destroyers, and it immediately was enveloped in white smoke. The enemy destroyers made radical maneuvers and began to withdraw, but continued their fire on this vessel and other ships of the force. A friendly destroyer crossed our stern at about 500 yards and made smoke, and closed the Jap destroyers as she approached. Firing of the 5-inch gun was ceased. . . .

A TBM aircraft, believed to be from the USS *St. Lo* that had been circling the formation, made a steep glide astern of the ship and strafed in the wake of the ship about 100 yards astern, exploding two torpedoes which had been fired from enemy destroyers. The explosion of the torpedoes was only a short while after the enemy had ceased surface shelling of the force. This was the first warning of a torpedo attack being launched against this ship. Immediately after these torpedoes were exploded, another torpedo was sighted directly astern in the wake of the ship. It appeared to be broaching [breaking water]. The 5-inch gun on the fantail opened fire at a depressed elevation . . . and a shell exploded approximately 10 feet ahead of the approaching torpedo; it was next observed veering to port. At least 12 other torpedo wakes were sighted on parallel course on both sides of the ship. After the torpedo attack the entire enemy surface force retired to the northward. . . .

Oddly enough, for what they had put forth against this virtually undefended American force, the Japanese were not scoring very well at all—certainly not in the tradition of those days in the South Pacific when the Japanese shot well and often, and their torpedoes gained the deadly name, "long lances," and the deserved reputation of being the best, by far, in the Pacific.

The *Kalinin Bay* was anything but destroyed, although she had taken some heavy punishment. The *Fanshaw Bay*, in the first line on the starboard side, took a hit from a 6-inch shell at 0850—but it was the only shell of a salvo of 5 to hit. She was hit again eight minutes later, and jettisoned her fire bombs, just in case. Some fires were set in the forecastle, and some damage was done to gas tanks, which began to leak and caused some worry. At about 0855 she was under fire from two cruisers and destroyers and took another hit on the forward end of the flight deck, and then at about 0911 she, too, noticed the torpedo attack, but by 0930 they were all gone, torpedoes and Japanese, and she was safe. It was, however, an indication of what she had been up to that, twenty minutes later, the engine room reported that they had better slow down because their stacks were overheating from the constant flank speed, causing a fire hazard. Now they could slow down. Altogether they had taken six shells, four direct hits, and two near misses. Four men were killed and five were seriously injured.

The *White Plains*, in the center of that forward line, was not hit at all, saw no torpedoes, and did not think much of Japanese gunnery.

The results may indicate that the Jap surface gunnery is not very good as all 13 of our ships involved should have been sunk by the number of projectiles thrown at them. This ship was not hit but it received so many straddles that by the laws of chance it should have been hit several times. One . . . salvo . . . 14-inch . . . was almost the gunners' delight with four close overs and two close shorts. . . . The laws of probability and chance were not operating in favor of the Japs that day. The shooting was good but the percentage of hits was very low, at least on this ship. No accurate estimate of total number of rounds fired can be given but photographs taken from this ship show about 180 splashes. . . .

The *Kitkun Bay* took eight salvos from Japanese ships within 1000 yards, but only one shot came close enough to do any damage at all, and that landed 50 yards astern. The *St. Lo* took innumerable straddles and near misses, mostly from the destroyers that came in on the starboard side of the formation (she was the starboard ship in the second line) but not a single hit was observed, and only three men were injured, all from flying shrapnel that causes superficial wounds.

But there was a more tragic story: that of the *Gambier Bay*. It would seem impossible that the Japanese could come down like wolves on the fold and not manage to do any destruction to the targets they sought, and they did sink the *Gambier Bay*.

Here is the story of the sinking of *Gambier Bay*, from the ship's action report and the Captain's recollections:

Captain W. V. R. Vieweg ordered the launching of planes as soon as he learned of the arrival of the Japanese on the scene, and the crew moved quickly. But there were problems because of the changes in course to try to escape the Japanese.

. . . When my planes were brought up on deck we had very little relative wind movement over the deck. According to the tables we didn't have enough wind to launch a fully loaded and fueled torpedo plane. The first torpedo plane to be launched with a torpedo in it was accordingly launched with only 35 gallons of gasoline in it. This plane subsequently launched a torpedo successfully against the enemy and then, of course, was lost.

When that plane got off, the second plane was launched with a full load of gasoline. There were two more planes —one got off successfully, but as for the second:

We had changed course a little more to the south which brought the wind almost directly astern of us and there was only a 5-knot relative wind over the deck and I knew that was certain death for the crew to catapult it and hence I pulled the crew out of the plane and catapulted the plane without a crew as a means of jettisoning it, since we were by that time threatened with hits. Salvos were falling pretty close.

Gambier Bay's trouble was that she was on the windward side of the formation, which meant her smoke and that of the destroyers blew away quickly, leaving her the most exposed and readily visible of the carriers.

I maneuvered the ship alternately from one side of the base course to another as I saw that a salvo was about due to hit. One could observe that the salvos would hit some distance away and gradually creep up closer and from the spacing on the water could tell that the next would be on if we did nothing. We would invariably turn into the direction from which the salvos were creeping and sure enough the next salvo would land right in the water where we would have been if we hadn't turned. The next few salvos would creep across to the other side and gradually creep back and would repeat the operation. This process lasted for, believe it or not, a half hour during which the enemy was closing constantly.

The first hit came at 0810. Thereafter she was hit almost continually on the flight deck and in the spaces above the waterline. The shells killed and wounded a number of men, and caused fires, but they were quickly put out. As far as they could tell, the men of *Gambier Bay* were being fired upon by no fewer than three of the cruisers.

The disastrous shell came at 0820. Apparently a salvo aimed for the flight deck (for that's what the Japanese were trying to knock out first) fell short and lit in the water just off the port side of the ship, exploding so near the plates of the forward engine room that they were holed. The engine room flooded so rapidly it had to be secured, and one engine stopped. Speed dropped from 19½ knots to 11 knots, and the *Gambier Bay* was a sitting duck among sitting ducks. Even if the Japanese could not shoot this day, all they had to do was come up and fire point-blank at the stricken carrier, which dropped astern of the formation.

The Japs "really poured it on then," said the Captain, and they were hit by nearly every salvo, or some shots from each salvo. "During the period from the first hit, which was around 8:20 in the morning, until we sank, which was about 9:10 in the morning, we were being hit probably every other minute."

The shells that struck high did not explode and did little damage. The damage came from the shells that struck alongside the ship, by and large, or came in just below the waterline. It was not long before the second engine room went out, and the ship was dead in the water. Then the fires, which had been kept down, began to flare up, and there was no water pressure. Soon every hit caused a fire, and the fires grew in intensity. There was one plane left on the hangar deck and it caught fire and the gasoline burned fiercely.

At about 0850 with the ship helpless in the water and with this division of cruisers passing close by and other ships of the main formation passing close by on the other side, and being fired at from all sides, I ordered the ship abandoned [said Captain Vieweg]. As we were abandoning ship the enemy ships in various directions were still firing.

Here is Captain Vieweg's story of his escape from the ship:

I remained on the bridge until everyone was off the bridge and the navigator, who had the deck, and I remained up there and we saw that abandoning ship process was continuing successfully and people were getting off and at that time I directed the navigator to leave the bridge and look out for himself, which he proceeded to do by clambering down the life lines which led from the open bridge.

The Captain decided to take a look for others, and went down through the interior structure, but was almost overcome by black noxious smoke.

. . . I found myself in the rather embarrassing position in that I couldn't go back up on account of the smoke which was really climbing up through that area. And about that time another salvo went through the bridge structure, which urged my departure. I continued, however, down to the flight deck and when I reached there the gases were so hot and black that I couldn't see.

I managed to feel my way aft along the island structure, hoping to reach the catwalk and perhaps get aft and below that way. However, instead of walking down the ladder into the catwalk gracefully, I fell into it, not being able to see, and I couldn't make out for certain where I was. In fact I was so confused at that moment that I thought I might have gone further aft than I had and had fallen into a stack, so hot and so black were the gases. However, I reached up instinctively. At this time I was probably prompted solely by instincts for self-preservation and grabbed ahold of the upper edge of what I was in and pulled myself up and over and started falling and a few seconds, perhaps a fraction of a second later, I broke into clear air with water beneath me. I fell about 40 feet and hit the water with quite a smack.

I had on me at that time my helmet and my pistol, which seemed to help very little since it gave me a good jab in the ribs and my helmet, being secured at the time, almost choked me as I hit the water. However, I came up quite rapidly and the cold water seemed to revive me quickly and I felt in perfectly good health except for my somewhat crippled right side which prevented me from using my right arm very much.

He had come off the starboard side. He tried to swim away from the carrier but it was drifting to starboard. So he swam aft.

About the time I got aft to the starboard quarter, another salvo went through the ship and at that time the ship was almost ready to roll over. The port side was in the water to the extent where the hangar deck was under water. I got about 100 yards off the port quarter at which time the ship very slowly rolled over to port and very slowly sank, and there was no serious detonation. . . .

At that point there was a Japanese cruiser about 2000 yards away, still pumping shells into the unfortunate *Gambier Bay*. But soon all the Japanese left—all but one.

However, perhaps the most alarming thing of the whole operation, from my point of view, was the fact that very shortly after we sank I observed a large Japanese ship dead in the water about three miles to the eastward. We were pretty low in the water, hanging onto a life raft, bouncing up and down and not feeling too well.

[They thought the ship was a *Kongo*-class battleship, and it worried them considerably lest they be captured.]

At any rate this ship remained dead in the water until about sunset at which time it gradually picked up steerage way to change course to the north and disappeared from sight. This ship was at all times attended by a destroyer, a two-stack destroyer, which during the early stages would seem to disappear and reappear and we couldn't quite figure out what it was doing, whether it was picking up people or what.

Captain Vieweg was grateful when it disappeared. Capture at this stage would have been just a little too much.

When he found the first raft Captain Vieweg had begun to assemble his people, but when he had 150 or so of them together he saw the big warship and stopped, lest he attract attention and the Japanese come to get them. Actually some 700 or more survivors of the carrier assembled on various life rafts and flotsam in the area, but they did not ever get together in the hours that followed before rescue. Some died of their wounds. Some were eaten by sharks, as was Lieutenant William H. Buderus, who saved a number of men before he was attacked. There were many heroes of these days and nights, and most of them remain unknown.

It seemed odd to all concerned that the Japanese turned around after those two and a half hours of battle, and deserted the force they could have annihilated. And yet, certain things were happening, particularly from the air, that the Japanese could not have liked at all.

Early in the morning, before the Japanese were sighted bearing down on the escort carriers, those baby flattops had been assigned various tasks. Some pilots, for example, were carrying supplies, particularly water, to troops ashore who were pinned down by Japanese units. Some ships had been assigned to send their pilots out after the ships of Admirals Nishimura and Shima that were moving back westward through the Sulu Sea, or lying hurt in Surigao Strait. Some were assigned to support missions ashore, to bomb and strafe enemy troops.

Of the ships of *Taffy* III, the unit under attack, the *Kalinin Bay* was able to throw heavy air strength against the enemy because it did not have morning commitments. The story of the *Kalinin Bay*'s planes and air crews is indicative of the bravery and daring that was shown that day. Here is the story of part of those planes.

As noted, the planes took off loaded with bombs, rockets, and ammunition to attack the Japanese. Lieutenant Commander W. H. Keighley set the rendezvous, but when he got into the air he found that he had radio failure, so he turned the leadership of the torpedo planes over to Lieutenant Patsy Capano and formed up on him. Also along were Lieutenant (jg) James E. Merchant, Lieutenant (jg) John J. Perrell, Jr., Lieutenant (jg) Elbert J. Green, and Ensign Richard G. Altman.

They flew through squalls and smokescreens, and at about 0740 they found the enemy: they saw 4 Japanese cruisers, 2 battleships, and a lot of destroyers. They were at 8000 feet, when the signal was given to attack.

Lieutenant Commander Keighley picked the second cruiser in line, a *Tone* class, as his target in a dive bombing attack. His six centuries [100-pound bombs] straddled the stern, going from the starboard quarter to just aft of amidships on the port side. Three bombs were direct hits, and the others were short or over. Ensign Altman glided down to about 5000 feet and when he was directly over a *Nagato*-class BB [battleship] he pushed over, firing four 5-inch . . . rockets and releasing two 500-pound general-purpose bombs. The rockets hit directly amidships causing an explosion and black smoke. The 500-pound bombs hit on the port side of the ship, one hitting the bow, one about 25 feet from the bow. Lieutenant Patsy Capano, leading the flight, was observed going down on the leading cruiser. . . . Lieutenant Perrell, having been launched without bombs, broke off from the formation before the attack was made and went south to another CVE group to see if he could be loaded there.

After the bombing, Keighley joined up with Lieutenant Capano for a strafing run on a *Tone*-class cruiser. It was about 0750. They went into AA fire and Capano pulled out to the left and Keighley to the right.

At 0800 Lieutenant Commander Keighley joined up with Ensign Heinmiller in a fighter for a strafing run on a *Nachi*-class cruiser. Ten minutes later Keighley picked out another fighter and they made another run on the same cruiser. Keighley made two more runs on this cruiser before his ammunition was expended. ARM1c Keighley's radioman strafed on all five runs. Then the turret gunner, ARM2c J. W. McBride, asked for permission to get into the fight, and Keighley circled the *Nachi*-class cruiser while McBride fired 200 rounds of .50 caliber at the ship.

After Ensign Altman recovered from his bombing attack he pulled up to 1000 feet and attacked a *Nachi* cruiser, scoring two hits below the bridge with 5-inch rockets. He then strafed with .50 caliber ammunition, and his crewmen strafed the bridge and gun galleys as they swooped in.

Lieutenant Perrell had gone off to find something to fight with, and he landed aboard CVE 77 (the *St. Lo*) at 0815 and was loaded with a torpedo. He took off with five other TBN's from that ship at 0915 and they found the Japanese from 7000 feet. They also found very heavy anti-aircraft fire. Lieutenant Van Brunt, of Squadron 65 from the *St. Lo,* led the attack. Perrell followed him in. The object was a battleship. Perrell had a full beam shot. He pulled out and strafed a *Tone* cruiser on the way, and so did his crew. He reported a direct hit on the battleship with his torpedo. The AA became heavier, and he jinked over the outer screen of destroyers, pulling up into the clouds about 800 feet above the enemy ships. He landed, then, on the *Fanshaw Bay.*

Lieutenant Commander Keighley landed at Dulag airfield.

Ensign Altman, after using up all his ammunition, landed at Tacloban, where things had gotten organized, and found two 250-pound general-purpose bombs. He also teamed up with two fighters from the *Fanshaw Bay* who had also landed there, and they found themselves a *Nachi* cruiser. The fighters went in strafing, and Ensign Altman went in bombing, scoring two hits, and knocking out a forward turret. On the recovery one of the fighters shot down a Jake (float plane) which belonged to the Japanese force and was obviously observing gunfire for the cruisers.

A second group of dive bombers and torpedo bombers from the *Kalinin Bay* was led out by Lieutenant Walter D. Crockett. Following him were Lieutenant (jg) Earl L. Archer, Jr., Ensign James B. Zeitvogel, and Ensign G. Neilan Smith. They went to 7000 feet and got into clouds, but about a mile astern of the Japanese fleet they came down through a hole in the cover—only to discover the hole covered by Japanese AA fire. Crockett chose what he thought was a battleship and moved in on it from stern to stem, bombed, and pulled up into the clouds. As he was diving, from the corner of his eye he saw one bomber hit by AA and crash into the water. His gunner saw another plane go down, smoking.

Crockett zoomed down out of the clouds and made a strafing run, but his rockets were short. His target was a destroyer.

Lieutenant Archer came down with Crockett but he took the last two destroyers in the column as his targets, and strafed from 6000 feet to 500 feet, then pulled up and looked for a target for his rockets. He joined a flight of 7 torpedo planes and 10 fighters going after the cruisers.

Archer was third man down on these ships, and attacked the second cruiser in a line, dropping his bombs and then continuing into the leading cruiser, which he shot at with his 8 5-inch rockets, walking them up the deck from low level. Two hit the bridge, he said, knocking part of it off the ship.

Ensign Smith joined Crockett and took on a *Tone*-class cruiser, the one closest to the carriers. He came in and surprised the Japanese, who did not even fire at him until he began shooting his rockets. He dropped two 500-pound bombs, and let go the rockets. He saw the rockets hit the superstructure of the cruiser, but the bombs missed—one 30 feet off the bow and one close off the stern.

Ensign Zeitvogel joined up with Crockett around 0750 and then lost him again when he made a steep climbing turn to avoid some AA fire from destroyers and cruisers below. A fighter from the *Fanshaw Bay* joined him then, and Zeitvogel pointed to one of the cruisers and the pilot nodded. They went in together, Zeitvogel strafing, and then he lost the other plane, which he thought must have been knocked down by AA fire. Zeitvogel climbed to 5000 feet and then swooped down to attack a destroyer with rockets. He selected the trailing DD of the formation that was coming in on the starboard side of the carriers, fired all the way down with machine guns, and let the rockets go at 1500 feet. The first two hit aft of amidships, the second two hit the water to port of the ship. He pulled out below 500 feet, strafing other ships as he went by, and turning to starboard. He strafed other destroyers, then, having spent all his ammunition, Zeitvogel joined up with three other bombers from the *Gambier Bay* and landed at Tacloban.

The field at Tacloban was a definite liability that day. Planes were crashing in soft spots in the runway, and loaded planes could not take off because the condition was so poor. Zeitvogel did not get off again that day.

Crockett landed aboard the *White Plains*, and so did Ensign Smith. Lieutenant Archer also landed at Tacloban, and could not get away until the next day. Then he went to Dulag, and found that field in such poor condition that he volunteered his services as landing officer, and broug't in carrier planes as though they were coming into their own ship. He was two days getting back to a ship, and then it was the *Manila Bay*, not his own.

That took care of most of the pilots of the bombers of the *Kalinin Bay*. The fighters also did their share that day. Lieutenant John W. Murphy took off with Lieutenant Charles G. Simmons, Lieutenant Leonard H. Porterfield, Ensign Pete Goodman, and Ensign Charles T. Green. Murphy led them right at the Japanese cruisers which were threatening *Taffy* III so sorely.

They went after the two Japanese cruisers closest to the carriers. They started at 10,000 feet, and began firing at 6000 feet, using dives at an angle of 65 percent. Murphy went first, and the others peeled off after him. The effect on the cruisers was spectacular—for these were only five fighters, firing .50 caliber ammunition which would bounce off the sides of those ships—yet after their first run the Japanese carriers began zigzagging, which they had not done before.

The anti-aircraft fire also grew more intense, so Murphy kept his planes out of formation, to lessen the danger to any of them.

Here is how the combined efforts of *Taffy* III and *Taffy* II were working that morning:

> After the conclusion of the third run about ten friendly fighters were observed attacking the cruisers. Our planes made three more runs on the leading cruiser and after Lieutenant Murphy had expended all his ammo, he tried to locate the rest of his division, but this was impossible at this time as the air was filled with FM-2's and TBN-1c's making runs on the enemy fleet units.

> Murphy and Ensign Goodman then went to Tacloban and landed safely. But they were stuck like so many others by the bad condition of the field. They were out of it.

> After the second run by Lieutenant Murphy's division, Lieutenant Simmons stayed up and was joined by an un-

identified fighter. Together they made a strafing attack on a Japanese cruiser that was shelling the escorts.

Simmons made three strafing runs, and as he was on the last one, he noticed that the AA was quieting down. He made three runs on the leading cruiser, and then four more on 2 enemy cruisers, pulling out at 800 to 1200 feet before three of his guns jammed. He climbed to 8000 feet and tried to clear the guns but could only get one to work. While up there he saw one Japanese cruiser dead in the water. He circled, and joined up with Lieutenant (jg) Samuel Francovich and Ensign Geoffrey B. King for one more run on the cruiser. He looked around, and saw that not only was *Taffy* III under attack, but *Taffy* II as well —so he went to Tacloban, long out of ammunition and with 20 gallons of gas. He landed at 0945.

Meanwhile, Lieutenant Kenneth G. Hippe took off at 0750, and was joined by Ensign James I. Murphy and Ensign George A. Heinmiller. His group climbed to 4000 feet, and Lieutenant Hippe led three effective strafing attacks on a *Tone*-class cruiser. The group rejoined and took on a *Kongo* battleship. Then came word from fighter direction to concentrate on the closest cruisers to the escort carriers. Lieutenant Hippe made four runs on the closest cruiser, and also looked for Japanese spotting planes but found none. His technique on attack was to climb to 7000 feet, nose down, firing, and pull out at 500 feet or less. He liked that approach, feeling that the longer he waited to pull out, the less AA he encountered.

When he ran out of ammunition he headed to Tacloban, and landed with seven gallons of gas. He regassed and rearmed there, but it was the same story. There had been too many accidents and the field was in rotten shape, so he was stuck until 1145, when he took off and landed at 1315 on the *White Plains*.

Ensign Heinmiller had come in with Lieutenant Hippe, but he lost him after the second run, so he joined up with anybody who came by to run in on the cruisers. Finally he joined forces with Lieutenant Commander Keighley and made three runs on a cruiser. Then he lost Keighley and made two more runs alone. His plane began heating up, and he climbed to 10,000 feet to cool it. He called fighter direction for instructions and was ordered to the beach, so he headed toward land. About 20 minutes later he sighted a number of Japanese Vals and Zekes [Zeros] heading toward the fleet. He saw one Val that seemed to be struggling, and since he had 150 or so rounds of ammunition he made a pass at him, an overhead run ending up on his tail, coming out of cloud cover. "When last seen the Val was smoking, in a dive out of control." The Zekes were about 5 miles behind the Vals, so Ensign Heinmiller dived for the water and headed south. He was not pursued and at 1140 he landed on the *Ommaney Bay*.

Lieutenant James I. Murphy was also with Hippe, but lost him after the third run on a cruiser, and Murphy kept on making runs on that cruiser. After four, he joined up with Lieutenant Leonard H. Porterfield, they made another run and then Porterfield signaled that he was out of ammunition, so he headed for the beach while Murphy kept on fighting. He was joined then by Ensign Paul Hopfner, and they heard a request from Bendix Base (fighter control) to hit the Japanese destroyers, which were attacking the escorts. Then he lost Ensign Hopfner, but made another run alone on the destroyer. He finally joined up with another fighter and they started for Tacloban, but learned from operations there that the field was closed because of crashes, and headed for the fleet. He landed finally on the *St. Lo*.

Lieutenant (jg) William C. Coughlan joined up with the TBM's led by Patsy Capano and with four other fighters from another carrier, after he missed the fighter formation that was moving in on the cruisers. When the word came from control to attack the nearest cruisers, Lieutenant Capano sent Coughlan in on a strafing run and he made several, going ahead of the bombers to draw fire. He made seven runs, and saw planes getting hits with bombs and rockets on cruisers. At 0900 he was out of ammunition and headed for Tacloban. He hit a soft spot in the runway and damaged the plane.

Lieutenant (jg) Samuel Francovich was launched at 0710 in a rain squall and lost the planes that had preceded him. He joined up with four fighters from other carriers and then Ensign King joined them, reporting he had just destroyed a Val. They followed the other fighters which circled the fleet, but became impatient, broke off, and attacked a *Kongo*-class battleship under heavy anti-aircraft fire. They were ordered to hit the advanced units, the cruisers and destroyers that were doing the damage to the escorts. They went in on cruisers and destroyers until they ran out of ammunition, and landed at Tacloban at 0930, rearmed and regassed, and took off again. King damaged his port wing on takeoff on the bad field, and headed back. Francovich accompanied him part way, and then headed off.

One tragedy was that of Lieutenant Patsy Capano, who had led the bombers in in the beginning. He had landed at Tacloban, but his plane was so badly shot up that it was unusable. He was eager to get back to his ship so he borrowed a TBM from a wounded pilot from the *St. Lo.* He boarded with his crew, ARM1c Malcolm J. Gordon and TBM1c Gordon E. Galloway. They also took along Ensign Paul Hopfner whose plane had been damaged and who also wanted to get back to the *Kalinin Bay*. But Capano came in when the CVE's were under heavy attack, and they sent him back to Tacloban. He never arrived.

Thus Capano and his crew were missing in action. And so, ironically, was Ensign Hopfner, who had survived his mission. Lieutenant (jg) Robert T. Sell made a forced landing off Samar but was picked up later. Lieutenant Porterfield crashed trying to take off from Tacloban, and was injured. The plane was wrecked. Ensign Geoffrey King crashed on landing at Dulag and wrecked his plane, but he was safe, if injured. Lieutenant Coughlan nosed over on landing at Tacloban, but was not hurt.

That was the story of one squadron. There were many such stories and the Japanese commented on the fierceness with which the Americans fought in the sky and on the sea this day. Admiral Kurita's operations officer had this to say:

> The attack was almost incessant but the number of planes at any one instant was few. The bombers and torpedo planes were very aggressive and skillful and the coordination was impressive; even in comparison with the great experience of American attack that we had already had, this was the most skillful work of your planes.

And here is what the squadron had to say about itself, in the action report prepared after the battle:

It is impossible to single out a group of individuals whose exploits stand out as being particularly noteworthy. The entire action was remarkable, conducted by our airmen without the slightest regard for personal safety. They pressed home their attacks determinedly, unremittingly. Their conduct was exemplary, and writes another chapter in the glorious history of naval aviation. Devotion to duty in the highest traditions of the naval service that day was commonplace.

If those words had been used often before in the history of naval operations, they were still certainly true of the naval aviators and destroyer and escort men that day. When their carriers were threatened they swarmed like angry bees, and it would seem that they drove off the Japanese because, suddenly, before 1000, the Japanese broke the action and moved north.

That, however, is another story.

18

THE BATTLE OF
SAN BERNARDINO STRAIT—
PART III

The sighting of the American force, and particularly an American force that fled from the Japanese fleet, very nearly unnerved Admiral Kurita. No question about it— it even shows in the action report of his force. A lookout saw masts: "It was subsequently definitely established that the masts belonged to ships of *a gigantic enemy task force* including six or seven carriers accompanied by many cruisers and destroyers [italics added]."

With the almost complete lack of intelligence that Admiral Kurita had received in the last week, and his gradual and growing knowledge over the period that Radio Tokyo and Imperial Navy Headquarters had been vastly overestimating the amount of damage done the Americans off Formosa, it is small wonder that he was confused. Perhaps a Togo could have overcome all these factors and figured out immediately what to do—not knowing what lay ahead, behind, or on his outside flank. It suffices to say that Admiral Kurita was not a Togo. He was a brave, loyal, and trusted officer of his Imperial Majesty, but he was not a master strategist.

Furthermore, the Japanese were definitely on edge. Scarcely an officer in the fleet did not know or suspect that theirs was likely to be a suicide mission. They were determined to take as many of the enemy with them as they could, and they wanted to make every action count. It was no good going on a suicide mission to end up on a reef, or in a POW camp. Besides, the sighting came at the most inopportune time: when the fleet was changing from night disposition to morning anti-aircraft formation. Immediately Admiral Kurita ordered an attack formation, but the result was that it was some time before matters were straightened out and in the meantime the world of fishes and the enemy was treated to the sight of battleships very nearly crossing one another's bows, and destroyers and cruisers exhibiting thorough signs of confusion.

As the action began, Admiral Kurita was turning over in his mind all he had learned. What was this force? He knew that Admiral Nishimura had been hard hit the night before by some force. Were the Americans ubiquitous? It was enough to challenge any man's imagination.

At the moment of sighting the Americans, Kurita and his staff noted down their estimate of the situation they faced.

1. The enemy was encountered at a time when neither he nor we expected it.

2. Employing every trick known to him, the enemy would try to put distance between himself and us (if possible maneuver himself to the windward of us) so that he could carry out a one-sided air action against us.

3. So that we could take advantage of this heaven-sent opportunity we should take after the enemy in present formation and at top speed. We planned first to cripple the carriers' ability to have planes take off and land on them and then to mow down the entire task force.

Thus the battle plan was made, based on the assumption that these were fleet carriers and light carriers of the type the Japanese had encountered at Coral Sea, Midway, and the First Battle of the Philippine Sea off the Marianas. That was a basic mistake, and it colored Admiral Kurita's philosophy completely. He simply did not understand that what he had before him were slow-moving auxiliary ships built for the purpose of anti-submarine patrol and landing support.

Here is the engagement from the Japanese point of view:

As befitted the flagship, the *Yamato* opened fire, she said, at 0658 that morning. Two minutes later she announced to the fleet that there were three enemy carriers. Two minutes after that Admiral Kurita ordered the Third

Section (Admiral Nishimura and Admiral Shima) to join
and reported that he was engaging the enemy. (What that
order meant is confusing, because Kurita knew that Nishimura had been hard hit. Perhaps he hoped that Nishimura
could still make at least a diversion to the south. Or perhaps the order to Nishimura was simply pro forma, for the
benefit of Imperial Headquarters.)

Admiral Kurita ordered the cruisers to move in on the
carriers and take them, and the destroyers to move in so
they could conduct a torpedo attack. Squalls and bad
weather upset the visibility, and the Japanese radar was
not equal to the task of blind fighting. Radar or not, the
Japanese depended far more than the Americans on visual
aids in fighting a naval battle. Radar was too new to them,
it was not as well developed, and they simply did not
have the equipment or experience to compete in this field.

Also, for some reason in this battle, the Japanese went
far beyond the usual number of errors in overexaggerating
the effects of their weapons on the enemy. The Americans
did it—in the heat of battle mistakes in identification and
hopeful errors in assessment of damage were routine—but
intelligence officers had been taught caution; the Japanese
intelligence officers seemed more eager to tell their superiors what they wanted to hear.

Probably as good a summary of the Japanese view of
the battle as could be found lies in the report of the
Seventh Cruiser Division which carried much of the action
for the Japanese fighting force that day, and which lost 2
cruisers in this fight.

At sunrise the cruisers were standing by at 28 knots,
with engines to be ready for maximum battle speed in 20
minutes. Then they sighted the Americans. *Chokai*, the
cruiser, saw them first and the *Suzuya* and the *Kumano*
were not far behind. At 0703 Admiral Kurita ordered the
cruisers to attack, and cruiser flagship *Kumano* relayed the
order to the others. By 0710 Admiral Kurita had discovered
that there were 6 carriers and they were to be the primary
targets. On went the cruisers with their attack.

At 0715 the Japanese reported they had set fire to one
American carrier. The cruisers and the carriers and destroyers of both sides were in action now, the Americans
making smoke, and the Japanese firing through it.

At 0724 three torpedo tracks were sighted off the starboard bow of the *Kumano*, torpedoes fired by the American destroyers in their attack. One hit the Japanese cruiser's bow, severing a section of it, and reducing the cruiser's speed to 14 knots.

At that same moment one of the carrier planes struck home, too. A near miss came in on the *Suzuya*, made her port inboard shaft unusable, and caused leakage of the sea water into the after fuel tanks. This reduced her usable fuel supply to 800 tons and her maximum speed to 23 knots. She was hurt, no doubt about it.

As the flagship *Kumano* lost speed, the *Suzuya* took command, although she was hurt. But the attacks never ceased. At 0744 "3 torpedo planes followed by 5 bombers, attacked *Chikuma* and *Tone*. AA action. *Chikuma* evaded by wide turn to starboard while *Tone* evaded by wide turn to port. Both ships returned to former courses and continued advance eastward, separated by a gap of 6 kilometers. . . ."

Ten minutes later, the *Tone* was under attack again. At about 0800 the flag and the staff of the division moved over to *Kumano* [the Admiral, 4 staff officers, 2 attached officers, 2 petty officers].

All this while the Japanese were talking excitedly about *Independence*-class carriers (fleet carriers) and *Baltimore* cruisers, when they faced nothing so serious. But the fight was serious, no doubt about it. At 0828 the Captain of the *Tone* was wounded in one of those strafing attacks by the planes above. And the *Suzuya* was having her troubles. Her captain tried to raise the speed to 24 knots, but she vibrated so badly she had to drop back. At 0838 the *Tone* claimed to have sunk a *Ranger*-type carrier. (This was the *Gambier Bay*.) At 0845 the *Tone* fired torpedoes at an American destroyer she thought was a cruiser. She was taking serious damage from shellfire, from the destroyers, too. The *Tone* also claimed one of the American fighting ships, "an enemy light cruiser, which took heavy list, and then blew up and sank."

At about 0853 the *Chikuma* moved up. Just at that time 30 American carrier planes attacked the *Chikuma*, *Tone*, *Haguro*, and *Chokai*. Here is the report as the Japanese had it:

Four torpedo planes executed extremely low-level attack on *Chikuma,* 2 from each side. Several enemy fighters simultaneously were over the ship. *Chikuma* observed firing at enemy planes with all her guns (seen from *Tone* at distance of about 5 kms.).

One torpedo plane and one fighter shot down off *Chikuma*'s starboard side.

Torpedo hit on *Chikuma* observed from *Tone* as follows: While *Chikuma* was maneuvering to evade the two torpedo planes which attacked first from the starboard side [she evaded by turning toward the planes], two other torpedo planes made an extremely low-level attack from the port side. Shortly thereafter a torpedo apparently hit the stern. There was a burst of flame and simultaneously a column of water almost as high as the length of the ship shot up into the air. The after deck single-mount machine gun and other gear were seen blown into the air. The after half of the after deck was apparently heavily damaged, and settled in the water, but the ship continued to move at slow speed and her guns kept on firing. She circled around, flying a signal indicating that her rudder was knocked out. No marked external damage other than the stern was observed.

By 0854 the cruisers were talking about "a strong enemy force located off the starboard bow, within 10 kilometers, but hidden by a squall." (It seemed inconceivable to the Japanese that the Americans had not yet produced any battleships.) The observers could see some results of their shooting, straddles, and hits on the carriers, but the American smoke-making was very effective and most of those carriers succeeded in spending a good deal of time hiding. Each time the cruisers would move around to get a view, the carriers would duck into smoke or squall and the destroyers and escorts would make more smoke.

Meanwhile, the *Chokai,* another cruiser, had been smashed by bombs or torpedoes and was in worse shape than the *Chikuma.*

At 0810, when everything seemed to be going well for the Japanese, the *Haruna* sighted a second group of carriers to the southeast, and this naturally got the Japanese to considering what they might face ahead. Here were 6 "fleet" carriers, and down below were more carriers. How many carriers did the Americans have and where were the destroyers and the battleships? Admiral Kurita put up 2 of his fleet's slender supply of float planes for observation. The fate of one of them was described by the aviators of the *Kalinin Bay*. The fate of the other was the same: the Japanese got no comfort from their float planes, and precious little information, before they disappeared from the scene.

The *Tone* and the *Háguro* of the Japanese Seventh Cruiser Division were really closing in on the Americans, but they were the only ships that were. The others seemed much more halfhearted, and the battleships were virtually out of it. One reason was that one of the American destroyers fired a spread of torpedoes at the *Yamato;* to evade them, she turned and ran 7 miles from the battle before she could lose them, and thus was well out of it —putting Admiral Kurita out of it too, with bad radio communication, bad visual communication, bad radar, and no spotter planes.

At about 0905 the Japanese destroyers launched their torpedo attack, but from almost 15,000 yards, which was hardly very daring, and no hits were made.

As for the Japanese, the *Tone* was hit, the battleship *Kongo* was harried, the *Chikuma* and the *Chokai* were out of it, and the *Kumano* was badly damaged. But the Japanese were still as strong as a gang of foxes in a henhouse. Thus it came as a surprise to the commander of the *Tone* and to others when, at 0914, Admiral Kurita ordered all ships to reassemble and head north. The *Tone* was then talking about a torpedo attack to the *Haguro*.

Tone estimated that continuation of the pursuit attack on the enemy carrier group would be extremely effective and that this favorable tactical opportunity should not be lost. However, in view of the 0914 reassembly order from Flag . . . and also the necessity of regrouping the force for the penetration into Leyte Gulf, she broke off the pursuit and followed. . . .

Admiral Kurita's second float plane had gone out of contact at 0904. It had taken him only 10 minutes more to order the regrouping, retirement, or whatever one wanted to call it. Whatever was ordered, the *Yamato* swung around to the left and Kurita headed north. Reluctantly, other units did the same. The foxes were leaving the henhouse, and much as they could not believe it, the Americans were saved.

19

THE LOST CHANCE

Perhaps better than any other source, the diary of Japanese Admiral Ugaki gives a feeling for what happened in Admiral Kurita's fleet during that fateful morning of October 25. That, coupled with the story of certain events occurring outside the fleet itself, shows the extent of the lost opportunity. For although the Japanese would not know about it for some time, they had come within an ace of doing precisely what they set out to do in the Sho plan: disrupt the American invasion of the Philippines.

As they chased the Americans—herded them south toward Leyte Gulf, as it were—the Japanese caught many American transmissions.

We were told that the enemy had requested aid from friendly forces by plain-language telephone and that the reply was it would require two hours. [That was Oldendorf's force to the south, which was sixty-five miles away.] From this it was concluded that there was an enemy force nearby. The question now was, for which force should we head?

Meanwhile, Admiral Kinkaid was as worried and upset as a commander whose whole force is endangered could possibly be, and his state of mind was certainly not helped by the fact that there was literally nothing more he could do from his flag plot on *Wasatch*. Admiral Wilkinson described the situation aptly later in a letter, when he said he sat in Leyte Gulf feeling like the girl whose fair white body was being fought over by the good guy and the bad guy.

Here is Admiral Kinkaid's recollection of the events:

> The CVE's [escorts] were being driven south by the Japanese cruisers. I had a dispatch from Sprague asking for permission to enter Leyte Gulf. I sent back a negative reply. To enter Leyte Gulf meant that they would be in confined waters. They'd be easy marks for Jap air, and if they got as far as the entrance of Leyte Gulf, he would be joined by my surface ships for cover. The message I sent to Oldendorf, as soon as I had the report of our CVE's under fire, was to assemble all of his ships at the northern part of the entrance to Leyte Gulf, get them all there as quickly as possible.
>
> That was followed a little bit later by an order to divide his ships into two groups, and to send one group outside to buoy . . . a marker buoy to our entrance to Leyte Gulf. I didn't want to send those ships outside of Leyte Gulf, although at that time the CVE's were in dire need . . . but I couldn't let them be hammered to pieces without doing anything, so I gave these preliminary orders.

Meanwhile, Admiral Kinkaid was trying very hard to find out what help he could get from Halsey. He did not know precisely where Halsey was, and he sent a string of messages, some of them in the clear. What he wanted was Task Force 34, those fast battleships, which could clear Japanese waters very quickly if they could be brought into position.

But he did not get them. In fact, until after the great battle was over he did not get anything from Halsey because that admiral was too far north and east, engaging the Ozawa force. Just at about the time Halsey discovered that Kinkaid was under attack by a force that had, after all, turned back and steamed through San Bernardino Strait, his planes found Ozawa and the action began up north.

Kinkaid was insistent. He called for aid from the fast battleships again. He called for a strike from Task Force 38, the carrier force. Unfortunately there was not a carrier unit within range of the problem; Admiral McCain was closest and he was dispatched to help Kinkaid, but he did not arrive until the afternoon, when the matter of the battle between Kurita and the CVE's was long resolved. What did happen with Kinkaid's insistent calls was that Washington and Pearl Harbor, where they were listening in to the messages, became alert and outraged that Halsey would desert San Bernardino Strait. Admiral Nimitz interfered by sending a message to Halsey asking what had happened to the fast battleships—and changed therefore the course of the battle. But as for help from Halsey to Kinkaid, it did not come, and forever after Halsey maintained that he had no responsibility to defend the Seventh Fleet tactically—that his was a strategic defense and he had headed for the carriers, taking the calculated risk that Kurita might come through.

Yet, all this interchange of messages, some of them in plain English, had a sort of reverse-English effect on the Japanese. Admiral Kurita was not sure what the real purpose of these messages was, but he gathered that there were strong forces afloat elsewhere than in the Leyte Gulf area, and he began to have second thoughts about his own mission. He also thought Admiral Kinkaid might be trying somehow to trick him.

What happened to Kurita, in the beginning, was that he lost tactical control of his fleet when the surprise came of seeing the Americans, and he never did regain it fully. The attack of the destroyers was sloppy, and the cruisers, particularly after 3 of them were put into a sinking or badly damaged condition, were not working together well. So, said Admiral Ugaki:

It was decided, first of all, to go down the center and destroy the group of carriers, and then it was decided that the fleet should head for the enemy off to the east. [That meant the Halsey force, if they could find it.]

We accordingly changed course to SSE and headed in that direction but it was already too late. We were unable to locate the aforementioned carrier group. Headquarters [Kurita] heard DesRon 10 ordering attack [its abortive torpedo attack] and directed all ships to gradually assemble to the north. We changed course to north. The time was 0924.

As they moved, the cruiser *Chokai* transferred her crew to a destroyer, and was abandoned. Then she was sunk. The *Haguro* moved north and tried to repair the bomb damage to her No. 2 turret. The *Suzuya* was lagging. The *Chikuma* got out of line, and she and her destroyer escort, the *Nowacki,* lost the formation forever.

While heading north, flashes were sighted in direction 280 and the fleet headed in that direction while continuing to assemble. Sighted scattered patches of water colored by dye loaded shells and a considerably large area of darkish red water. Immediately beyond the latter were enemy survivors, some clinging to damaged cutters and some just drifting. I wonder what these survivors thought on seeing our fleet sweep boldly by in pursuit? Even though they were in need of help they gave no indication of it when they saw who we were.

While the Japanese moved about, indecisively, American planes continued to bomb, and at 1014 smashed the *Suzuya* again. She began to waver and became unnavigable, the fire reaching her torpedoes. Cruiser Division Seven flag was transferred to the *Tone;* the *Suzuya* was abandoned and sank.

To follow the Kurita force for the remainder of that day: A destroyer was damaged in that air attack at 1014. ("The enemy survivors who witnessed this spectacle from afar must have given three cheers.") Then, at 1120, Admiral Kurita decided to go back into Leyte Gulf again and gave orders. But at 1215, while steaming south, the force was hit again by 30 planes. This time they moved into their circular anti-aircraft formation and drove off the Americans without substantial damage. At this time, too, Admiral Kurita apparently saw something else that unnerved him: a *Pennsylvania*-class battleship mast. Now there was no *Pennsylvania*-class (nor any other) battleship in the area, but there had been talk about it taking two hours to bring help and this was more than two hours later, so Admiral Kurita, without air eyes or any useful intelligence, had to rely on imagination. The battleship *Pennsylvania* was the result of good imagination. The fleet launched another float plane, but apparently it was shot down, or at least gave no sufficient information for action.

Kurita wavered. At 1313 he decided that he would not go into Leyte Gulf, and changed course to due north. They were attacked again by American planes at 1316. Kurita seemed to be unsure. He was not a man to take much advice and had made these previous decisions rather quietly. Now Admiral Ugaki, who had been quiet himself, stepped forward and suggested that they head slightly eastward rather than directly north, and thus get out of the bad weather that was hugging the Samar coast. Admiral Kurita accepted the idea.

Somehow, through a combination of intelligence and bad observation during the fight off Samar, the Japanese persisted in the idea that they had been fighting light carriers and fleet carriers and not escort carriers. Admiral Kurita had the idea that his ships could not catch up to the carriers because the carriers could make 32 knots. This was arrant nonsense, but intelligence and communications this way were not the Japanese forte. One might use intelligence in both senses here, except that it suffices to say that Admiral Kurita simply *did not know,* and not knowing, he decided not to risk his fleet's existence by going into the unknown of Leyte Gulf, no matter what his orders. The Japanese army would have applauded that decision had they been party to it; they had been telling the navy this same thing for weeks.

Kurita also knew that the American planes were shuttling between their carriers and Tacloban and Dulag. This meant to him that they were immensely dangerous. He did not know the condition of Tacloban and Dulag fields. Also he had so many fragmentary reports of American forces in so many places, that he simply had to do what he thought best under the conditions, and he chose to try to join Ozawa and take on Admiral Halsey and destroy the Third Fleet.

Not all of Admiral Kurita's officers agreed with him, had he bothered to ask. Admiral Ugaki did not. He wrote in his diary:

If battles could be waged by hard and fast rules, there would be nothing to them. At times, however, there are errors and unforeseen events. In particular with the friendly air forces carrying out the attack, I thought that we should have at least pursued the enemy. In general the will to fight and the ability to act promptly are not all that they should be, and standing on the same bridge, I have experienced considerable irritation [with Kurita]. If fuel is the primary consideration then it is only natural that we head for San Bernardino Strait. But if the enemy is destroyed, you can fuel the destroyers from the battleships at night. . . .

So the ships headed back for San Bernardino Strait, the final analysis coming under more air attack. The reason for the retreat was that Kurita was unable to find Halsey's task force quickly, and he did not want to waste fuel. They entered the Strait just about at dark, "not even zigzagging in our haste to return. When one is being pursued there is nothing like putting in distance between one and the enemy, so this was not unreasonable," said Admiral Ugaki. They passed through the Strait at 2100.

"There was a radiogram that when the battle situation report was made to the Throne today, His Majesty expressed satisfaction with the actions of the surface forces, which are attaining battle results despite all the difficulties. We also received stirring praise from Commander-in-Chief, Combined Fleet, and I can't help but feel that these eulogies are not in conformity with the situation . . ." wrote Admiral Ugaki.

Understatement? Indeed it was. Combined fleet was shocked to learn that Kurita had turned back, and issued an order telling him to conduct a night action if that was possible. It was hardly possible. On receipt of the order Kurita was already on his way back, having missed one of the great chances of the war to create havoc in the American fleet. The eulogies certainly were not justified by the situation.

In his diary Admiral Ugaki gives a hint, no more than that, of what was going on in Japanese air on this fateful day, October 25.

On October 25 the Shikishima unit of the new Kamikaze Corps flew out from Mabalacat at 0725 looking for the enemy. So did other planes of the Japanese, but these Shikishima planes were different. Their pilots were dedicated to crash-diving on the American ships and sinking them at the cost of the pilot's life for each plane that dived.

The Japanese were not fools. The men in charge of the kamikazes would not allow the best pilots to waste themselves. Each pilot's success or failure was to be observed by someone who lived, and the pilots of the suicide planes needed escort to the targets, to assure the best chance of delivering their deadly weapons.

At 1000 on the 25th, Lieutenant Yuko Seki began to make history. He was flying a Zero with a bomb under each wing, when at 1010 his force sighted the American escort carriers, which had just broken off from the action with the Japanese fleet of Admiral Kurita less than an hour before. There were 5 kamikaze planes, escorted by 4 Zero fighters, and as soon as they were in position and each man had chosen his target, they peeled off and let go.

Here is what happened next; from the action report of the escort carrier *St. Lo:*

At 1040 Lieutenant James Murphy of *Kalinin Bay,* whose exploits have been described earlier, landed his fighter on *St. Lo,* which had agreed to take him, as well as planes from other beleaguered carriers.

Then:

At about 1051 AA fire was seen and heard forward and General Quarters was sounded. Almost immediately thereafter, numerous planes believed to be both friendly and enemy, were seen at 1000–3000 feet ahead and on the starboard bow. These planes moved aft to starboard and one of them, when about abeam to starboard, went into a right turn toward the *St. Lo.* The after starboard guns opened on him, but with no apparent effect. This plane, a Zeke 52, with a bomb under each wing, continued his right turn into the groove, and approached over the ramp at very high speed.

1053. After crossing the ramp at not over 50 feet, he appeared to push over sufficiently to hit the deck at about No. 5 wire, 15 feet to the port side of the center line. There was a tremendous crash and flash of an explosion as one or both bombs exploded. The plane continued up the deck leaving fragments strewn about and its remnants went over the bow. There is no certain evidence as to whether or not the bombs were released before the plane struck the deck.

The captain's impression was that no serious damage had been suffered. There was a hole in the flight deck with smoldering edges which sprang into flames. Hoses were immediately run out from both sides of the flight deck and water started on the fire. He then noticed that smoke was coming through the hole from below, and that smoke was appearing on both sides of the ship, apparently coming from the hangar. He tried to contact the hangar deck for a report, but was unable to do so. Within one to one and a half minutes an explosion occurred in the hangar deck and, he believed, bulged out the flight deck near and aft of the hole. This was followed in a matter of seconds by a much more violent explosion which rolled back a part of the flight deck, bursting through aft of the original hole. The next heavy explosion tore out more of the flight deck and also blew the forward elevator out of its shaft. At this time, which he estimated as still shortly before 1100, he decided that the ship could not be saved. With the smoke and flame, he was even uncertain as to whether the after part was still on the ship, though later he had glimpses of it. All communication was lost except the sound-powered phones which apparently were in for some time although no reports could be obtained from aft. . . .

The *St. Lo* was abandoned, and sank before 1125—less than an hour after Lieutenant Murphy had landed with such relief on this carrier, back on his ship after an exciting day.

The story of the *St. Lo*'s sinking is a story of heroism, but its relationship to the death of the Japanese fleet is a very special one, part of a story that was told that day over and over.

Earlier in the morning, the escort carrier *Santee* had

been hit by a plane that either crash-dived on the carrier or fell into it, probably the latter, for no bomb explosion was felt and that saved the *Santee* from more damage than she suffered (43 casualties). She was very nearly hit by another plane, whether a true kamikaze or not is debatable. Then the *Petrof Bay*, another of the carriers of Admiral T. L. Sprague's *Taffy* I, suffered a near miss from a plane. The *Santee* was also hit that morning by a torpedo from a Japanese submarine, the *I-56*. The *Suwannee*, another escort carrier of *Taffy* I, was hit by a plane carrying a bomb (probably kamikaze) but in two hours she was taking planes again.

At the same time the *St. Lo* was hit and sunk, kamikazes of Lieutenant Seti's unit also dove into the *Kitkun Bay*, and tried to get the *Fanshaw Bay* and the *White Plains* but were shot down. Yet another plane exploded just off the *White Plains* and did serious damage. The *Kitkun Bay* and the *Kalinin Bay* were both hit again by kamikazes.

This was a new experience for the Americans. Occasionally damaged planes, or planes flown by mortally wounded pilots, had crashed into ships before (the *Australia* took one on October 21) but this was an entirely different matter, and the American sailors knew it well. Here is the initial reaction from the *White Plains* that day:

DEVIL DIVER TACTICS
(a) Devil Diver Attack from Astern:
It was noted that in every case of attack by devil divers against this Task Unit on ships of this class the devil diver circled from ahead to start his dive from astern. It is probable that this method is used by the devil diver because AA defense close aboard astern is least effective on this class vessel.
(b) Maneuvering to Avoid Suicide Divers.
This vessel avoided a direct hit aft by a hard left turn executed at the commencement of the dive. It is believed that the most effective avoiding maneuver to combat suicide attacks by more than one aircraft vessel of this class either during day or night would be an emergency zigzag of about 25 degrees to the right and left of the base course effected by about 25 degrees of rudder on each turn. At least 18 knots is

recommended to give quicker effect to the rudder and compensate for loss of speed.

These advices were to be combed and followed and improved upon in the months to come, because the Japanese, in failing to penetrate Leyte Gulf in the Sho operation, still had created a desperate new weapon that was to replace the Japanese fleet as a fighting force.

Admiral Kurita, of course, had no knowledge of the desperate measures that Admiral Ohnishi had begun.

That day, the Seventh Fleet forces fought off many air attacks, both conventional, from forces of the Second Air Fleet, and suicide from the forces of Admiral Ohnishi's First Air Fleet. The Japanese made several more submarine attacks, too, including a night attack on the *Petrof Bay*. The next day the *Suwannee*, an escort carrier, took another kamikaze, causing some 250 casualties, but not sinking the ship, and the destroyer escort *Eversole* was sunk by torpedoes from a submarine. (Submarine *I-45* was sunk a few days later in these waters.)

In a few hours, the kamikazes had done tremendous damage. Had they been able to correlate their attack with Admiral Kurita's—had Kurita even been given the benefit of the information that he was going to have any air support at all—things might have gone differently at Leyte Gulf and Samar. But as it was, the heart of the Japanese fleet, the Kurita force, was sent staggering back home to Japanese waters, having suffered badly in its attempt to reach the American force, and having failed. The mystique of the Japanese as never-say-die fighters was shattered once and for all.

20

THE BATTLE OFF CAPE ENGANO

Even if for the wrong reasons, Admiral Halsey and his
staff had the right idea about Admiral Kurita's center
force. As the Third Fleet steamed at high speed northward
during the night of October 24 to engage Admiral Ozawa's
decoy force of carriers and heavy ships, Halsey and his
officers were certain that Kurita would not fight, or if he
fought, that he would not fight effectively.

With the belief that the Japanese southern force was
doomed [which proved to be true], with the conviction
that the center force had been so heavily damaged
[wrote Admiral Carney later] that although they could
still steam and float they could not fight to best advantage, it was decided to turn full attention to the
still untouched and very dangerous carrier force to the
north, not only for the immediate purpose of this engagement, but with a very definite view to eliminating
them in view of the projected operations of which we
knew—the occupation of Mindoro and the occupation of Luzon.

It was, as everyone from Halsey on down knew, "a big
chance" they were taking by leaving San Bernardino Strait,
and it was a calculated decision, not a spur-of-the-moment
hothead idea as has sometimes been indicated.

Admiral Halsey decided against dividing his fleet by
leaving surface forces at San Bernardino and taking

aircraft carriers north because that would expose the surface forces to air attack from land-based air without adequate covering. He decided that a fleet in being in the long run was the best guarantee to successful winning of the war and he knew that Admiral Nimitz also had strong views along these lines.

So they all headed north at high speed. McCain was farthest away, he who had been on his way to Ulithi to replenish, but they expected him to close up later.

Here is Commodore Arleigh Burke's recollection of the spirit of the next few hours:

At 2029 that night word was received that Task Group 38.3 [in which Mitscher and Burke were riding on *Lexington*] would join 38.2 and 38.4 in latitude 14°28′ North, longitude 125°50′ East, and that all three task groups would attack the enemy carrier force.

At about 2330 the task groups were rendezvoused. Admiral Mitscher took tactical command, came to course north, speed 25. At 2400 course was changed to the northeast, speed 16. At 1230 (0030) the *Independence* [night carrier] launched a night search to the north. . . . At about 0205 one of these planes made a radar contact. About thirty minutes later this same plane made a contact with the second group of six large ships which was slightly to the east of their original contact, which put the closest enemy group to us almost due north, about 80 miles away. [Ozawa, it will be remembered, had split his force, and the scouting force was trying to get back to him this night.] This was going to be good, this battle was going to be fought close enough. . . .

But then, as so often happens in war, fate took a hand. The Americans were moving in steadily on the Japanese; they had a tracking plane out—and the tracking plane developed engine trouble at 0300 and had to return to the *Independence*. Frantically, other planes were sent out. "We had this tremendous task force," wrote Admiral Burke, "our tracking plane had to return. The other planes, the other night planes, had radar trouble and we never regained radar contact during darkness."

Thus go the best laid plans of men and nations, even when they possess the utmost physical superiority.

Just before the tracking plane failed, the battle line was formed. Admiral Halsey had a definite plan for fighting this battle:

> The commander . . . had conceived an interesting scheme of battle in the employment of carriers and surface forces and the crux of it was that powerful surface striking forces were to be advanced in the direction of the enemy so that they could hump him as quickly as he had been slowed or damaged by the air strikes. This had been done during the night and a fast, surface striking force was bearing down on the enemy formation. . . .

Just before dawn, the fleet armed its planes, and at 0555 the search for the Japanese began. "We took a chance after we launched our search," said Commodore Burke. "We launched our attack with every plane we had available immediately following. We told the attack groups to take station fifty miles ahead of the task force on a bearing true north on the way to contact."

They thought they knew where the enemy force was located, but they could not be sure, so it was a definite chance. This decision was Admiral Mitscher's, for he had tactical command. It has been said that Halsey ran the whole show, but this was not totally accurate. Halsey supervised closely, as he said, and he set up the operations, but then he let Mitscher undertake the execution.

The reason for the quick movement was to get the attack planes off the decks and into the air "so they could strike the enemy very quickly, and if the enemy did strike us they would not catch our planes on deck," as Burke said. For it must be remembered that, although after the battle it became apparent that the Japanese did not have any planes to speak of on their carriers (about 30 at this point), Halsey's force did not know that, and on the basis of previous performance they could be ready for strong Japanese attack even if they did know that Japanese pilot attrition had caused a situation in which the current batch of fliers were not as skillful as the old ones had been.

At 0730 [said Burke] our planes sighted the enemy carrier task force consisting of 1 carrier, 3 light carriers, 2 old battleship carriers, 5 cruisers and half a dozen destroyers. . . . The enemy had changed course to about 010 [nearly north] and was going as fast as he could possibly go. Apparently he got warning when our night plane had made radar contact on him and he started getting out of there fast.

That remark, certainly believed by Commodore Burke at the time, represented the success of Ozawa's mission in a way. He had been sent to lure the Americans north, away from Samar and Leyte Gulf, so that Admiral Kurita could "get into the henhouse." So far, Admiral Ozawa's mission was a total success, one might say. He was luring the Americans north. He was not to know until later of the absolute failure of Nishimura and Shima to set the lower half of the pincers, and the knocking about that submarines and carrier air had given Kurita in the past few days, a beating that destroyed his judgment and his faith in the Sho plan so that when the time came to execute his part of it he backed away rather than move into Leyte Gulf and what seemed to him almost certain annihilation.

At 0840 that morning the first attack groups struck the enemy. Admiral Halsey and his officers were feeling very confident of the future. They had received Admiral Kinkaid's message at 0400, the one sent on the advice of Commodore Cruzen. The message had told of the action at Surigao, or the beginning of it.

Our surface forces now engaged enemy surface forces Surigao Strait entrance to Leyte Gulf. Enemy force sighted in Strait by PT boats about 0201 arrived entrance gulf about 0301 consists of 2 battleships, 3 cruisers, and destroyers. Question. Is TF 34 guarding San Bernardino Strait?

But they had not received the message until 0648, just 10 minutes before Admiral Kurita's battleships and cruisers opened fire on the escort carriers off Samar.

At 0705 Halsey replied that Task Force 34 was not guarding anything but was with the carrier groups getting ready to engage the enemy carrier force.

Then Halsey began to learn from the messages what was happening off Samar. The first word was that "Ziggy" Sprague reported enemy battleships and cruisers firing on him. That came in at 0822, even while Halsey was pondering an unpleasant word from Admiral Mitscher telling him that contact was lost with the Japanese force of Admiral Ozawa. Two bits of bad news, enough to give a fleet commander a few more gray hairs.

Then the messages from Kinkaid came thick and fast, and completely out of sequence. That was the problem of communications. Here is how they were received.

The first word came at 0822:

FAST BATTLESHIPS ARE URGENTLY NEEDED IMMEDIATELY AT LEYTE GULF.

That was all it said.

Why they were needed was not explained. For Kinkaid had been sending messages for an hour, explaining everything, but those messages stacked up while this one got through. And this one came while Halsey was very much occupied with the fight against Ozawa, which had begun.

Next message came at 0838, and it explained a lot more. It was from "Ziggy" Sprague, in the clear, to T. L. Sprague.

UNDER ATTACK. . . . ENEMY COMPOSED OF FOUR BATTLE-SHIPS, 8 CA MANY DESTROYERS.

But this was informational, not terribly upsetting, particularly when, just four minutes earlier, Halsey had ordered the fleet to close on the enemy—meaning Ozawa.

Then came another plain message which Halsey received at 0900, explaining more:

ENEMY FORCE ATTACKED OUR CVE'S COMPOSED OF 4 BB'S 8 CRUISERS AND OTHER SHIPS. REQUEST LEE PROCEED TOP

SPEED COVER LEYTE. REQUEST IMMEDIATE STRIKE BY F. T
CARRIERS.

Since Lee had just been ordered along with the others to
close Ozawa, it seemed most unlikely information, and
Halsey devoted most of his attention to his own battle.

At 0921, while getting reports of his own fighters, Halsey
had another copy of a plain-English message from "Ziggy"
Sprague to everyone, Kinkaid, himself, Nimitz, and T. L.
Sprague—well, everyone who counted in "Ziggy" Sprague's
book at that moment:

STILL UNDER ATTACK AT 0830.

Halsey responded at 0927 to all these messages by sending one message to Kinkaid: "Am now engaging enemy
carrier force. TG 38.1 with 5 carriers and 4 CA's [cruisers]
has been ordered to assist you immediately. My position
with three other carrier task groups [and here he gave
information that should have shown Kinkaid he could not
possibly help him with the fast battleships]."

So, Admiral McCain, on his way to join up, was being
diverted, and that was all Halsey thought was needed.

Halsey was digesting the information about the success
of his own attacks on the Ozawa fleet right then.

Then came two rockets.

The first was from Admiral Nimitz, Halsey's boss, off in
Pearl Harbor:

WHERE IS TASK FORCE 34? THE WORLD WONDERS.

The second was received three minutes later; it was
from Kinkaid:

MY SITUATION IS CRITICAL. FAST BATTLESHIPS AND SUP-
PORT BY AIR STRIKE MAY BE ABLE PREVENT ENEMY FROM
DESTROYING CVE'S AND ENTERING LEYTE.

The combination of these two messages, coming as they
did, created a harrowing puzzle for Halsey. He had just
learned of a series of strikes on the Japanese fleet of
Ozawa, and he was confident that in a few more hours

the Japanese could scratch one carrier force altogether. It would be one of the most spectacular victories of the war.

Here, from the pages of the action reports of Air Group 15, which was stationed aboard the Carrier *Essex* in Admiral Sherman's Task Group, is an indication of what was happening in Halsey's area.

Searches were launched at dawn on the 25th to regain contact with the enemy's carriers. In addition to the regular search teams a 4 mm plane VF [fighter] division on CAP [Combat Air Patrol] over the disposition led by Lieutenant J. J. Collins . . . was diverted to a high-speed search mission. At 0710 just as this fighter search made a turn at the end of its northern leg, the enemy was sighted 18 miles beyond by Lieutenant Collins' wingman, Lieutenant (jg) H. B. Voorhest. Voorhest directed Collins' attention to the enemy disposition. Lieutenant Collins then reported the contacts, retired, gained altitude, and returned to observe the enemy from 18,000 feet until forced to return to base because of low fuel at 0840 at which time all attacks of Strike 1 had been completed.

The 14 fighters of Air Group 15 were led by Commander David McCampbell, who had distinguished himself so much the day before in aerial combat. They went out on search, and found nothing, but when Collins found the enemy the strike group was only 50 miles away from the Ozawa fleet. They headed in, 10 of them carrying 500-pound bombs, 4 planes flying high to cover the others. This time McCampbell flew high and coordinated the strikes from above. The 10 bomb-carrying fighters swooped down on a steep high-speed dive and then strafed as they pulled out. They concentrated on the destroyer screen, and on AA, which was very strong.

During the first strike, one of the enemy's northernmost carriers was able to launch fighters, about 18 or 20 Zekes, which 4 of our VF's engaged and shot down 8 and probably 3 more of the Zekes. One of our pilots, Lieutenant J. R. Strane, was shot down in flames, managed to bail out, and was picked up by DD 669 late in the afternoon. All but this one F6F returned to base.

The Japanese were still tough fighters, in the air and on the sea. Lieutenant Strane's experience shows the ability and dedication of both sides:

After recovery from bombing and strafing the carriers, Lieutenant Strane noticed five or six Zekes 10 o'clock up at 9000 feet. The VB's were retiring below so Strane's team followed and covered, climbing, but did not turn toward the Bogies until they started a run.

On the first contact he flamed a Zeke as it was pulling off from his attack, getting in full deflection bursts from 3 o'clock down, and saw this plane crash in the water along with two other splashes. Next thing he noticed was his wingman start a diving turn to the left, and as he rolled over he saw 2 Zekes firing at the wingman. He continued in his dive and was in excellent position astern and above both, and flamed them both, one 0500 the other from 0700, with only short bursts in each. Both crashed. At this time he saw his wingman recovering to the left ahead and looked back for his section but did not see them. He did see, however, many Zekes. He turned into the closest one and fired a short burst that started smoke and flames but he did not see it crash as he was hit at the same time by another Zeke firing from ahead. He tried to roll onto this one for a shot but could not quite make it before the Zeke had flown directly in front and over him. His power then failed. . . .

His F6F-3 started smoking badly, then burst into flames, and another Zeke made a run on him hitting his port side many times and breaking loose the instrument panel. He considered trying to put the fire out in the cockpit so he could ditch, but it was beyond control, and he prepared to bail out after giving his position over the radio, luckily undamaged. His equipment twice caught on the cockpit enclosure, causing anxious moments, and he left the plane at

2500 feet. Two Zekes were circling so he delayed opening his chute until as late as possible. He almost opened his chute too late, for upon its opening he made but one swing when he hit the water. He swallowed considerable salt water, while getting disentangled, but he lost it all with no trouble when in his raft. Throughout the day he fired 3 Very cartridges at low flying search planes with no success (the sun was very bright), watched over 350 planes attacking the enemy disposition, stayed out of the sun and dozed. About 1600 he sighted a friendly surface force and succeeded in getting a Roger from a DD (669) at 9000 yards with his mirror, and was picked up. He then had the pleasure of watching, from the bridge, the polishing off of the enemy carrier he had hit previously as well as the sinking of an enemy cruiser in a night action.

Here is the account of the dive bombers in action:

Fifteen Helldivers, led by Lt. John David Bridgers, rendezvoused with VF [fighters] and VT [torpedo planes] and were vectored to a point fifty miles north of base where they orbited at 12,000 feet and were joined by air groups from other carriers. Upon receipt of a contact report from communication relay planes the group departed for the enemy fleet, climbing to 14,500 feet en route. At this time one VB returned to base because of engine trouble. The Target Coordinator sighted the fleet and assigned the *Essex* group a CVL [light carrier] of the *Chitose* class, then . . . on the starboard quarter of the disposition as if in the process of launching planes. As soon as the VT reached their desired position the dive bombers started their high-speed approach from the south, attaining a speed of 240 knots prior to the break-up at 11,000 feet up sun from the target. These were the first planes to reach and attack the enemy disposition. The heavy anti-aircraft fire was intense during the approach, as many batteries were concentrated on the one formation. Dives were made from the northeast, and of the 12 bombs released on the CVL eight were observed to be direct hits. The CVL began a slight turn as the attack started but resumed its course without further evasive action. The VB attack left the carrier burning fiercely, exploding and in sinking condition.

And here is the report of the *Essex*'s torpedo planes:

12 VT [torpedo planes], loaded with torpedoes and led by Lieutenant Commander V. G. Lambert, were launched at 0615 to attack units of a Jap Carrier Task Force reported some 250 miles east of northern Luzon. With . . . VB in the lead and VF flying cover . . . orbited . . . word came in thirty minutes or so that the force had been sighted. . . .

While en route to the target and while some 30 miles away, the heater system in Lieutenant (jg) C. G. Hurd's plane caught fire. He was forced to return to base after jettisoning his torpedo.

As the attack got under way, general disorder among the ships prevailed and it is extremely difficult to determine where one ship was in relation to another. The first reaction of this force, however, was a turn . . . to complete a circle. . . .

The VT . . . were ordered by the Target Coordinator to make a coordinated attack with the VF and the VB on the CVL [light carrier] on the starboard side and aft. . . . An immediate let-down was made from 10,000 feet to between 6000 and 7000 feet and Lieutenant Commander Lambert split his flight so that they could attack from either side of the disposition. . . .

Dive bombers were already attacking as the VT went into their runs—and in a matter of seconds had scored numerous hits on the flight deck. Because of the fact that his ship was burning and obviously out of action, the Target Coordinator called to the VT and directed them to shift to the XCV-BB [*Ise*] which was close aboard to the port. . . .

Four pilots, however, had already committed themselves to the CVL. The ships had turned hard to starboard. . . . Three pilots attacked from the southwest, giving them shots on the starboard side. . . . The fourth attacked from the east, giving him a shot on the port side. . . .

Lieutenant (jg) M. P. Deputy dropped his torpedo. It ran hot.

Lieutenant (jg) L. G. Muskin dropped his. It ran hot.

Lieutenant (jg) J. C. Huggins dropped his. As he was retiring his crew reported two large explosions near the bow.

Ensign Kenneth B. Horton dropped his torpedo. He and his crewmen saw it run hot and explode aft on the port side of the carrier.

The carrier sank at the end of the strike. She was believed by the pilots to be of the *Chitose* class.

Meanwhile, other pilots diverted their runs to the hermaphrodite battleship *Ise*. Lieutenant ((jg) H. D. Jolly dropped on the starboard bow and believed he got a hit. Ensign P. J. Ward dropped below the No. 2 turret and saw two explosions, one of which he thought was his. Lieutenant (jg) J. Smith dropped on the starboard bow, and thought he got a hit.

When the first target was abandoned by the Target Coordinator, other pilots turned toward another carrier, a *Zuiho* class, they said. Lt. Charles Wm. H. Sorenson dropped his and his wingman, Lieutenant (jg) L. R. Timberlake, dropped his torpedo—and they believed that both ran hot and true and exploded. Lieutenant (jg) Holladay dropped on the carrier and thought he got a hit, too.

Then, flying by some Zekes that attacked but did not press the formation, they flew home. All the torpedo planes returned safely.

There, in the story of the first strike of one carrier air group, a reader can get an impression of what was happening to Admiral Ozawa's fleet. There were, remember, twelve carriers in the three groups attacking Ozawa, so the *Essex* story can more or less be multiplied by 12 to convey the impression.

Here is the way the action looked from Admiral Ozawa's point of view.

On the night of October 24—just about midnight— Ozawa sent a message to combined fleet headquarters summing up his knowledge of the actions of the day. He knew that Admiral Kurita had come under heavy attack, and expected more tomorrow for Kurita, so he was moving fast south to sacrifice himself and expose his fleet with its 29 airplanes to Halsey.

He had launched his strike on the 24th and had no idea of what had happened to the planes—not even whether they reached the target area. If they did, they were among those attacking Frederick Sherman's group, but that was never known certainly. That night, Ozawa knew he was being tracked until evening, but he did not know what happened after that, except that once sure the Americans were following, he began to draw them away from Kurita.

By 0400 on October 25, Admiral Ozawa was receiving disheartening news. He received a report of the Nishimura penetration, and at 0440 a report of Nishimura's almost complete annihilation (that was Ozawa's term). Next came reports from land-based air forces discussing so many different American dispositions that Ozawa must have been confused or disbelieving. For one thing is certain: the Japanese, throughout the Sho operation, had no real conception of the vast military resources they were facing in and around Leyte Gulf.

At 0720 Admiral Ozawa knew he was being tracked and so reported to Imperial Headquarters. He put up a combat air patrol of a dozen planes or so, but the pilots had instructions to avoid wasting themselves uselessly, and they followed them.

Admiral Mitscher's planes then began boring in, in waves, and they got hits, on the *Zuikaku,* the *Chitose,* the *Zuiho,* and on lesser ships of the screen. Here is part of the action report of the *Zuikaku,* the proud carrier of the fleet that was Admiral Ozawa's flagship and had humbled the Americans before in better times.

At 0100 the *Zuikaku* prepared to make 20 knots on 30 minutes' notice, which meant firing and readying her boilers and taking the chance of expending large amounts of the fuel, of which Ozawa was so short.

At 0530 the crew manned action stations, and half an hour later they prepared to make 24 knots immediately and flank speed on 15 minutes' notice. The tempo was increasing.

At 0613 Ozawa launched one bomber and 5 fighter bombers for attack, a third of the entire force of planes available to him. At 0622 the cruiser *Tama* reported sighting planes coming in; 3 minutes later, rice balls and other battle rations were issued to the men at their posts.

Then the Japanese waited.

They waited until 0713 when the *Hyuga* reported aircraft on her screen 170 kilometers away. Four minutes later, the *Zuikaku* launched 4 more fighters for air cover.

At 0734 Ozawa had the heartening information that Admiral Kurita had come through San Bernardino Strait and opened fire on 3 American carriers. Just then one of his search planes broke down with an oil leak, and headed for the land base assigned to it. One eye gone.

The Japanese waited, and prepared their anti-aircraft guns.

The Americans were reported 100 kilometers away.

At 0807 Ozawa launched another 9 fighters, and a minute later came a report of about 130 planes gearing in, 160 degrees to port at 6000 meters. Ozawa ordered the battle flag raised. He was going into the action for which he had waited all these days.

Just then the *Hyuga* reported another American formation on the radar, 90 kilometers away.

AND . . . the Americans attacked.

The air was filled with popping anti-aircraft, very accurate and heavy, and planes swooping down, apparently without order, but actually very well coordinated by Commander McCampbell, who circled high above the battle and directed his forces in like a gunner aiming his weapons.

0817	11 Grummans approached on bearing 220° divided into two groups
0821	Opened fire
0824	Speed 24 knots
0829	Enemy aircraft (40 bombers, 10 attack planes) making continuous dive bombing and torpedo attacks. Torpedo track on starboard beam
0835	Torpedo track on port stern. Bomb hit (250 kg.) on port side amidships

0837	Torpedo hit on No. 4 generator room (flooded). List to port, 29.5°. Secondary switchboard control panel, starboard low voltage switch panel, port switch room. No. 10 power line conduit and No. 8 power line conduit flooded. No. 3 foam pump unusable. Power supply for helm cut. Rudder disabled. Carried out direct steering. Port after engine room flooded and unusable. Impossible to remain in engine room due to heat
0840	Only starboard No. 2 shaft operable
0845	List corrected to 6° by speedy flooding of tanks. Helm restored by emergency power
0846	All transmitters out of commission
0854	Fire in upper and lower No. 2 hangars (extinguished) 8 enemy planes 20° to starboard
0854	Anti-air action
0859	Check fire
0923	Message from *Oyodo* "notify condition of your communications equipment." [It was very serious]
0927	Stow anti-aircraft gear

The first wave ended then, but if the Japanese thought it was the end of the action they were sorely mistaken. The second wave came in three minutes later. One can sense the rise and fall of optimism in the action report:

0950	Ammunition in aft magazine shifted to starboard side [Then came the second wave of planes]:
0953	Large air formation [about 30 planes] coming in 160° to port. [14 Curtiss carrier bombers.] Anti-air action. Full speed ahead
0958	Open fire. [10 bombers and 6–8 attack planes attacking this ship.] Two torpedo tracks on starboard stern
1008	Check fire. All enemy planes repulsed
1022	Unidentified aircraft [1 Grumman, 1 Curtiss] sighted
1032	Hove to for transfer of flag to *Oyodo*
1045	Submarine apparently 90° to starboard

1051   Commander [Ozawa] transferred to boat
1100   Flag transferred to the *Oyodo*
1102   Aircraft spotted through closed gaps
          Anti-air action. Full speed ahead. Open fire.
          All carriers of CarDiv 3 unable to recover
          planes. 9 planes of direct air cover landed in
          water

And so it went that morning. His communications out, Admiral Ozawa moved to the *Oyodo*. The destroyer *Hatsuzuki* picked up Lieutenant Kobayashi, the air-cover commander, and the others, at least 7 of them. The Japanese estimated they had shot down 6 Grummans and 3 bombers. And from the south came the heartening news from Admiral Kurita that he had sunk 3 or 4 enemy carriers and one cruiser by this time.

The third strike came in on the *Zuikaku* and the others at 1308. But before it arrived, the whole complexion of the battle had changed suddenly because of a message sent by Admiral Nimitz in Pearl Harbor.

At 1000 Halsey had received the strange message from Nimitz that both upset and infuriated Halsey. The message was unlike Nimitz—not because Nimitz would not question—because it came to Halsey's desk as: *Where is Task Force 34? The world wonders.* That last phrase seemed pure sarcasm and was so taken by Halsey at this moment when he believed he had a triumph on his hands.

Twenty-five minutes after the message arrived for Halsey, another one came—from Admiral Bogan to Admiral Mitscher—showing how well the fliers were doing in their attacks on the Japanese. Bogan's boys reported hitting a fleet carrier with a torpedo and three bombs, setting a cruiser afire, hitting a destroyer. The destruction of the Japanese fleet had begun, and Halsey was only about 50 miles away. He could move in with his battleships and cruisers and finish off the lot.

But that Nimitz message rankled.

Actually, the message represented a comedy of errors that was again a part of the communications problem that marked the battles of Leyte Gulf all the way through on both sides. It was the practice in the American Navy to guard secret messages with padding so the enemy code breakers could not, after the fact, reconstruct obvious messages by putting together word groups and letter groups, and thus break the American naval code. So when Nimitz wrote his message at Pearl Harbor, he was asking a question, purely and simply, in the best Nimitz form. Where, he asked, was Task Force 34, which Halsey had indicated would be formed if he decided to go after the Japanese.

But when the communicator in charge took that message, it was set up as follows:

There were four words of padding at the beginning— *Turkey trots to water*—then came the message—*Where is Task Force 34?*—then came the rest of the padding, to protect secrecy—*The world wonders.*

That single phrase could not have been more unfortunate, because it could be construed to make sense, to be a part of the message. When the message was received aboard the *New Jersey*, the normal procedure was to strip it of its padding at the two ends and give Halsey the actual message. But a tired, confused communications man stripped away only half the padding, leaving *The world wonders* for Halsey to wonder at. When an admiral receives such a message as that from his Commander in Chief, he had best make some response.

Halsey's response was to do what he thought the message indicated he do—break off part of his fleet and send it back to the San Bernardino area.

So Halsey sent the following message, in sadness and in anger:

At 1115 . . . TF 34 and CTG 38.2 [Bogan] reverse course. Retain as one part of TF 34 all bludgeons— *Biloxi, Miami, Vincennes,* DesRon 52. All other units now with TF 34 proceed to join their respective groups of TF 38. TF 34 and CTG 38.2 proceed south at 20 knots. CTG 38.3 and CTG 38.4 continue strike enemy force during daylight today. Drink at dawn tomorrow. Detail orders later.

So, although the task groups of Admirals Sherman and Davison would continue hitting Ozawa's fleet, the heavy surface units were sent back toward San Bernardino Strait. Two hours later Halsey had a message from Kinkaid announcing "situation looks better" and reporting that the Japanese fleet of Admiral Kurita had turned about and was retiring, although Kinkaid with his usual caution indicated they might return.

Halsey could have kicked himself.

21

MOPPING UP FROM LEYTE

Morning and afternoon of October 25, the Japanese went limping homeward from Surigao and San Bernardino straits, while to the northeast Admiral Ozawa stood and took the beating he had expected, and all to no avail because of the failure of Admiral Kurita to recognize his opportunity in the midmorning of that day.

To the south, the planes of the escort carriers sought the ships that had escaped. In the morning, the cruiser *Mogami*, sorely damaged, was being escorted homeward by the destroyer *Akebono* when, at 0727, 4 carrier planes attacked. The attack was driven off, but at 0830 the *Mogami* lost way completely, the fires gained ascendancy, and the bilge pumps stopped working. Without pumps, the fires could not be put out.

At 0902 17 carrier bombers attacked the *Mogami*, and she took a bomb on the bow and one on the stern. The bomb that struck forward penetrated the No. 1 gun turret and destroyed the oil tanks, starting another fire. The No. 1 powder magazine was soon in danger.

At 1030 the secret papers were destroyed, and the destroyer *Akebono* took off the crew. Her captain reported to Admiral Toyoda in Japan, and Toyoda gave the mournful order to destroy the cruiser. At 1230 the *Akebono* fired a single torpedo into her, and she sank. Her survivors were carried to Cavite and put ashore there. Her captain, executive officer, and navigation officer—and many, many others—had been killed in action that day.

The cruiser *Abukuma,* escorted by the destroyer *Ushio,* headed for Cagayan to undertake the emergency repairs that would bring her safely back to home waters. But the anchorage at Cagayan proved unsatisfactory when she arrived, and she went on to Dapitan, planning to go to Coron Bay the next day. But on October 26, when she was 20 miles out of Dapitan, the *Abukuma* was caught by some 20 B-24 bombers, and she sank 37 miles from Dapitan at 1242 that day. The Captain of the *Abukuma* was picked up by the *Ushio* which circled and looked for survivors. Altogether 26 officers and 257 men were rescued, 51 of the men wounded.

Of Admiral Nishimura's force, then, the only ship that returned to friendly waters was the destroyer *Shigure,* which went home with Shima.

Of Shima's force, the two cruisers, *Ashigara* and *Nachi,* made it to safety, and so did 3 destroyers.

The transport unit, which had headed south under such odd orders, was attacked by escort carrier planes in the Visayan Sea on October 26, and the *Kinu* and the *Urinami* were sunk.

So the survivors of the southern pincer were very few and far between. As Morison noted, by November 5 only the *Ashigara* and 5 destroyers of the Surigao Strait force were still afloat, the *Nachi* having been sunk in Manila Bay on that day. If one considered the Surigao Strait battle alone, it was a debacle for the Japanese at virtually no cost to the Americans.

Sunk were: the *Nachi,* the *Abukuma,* the *Yamashiro,* the *Fuso,* the *Mogami,* and three destroyers.

Next to feel the blows of the follow-up was Admiral Kurita's force, after it ceased steaming to and fro, undetermined, and headed back through San Bernardino Strait toward safety.

Once the escort carriers recovered from the shock of attack, and while they were under vicious attack by the new kamikazes, the planes went after Kurita. An indication of what happened then can be found in the reports of the members of Composite Squadron Five, the air group that served aboard the carrier *Kitkun Bay,* one of Rear Admiral Ralph Oftsie's two ships. His other was the *Gambier Bay*, which went down that day.

Ensign D. W. King took off with a flight at 1510 on October 25, with instructions to find the Japanese fleet and attack. They passed a cruiser dead in the water, orbited by a destroyer—and ignored it. They were under instructions to hit as many ships as possible and leave the cripples.

We were flying at 9000 feet toward the San Bernardino Strait when we sighted a very large oil slick. We followed this slick for about 30 miles before we found the Jap fleet. We sighted friendly planes coming to attack. The visibility was poor. The force was 150 miles from our base.

The Jap force consisted of 3 or 4 battleships, one of which was a *Nagato*, 3 or 4 heavy cruisers, one of which was a *Mogami*, and 6 to 8 light cruisers and destroyers.

The leader of the other group of planes, which were approximately 15 VF [fighters] and 12 to 15 VT [torpedo bombers] in number, announced that they would start their attack in three minutes. After about three minutes our leader announced to start our attack. Ens. Marchant and Ens. Fulton concentrated on a battleship on the after port side, and Ens. Kummerlin and myself took the forward port beam. We dove from 9000 feet. . . . My target was a heavy cruiser. My run was on a 45° angle bearing off the bow. I did not see the run of my torpedo as I made a turn immediately after making my drop. My radioman could not see the run either, as the plexiglass was broken out. I think that Ensign Kummerlin got a hit. The AA was heavy and intense. We joined up astern of the Jap force and headed for home.

I was hit by AA fire in my port bomb bay and my port wing. The port wing tank was streaming gas, and there was a large hole in the bomb bay door. The bomb bay doors would close only part way. My hydraulic system was completely shot out.

We found our ship just after dusk and made night landings.

Here is part of Lieutenant J. F. Kalb's report:

After passing by one battleship and one cruiser which were dead in the water, we sighted a *Tone*-class cruiser making right-hand circles approximately 4 miles southeast of the other 2 ships. We were at 8000 feet at that time. We waited until we were east of the cruiser and it was coming toward us in its circle. . . . As soon as we started our dive the cruiser took evasive action, first making a turn of 75° to starboard and then going on a straight course. By this time Lieutenant (jg) Andrews and Lieutenant (jg) T. G. Buttle were dropping their torpedoes, and Lieutenant (jg) Curtis and myself launched ours a few seconds later. The Jap cruiser then turned to the starboard to parallel Lieutenant (jg) C. S. Curtis' and my drops. As I pulled out of my dive, I saw two 500-pound SAP bombs, dropped by Lieutenant (jg) McDermitt, explode. The first one appeared to be a near miss on the starboard bow and the second appeared to be a hit on the bow of the Jap cruiser. Soon after the two bomb explosions I saw the wakes of the two torpedoes dropped by Lieutenant Andrews and Lieutenant (jg) Buttle. Both of these torpedoes hit amidships almost together on the port side. The Jap cruiser immediately lost speed, and in five minutes was dead in the water, listing slightly to port. . . .

As always in an air battle, it was not quite one-sided, as Lieutenant Buttle's report indicated, after he had made his attack:

. . . Five minutes later, while approximately 10 miles south from the cruiser, my gunner called my attention to a lone avenger making a glide bombing run on the *Tone*, which appeared to be almost dead in the water and smoking heavily from the port side. Just as I saw him he was hit, and went all of the way down to the water in a red ball of fire. My gunner is positive that he saw two parachutes open but I was unable to observe such. . . .

Here, taken from the action reports of the First Striking Force [Kurita], is an outline of what happened that day to the Admiral and his ships as they turned about.

At 1018, while Kurita was still debating his next move, he ordered all his damaged ships to head for San Bernardino Strait and home waters. At 1030 the *Yamato,* the flagship, sent a message claiming one carrier of the *Enterprise* class sunk and another damaged, plus 3 destroyers. There, of course, was further evidence of the Japanese failure to ascertain the nature of the force they engaged. By 1100, the destroyers had become cruisers, too, in Japanese thinking.

Here is Admiral Kurita's rationale for deserting the action that day:

Until about 1200 we were determined to carry out the plan to penetrate into Leyte Gulf in spite of repeated enemy air attacks. However, according to an enemy dispatch, the enemy 7th fleet was ordered to concentrate in position about 300 miles southeast of Leyte. The enemy was also concentrating its carrier based air strength at Tacloban and together with its surface task force, was disposing itself to counter the penetration into Leyte which is anticipated. Its preparations to intercept our force apparently were complete whereas we could not even determine the actual situation in Leyte Gulf. Moreover in view of what happened to the Third Section [Shima] and the Second Diversionary attack force [Nishimura] it seemed not unlikely that we would fall into an enemy trap, were we to persist in our attempt at penetration. The wiser course was deemed to cross the enemy's anticipation by striking at his task force which had been reported in a position bearing 5 degrees distance 113 miles from Suluwan Light at 0945. We believed that turn about, proceed northward in search of this element, would prove to be to our advantage in subsequent operations. . . .

All this while, Admiral Kurita was getting feedback of the Kinkaid and Sprague messages in the clear asking for help (coming from shore stations), and they added up to calls for help from a very strong force somewhere southeast of Leyte Gulf. Or so it seemed to Kurita.

So all plans were abandoned, and San Bernardino Strait and beyond became the goal.

That day, starting with the morning attacks, the Japanese force was subjected to eleven air attacks, and when they were over the *Kumano, Suzuya, Chikuma, Chokai,* and *Hayashimo* were either finished, or very nearly so. They were detached and ordered to make it or not by themselves with destroyer escorts. When the *Suzuya* sank, her crew went to the destroyer *Okinami* and when the *Chokai* went down, her crew went to the *Fujinami.* The destroyer *Nowake* was sent to help the *Chikuma,* and was never heard of again.

The rest were heading for Coron Bay. That night the last of the survivors passed through the straits.

Here, from Admiral Ugaki's diary, is the sad story of the retreat on October 26:

Today, before dawn, we passed north of Tablas Island, our battlefield of two days ago, and offered a silent prayer for *Musashi.* We proceeded southward along the west coast of Tablas and about 0800, just as we were approaching the northwest tip of Panay, about 30 planes which had followed our oil slicks, attacked. At 0834 50 more planes attacked, and at the end of the attack several torpedo bombers appeared. *Yamato* skillfully evaded the torpedo attacks, but *Noshiro* sustained hits and became unnavigable. A destroyer was assigned to tow *Noshiro. Yamato* sustained considerable damage when two bombs dropped by dive bombers hit her forecastle. At 1040, the third wave of planes came in—30 B-24's making their initial appearance. Flying at high altitude they leisurely maneuvered, and one group dropped its bombs between *Haruna* and *Kongo,* and another group on *Yamato. Yamato* skillfully evaded by right rudder, but water spouts and bomb fragments from 3500 kg near misses passed over the main battery fire control station with considerable force. One ricocheting small fragment pierced the Chief-of-Staff's right thigh.

Almost simultaneously with the B-24's, about 60 carrier aircraft attacked. *Noshiro* was torpedoed and finally sunk. This was the last attack made on our force, but our feeling was that we had had enough.

Although the *Yamato* was a huge enough ship that she could keep on fighting when lesser vessels would have gone to the bottom, she had been very seriously damaged in all this action of the past three days. One bomb had pierced the anchor deck and exploded deep below, smashing two large holes in the armor plating. One shell had blown away part of the armor of No. 1 turret. Another, through the top deck, had raised havoc in the crew's quarters. A bomb had made a large hole above the waterline near No. 1 turret, and water had come in through the various holes so heavily that the ship took on about 3000 tons, and then the Captain had to counterflood with another 2000 tons to correct. Even so the *Yamato* at the end of the action was well down by the bow and limping.

The *Nagato* was also damaged by bombs and fragments. The *Kumano* was attacked again and barely made Manila Bay, and her escort, destroyer *Fujinami*, which was carrying survivors of the *Chokai*, was sunk on the way to safety. "The enemy," wrote Admiral Ugaki, "with the victor's feeling of finishing off the cripples, went about this task in a most thorough fashion."

Some justification was given Admiral Kurita's decision to turn back by the fuel shortage—so serious that, although they planned to refuel at Coron Bay, several of the fleet's destroyers ran out of oil even before they reached Coron, and had to be given an emergency supply, a dangerous proceeding in what were now American waters.

By October 27, the Kurita force had reached the northern edge of the Dangerous Ground—which held so many sad memories for them from a few days before, when the *Darter* and the *Dace* had attacked near here. The Japanese had a serious problem: American planes could track them for miles because they were trailing a fleet-size oil slick, and every ship was damaged to some extent. Admiral Kurita decided to pass through the center of the Dangerous Ground as the lesser of two evils. And he and his staff indulged in a lively debate as to what course should be followed. Some felt that the fleet really ought to abandon its plan to return to Brunei Bay, which was now too close for comfort to American bases, and go on to Camranh Bay instead. They could make that the new base, at least for the moment until repairs could be begun.

But Admiral Kurita decided in favor of his original plan: to return to Brunei Bay. That was that. There were no attacks, and they could fuel their destroyers from the *Nagato* and the *Haruna,* although the process gave Kurita an anxious hour. In one way they welcomed the bad weather that descended, but moving through the Dangerous Ground in poor visibility was a very risky business and they were well aware of that problem. The main force lost contact with several destroyers this day; they had headed into Coron Bay for refueling, and did not appear. Kurita reversed course for several hours, but still they did not appear. Worrisome. But worries were lessened enough by now that the *Yamato* and the others could bury their dead, taking time for the civilized rites necessary to bury them at sea.

On the 28th the fleet was heading southeast, bound for Brunei Bay. Luckily the weather was foul and cloudy, and if there were American search planes and submarines about, the Japanese managed to evade them.

At 2000, the limping fleet entered the bay, during a squall, and proceeded to its anchorage. The *Yamato* became fouled with the anchor of the oiler *Yuho Maru,* when her anchor windlass gave way: another little bit of damage. Admiral Kurita secured then, but first ordered fueling so that, whatever happened, he would be ready to go out and fight again if necessary. The officers and men began to relax, and the survivors of the sunken ships reported in. Admiral Ugaki saw with pleasure that Captain Owada of the *Takao* and Captain Araki of the *Atago* had turned up on the flagship bridge to report on their woes. Yet, as he saw these gentlemen, he could not help but be sadly aware of the absence of Captain Iguchi, Commander of the beloved *Musashi,* the great sunken battleship that still haunted Ugaki.

The battle was over for Admiral Kurita, and he was

now assigned the immobile task of maintaining his "fleet in being." From Japan, Admiral Toyoda ordered that the ships remain at Brunei, even those ships that were streaming oil and needed dockyard repairs, because Toyoda was sending two and a half divisions to Morotai, and the presence of these ships (scarecrows though they might be) would give the Japanese about all the naval protection they might expect in these difficult days.

Admiral Ugaki relaxed, and took his first bath in days, and while doing so he mused on the negative fortunes that had overtaken Japan.

Admiral Kurita remained at Brunei for a time, as requested. The missing destroyers turned up (except for some that were sunk in Coron, as were some tankers). One tanker was sunk in Balabac Passage, one fled north, damaged, and one had a narrow escape in Paitan Bay. They were dogged by submarines, as Japanese tankers had been and would be for the rest of the war; indeed the days of the Japanese fleet would be numbered now, if for no other reason than by her inability to secure fuel for the fighting ships.

For a few days the ships were occupied with the repairs they could make, with loading ammunition, and with hospitalizing the injured and the sick.

Then they waited until the end of November, when the ships returned to the Inland Sea, the mighty *Yamato,* too. Most of these ships would never again move out of inland waters.

As for the northern force of Admiral Ozawa, it was lucky in a way. Admiral Halsey turned the battleships and cruisers around and sent them south. Yet Ozawa's troubles did not end, by any means, at 1115 on October 25, the point in time at which Halsey had executed his decision so reluctantly.

The action report of Admiral Sherman's task group gives an indication of the kind of punishment the Americans meted out during the rest of that day, ordered by Halsey to continue strikes against Ozawa:

Shortly after strike No. 3 took off at 1145 *Belleau Wood* target coordinator reported that the enemy ships were then in two groups. One to the south, thereafter known as "the cripples," was composed of an *Ise*-class XCV [battleship-carrier] one CL [cruiser] and 22 DD's [destroyers] all circling the second *Chitose*-class CVL [carrier] which was still dead in the water and burning as result of the first attack. The other group was some 20–30 miles northwest of the cripples. It consisted of *Zuikaku* [carrier flagship], *Zuiho* [carrier], the other *Ise* XCV, 3 cruisers and 2 or 3 destroyers. The enemy ships were approximately 102 miles . . . from our formation . . . and Task Group 38.3 planes were ordered to strike the northern group which was apparently still heading north at 15–20 knots.

Their attack at about 1310 put finishing touches on *Zuikaku* with nine direct 1000-pound and 2000-pound bomb hits. In addition one torpedo was put into the northern *Ise*-class XCV. Planes from Task Group 38.4 were soon to make several good hits on *Zuiho*, which was also left dead in the water burning badly. At about 1400 *Lexington* target coordinator watched *Zuikaku* founder. . . .

This coordinator was Commander Theodore H. Winters, Jr., of *Lexington*'s Air Group 19, and he had taken over on target from Commander McCampbell. Here is part of his account of what he saw below:

By the time I relieved him [McCampbell] as Strike Leader, and Air Coordinator over the targets, there were only three carriers left and about two battleships, exactly two battleships, and three or four cruisers. They were more or less spreading out, trying to get away . . . so we took our groups on up further north and hit . . . *Zuikaku* and the *Zuiho*.

I put my group, Group 19, on the *Zuikaku* and they really smothered her, she slowly burned for about two hours and I spent six to six and a half hours over the target so I watched these ships sink. The *Zuikaku* sank in about two and a half hours and the *Zuiho* . . . a little bit smaller than our *Enterprise* was very fast and maneuverable and it took several strikes on

330 EDWIN P. HOYT

her to sink her. Finally she rolled over and sank after about three hours of attack. There was no explosion or going up in a mass of flames or anything spectacular. . . .

An interesting note on these two fast carriers . . . two destroyers picked up the survivors on the *Zuikaku* when she sank and I marked down the two in formation to keep our eye on for future reference. And those same two went over and picked up survivors off the *Zuiho* a while later when she sank, and we got destroyers on these two cans and set them on fire from end to end before the day was over, and the slaughter must have been terrific. . . .

The third strike of the American force did not bother the "cripples" but at 1410 came a report that the *Hyuga,* and the other undamaged ships of the southern "cripples" force, were abandoning the light cruiser and heading north, so planes from the *Lexington* and the *Langley* were rushed to them to join a TG 38.4 attack. And the final air attack of the day was made at 1615:

Pilot reports, substantiated by photos, indicate that only ten vessels were still afloat—2 *Ise* XCV's, 1 unidentified CA [cruiser] 1 *Oyodo* or *Agano* CL [light cruiser]; 1 *Natori* CL, 1 unidentified single-stack CL, and 3 DD's, all under way plus the crippled *Chitose* class CVL dead in the water and abandoned by the other ships. A result of well-coordinated attacks, two torpedoes and six direct bomb hits were obtained on the XCV's. One of them slowed to 8 knots temporarily, but later was reported still heading north at 20 knots. A destroyer was confirmed sunk and one 250-pound bomb hit was obtained on the stern of a CA.

Here is more of the action report, couched very personally by Admiral Sherman:

"In the course of the day's strikes it rapidly became evident that there might be several Jap cripples which could best be finished off by ship gunfire or torpedo attacks after dark. At 1340 Sherman asked permission to or-

ganize a cruiser and destroyer attack after dark, and
Mitscher agreed but said he thought it might be difficult
with only one battleship in each group—and he did not
want any damaged ships to tow home. So Sherman made
plans for his attack, leaving Cruiser *Reno* and 4 destroyers
for screening, and telling *Essex* to put up two night fighters
for snooping.

"I felt that the tactical situation warranted this reduc-
tion in the carrier screen," said Sherman. "We ruled the
sea in our vicinity, there were no enemy aircraft in the
air to bother us, the enemy was in full retreat, and the
only remaining objective was to prevent his cripples from
getting away."

So 4 cruisers and 12 destroyers went out about 1615.
First they found the carrier, dead in the water, and opened
fire. The Japanese tried to return fire, but their ship was
too badly hurt to be effective. At 1700 the carrier capsized and sank.

The cruisers and destroyers found a force of two Japanese destroyers and a dead cruiser, and opened fire. The
destroyers had been picking up survivors—they fled, and
got away, moving north at high speed. The Japanese cruiser stayed and fought, and made speeds up to 26 knots in
her flight. Finally, she exploded and sank at 2055.

Here is Admiral Sherman's assessment of the accom-
plishment of the day:

> . . . The situation during the day had been ideal.
> We had wiped out the enemy air on the day before
> and we had him within striking range of our aircraft.
> We were proceeding toward him at 25 knots, he could
> not get away, and a good fresh breeze for air opera-
> tions was only 45° on my starboard bow. It was a
> happy situation. The enemy was between 80 and 100
> miles away, an ideal distance for aircraft strikes. We
> pounded him from dawn till dark with everything
> we had.

Commander Winters felt the same:

> The action on the 25th . . . impresses me as one of
> the most remarkable that I've ever heard about. We

sank 4 of their carriers, including their biggest, the *Zuikaku,* corresponding to our *Essex* class, and a couple of their cruisers and 3 or 4 destroyers and crippled 2 battleships, one so badly that it was later sunk by submarines, without the loss of a single ship in that part of the battle. . . .

Admiral Sherman summed it up from his point of view: ". . . The Japanese navy had been dealt blows from which it is safe to say they will probably never recover. . . ."

From the beginning of the day, Admiral Ozawa's force was really doing nothing but maneuvering to avoid as many bombs and torpedoes as possible. What else could Ozawa do? He was the sacrificial lamb, and he knew it. After the war he said that if Kurita had been able to get in among the American transports in Leyte Gulf and destroy them, he would have done all that Ozawa could have expected of him. At no time did Ozawa expect any help from Kurita or anyone else.

At 1100 on October 25, with the destroyer *Akazuki* sunk, the *Chitose* virtually dead in the water and the cruiser *Tama* badly hit, Admiral Ozawa ordered a retirement to the north. He reported to Tokyo that he had been hit, and that he was bringing the fleet north at 18 knots. Then came the third wave of American planes, and more damage.

In mid-afternoon, Ozawa assessed his situation.

He judged correctly that the mobile force then was encountering two American task groups, one in the south and one southwest of him. They were drawing nearer, he knew. He considered whether or not to continue to draw away or to plunge in with a surface attack. But what did he have to fight with? Against the American carriers and their supporting ships he had nothing but surface ships. "No aircraft available for use," said his summary. Even the cruiser's seaplanes had been damaged and could not fly. "Reconnaissance and attack capability nil."

Consequently, Admiral Ozawa did not know the American position, but he did know that he had done absolutely no damage this day to the Americans, and they had done plenty of damage to him. His decision was to "continue diversionary operations" until a "favorable opportunity arises" in which case "the main body will counterattack and destroy the enemy at any cost." He ordered all ships to join up and head north.

By 1500, Ozawa had the melancholy task of reporting that he had lost the *Zuikaku, Zuiho, Chitose,* and *Chiyoda,* the 4 carriers, and the destroyer *Akitsuki,* and that *Tama,* the cruiser, was so hard hit that he had ordered her to retire independently as best she could. (The *Tama* was sunk that night by the American submarine *Jallao* before she could arrive anywhere.)

By late afternoon, Admiral Ozawa still had 12 of his 17 ships afloat. He had reported the *Chiyoda* lost, and he was right, although she did not actually sink until about 1700, when plastered by cruisers and destroyers.

By 2000 the darkness was protecting Admiral Ozawa from further American air strikes. He had reports from the destroyer *Hatsuzuki,* which was rescuing carrier survivors, that she was under attack by surface forces. This was the cruiser destroyer force under Rear Admiral Laurence T. DuBose. The force chased 3 Japanese destroyers, in fact, and finally sank the *Hatsuzuki* just at 2100. By that time Admiral Ozawa had decided to go to the assistance of the destroyer and turned around with the two hermaphrodite battleships, a cruiser, and a destroyer to fight. The last word from the *Hatsuzuki* came at 2041, her captain reporting that she was engaging the Americans. Then there was silence. Ozawa heard no more nor found the American surface force.

He did, however, hear indirectly. At midnight, Ozawa made a situation estimate:

Searched for enemy force until 2330 but failed to ascertain his position.

1. While search was in progress, *Wakatsuki* rejoined and made the following report concerning the enemy situation: *Hatsuzuki, Wakatsuki,* and *Kuwa,* while rescuing survivors of *Zuikaku* and *Zuiho,* were attacked from the east at around 1900 by an enemy force of 10 ships. . . . *Wakatsuki* and *Kuwa* speedily retired. *Hatsuzuki* was seen engaging the enemy while

laying down smoke but was not subsequently heard from.

2. Estimate:

(a) Judging from the above information, together with the respective positions of our force and the enemy, and our own search course, it is concluded that the enemy either passed to the north or withdrew to the south while we were searching for him.

(b) The Mobile Force Main Body will again proceed northward and seek to engage the enemy.

It is doubtful if Admiral Ozawa was playing more than pro forma with this situation report, for at 2000 he had received a report from combined fleet headquarters that indicated the battle was over in the south. Admiral Toyoda had said that if a chance came for Kurita to make a night attack against the enemy he ought to do so, and so had Ozawa, but if no chance came, then Ozawa was to move north to refuel and return home. Ozawa, reading between the lines, knew that Kurita had given up his mission, and there was no further sense in any sacrifice.

On the morning of October 26, Halsey's Third Fleet had lost contact with Ozawa altogether. Two of the task groups fueled that day, and two concentrated their strikes on the retreating Kurita force with some effects as noted, but the battle was over for Ozawa. He headed for Amami-o-Shima where his diminished oiler force was waiting. They headed northwest, very carefully avoiding submarines and sticking to the coastline of the Nansei Islands, and entered their anchorage on October 27. That day new orders were received. The *Oyodo* and several destroyers would go to Manila where they would be made available for transport and guard duty for the beleaguered army troops, whose battle for the Philippines was just beginning. The damaged ships, such as the destroyer *Shimotsuki,* were ordered to the Inland Sea for repairs. Ozawa took his flag to the *Hyuga,* the hermaphrodite battleship-carrier, which was the best thing he had left, and on October 28 he took the sadly diminished remains of the main body back to the Inland Sea. On October 29 the force arrived. There was a brave general order to the effect that the *Hyuga* and the *Ise* would prepare themselves for battle once again, but no one believed it. The mobile force of Admiral Ozawa had lost 4500 men. Up until this battle Japan's navy had lost perhaps 40,000 men in all actions fought during the war, and although the total losses were never assessed, in the almost complete destruction of Admiral Nishimura's force, and the heavy punishment dealt Admiral Kurita in loss of vessels, the Japanese casualties for the battle must have exceeded 10,000 men, plus the ships they went out in, and in which they went down. As for pilots and planes, altogether in the days of battle that began with the assault by Halsey's fleet on Okinawa early in October, the Japanese must have lost more than 1000 planes, plus air crews in most cases. Army and navy figures were not evaluated together, but nearly half that many planes were lost in Okinawa, Formosa, and the Luzon battle alone.

Admiral Ozawa recommended the disbanding of the mobile force, and the reliance of the navy in future on land-based air unless something could be done to give the navy new carrier pilots (there still existed several operational carriers) and ships capable of making at least 24 knots, which the other fighting ships were not.

For the time being, at least, any use of Japanese naval power would have to be piecemeal, Ozawa indicated. What he did not say was that he and the other admirals knew that they had seen the effective end of the Japanese fleet.

AFTERWORD

The battles of Leyte are important in the scheme of naval and military history because of the many aspects of command with which they deal, and they are important in the study of war for what they teach about the defense of desperation. Even in their desperate Sho plan the Japanese naval authorities were following the normal processes of war, but when the Sho operation so obviously began to fail for want of air cover, then a new policy of desperation was begun. The kamikazes, the instrument of the suicidal war policy, showed the world in the next nine months just how dreadful war can become when a handful of men are literally ready to do anything to stop the enemy.

The battles of Leyte marked two turning points in the war against Japan. First, as noted, was the coming of the kamikazes, a policy to which the Japanese authorities were persuaded by a number of admirals and other officers, most notably Vice Admiral Takijiro Ohnishi. The logic of desperation is simple, if frightening: Admiral Ohnishi was sent to the Philippines to make sure that the Sho operation was a success, and success depended on the suppression of American air control of the Philippine waters while Admiral Kurita sailed down and Admirals Nishimura and Shima sailed up and closed the pincers on the Leyte beaches. When Admiral Ohnishi discovered that he had fewer than 100 planes with which to work, and when the Second Air Fleet from Formosa arrived so decimated that it had only 200 more planes, then he saw that only by making one plane do the work of ten could he possibly achieve his directive. Since he was on notice that success was imperative, his decision was quite simple. The morality of the kamikaze might be questionable (Ohnishi committed suicide with the failure of the war) but the efficacy was not. Of course, one must also reflect on what part the Western insistence on unconditional surrender played in the killing of thousands more Americans by Japanese suicide pilots in the months to come, when by the naval standards at the time of the Leyte battles, the victory was already won, and Japan must accept defeat.

Japan was already defeated in the autumn of 1944. Two months after Leyte, while the Japanese land armies were still fighting vigorously in the Philippines, one whole convoy was wiped out by the Third Fleet. And that was not a solitary instance: at least two other convoys of ten and a dozen ships were all but destroyed.

Those ships were lost before they could return to Japan. So it can be accepted from the Japanese figures that there was not enough fuel oil and gasoline in Japan to resupply the outlying parts of the Empire, or to operate the naval vessels. Suicidal policy and the fact of defeat are both shown overwhelmingly in the sortie of the *Yamato* and her little squadron in April. The Imperial High Command issued a comforting report which praised the dead of the *Yamato* (and themselves for ordering the operation), stating that it was a success because it let the kamikaze pilots concentrate on American ships while the pilots of the fast carriers were attacking the *Yamato* and the lesser ships. The facts do not bear out this contention. The *Yamato* "attacked"—that is, she came into action—on April 7. But on April 6 (she did not leave Japanese waters until 1500) 17 American ships were put out of action by kamikazes, while on April 7 only 6 ships were put out of action, two of those victims of mines, not air attack. The official Japanese argument does not hold up at all.

It made no sense of any kind, from the viewpoint of the West, that the *Yamato* should be sent out with only enough fuel for a one-way trip, or should be sent out at all. Yet it is not enough to look at the matter from the American point of view. From the Japanese point of view, at this stage of the war, normal logic could have no further effect on military counsels, because normal logic told the admirals that the war was lost and should be ended. It could not be ended because the Americans would not let it be ended on a basis that the Japanese could consider honorable. There is politics in war, and while the generals and admirals could discount Admiral Halsey's boast that he would ride Hirohito's horse down the streets of Tokyo, they could not discount the danger that the Emperor would be tried as a war criminal. God is not a criminal, and the Emperor was God. So Japan was forced—there is no question about that—to a policy of desperation, and the only way the most dreadful slaughter in the history of warfare was averted on the beaches of Japan was by the dreadful slaughter of civilians at Hiroshima and Nagasaki. Even that would not have stopped the war; Admiral Toyoda and others shrewdly guessed that the American supply of atomic weapons was extremely limited, and they would have gone on with war on the beaches. They had saved the gasoline; they had manufactured the kamikaze planes; they had other suicide weapons that would have decimated those beaches and the ships that stood off them. The slaughter of Americans and Japanese in a landing on Japan would have been enough to give even warriors pause, and the Japanese were ready, soldier and sailor, to die on those beaches for their country. They were saved only by an Emperor who realized that the submarines and the airplanes had already destroyed Japan's ability to fight a war to any conclusion other than suicide.

A change in the war shown at Leyte, then, was the turn from a policy of defense to a policy of military suicide to achieve defense. There were a few leftover actions of the old school by the Japanese: Admiral Kimura's "Christmas call" on Mindoro with his half-hearted bombardment of San Jose and the beaches represented the traditional in warfare; perhaps its failure underscored the need for change to the policies of absolute desperation. In any event, the Sho operation, even if it had succeeded in doing everything that Admiral Toyoda had outlined, would have meant the end of the Japanese fleet. The battle might have been different under certain circumstances: had Admiral Kurita stayed his course he would have destroyed perhaps another dozen ships, maybe even more. But Admiral Oldendorf would have gotten to him in two hours or so with the old battleships, the cruisers, and the destroyers. There would have been more ships sunk on both sides, more lives lost; but the fact was that the Japanese sent out 63 ships to oppose a vastly superior number. Under no conceivable conditions could the Japanese have done anything but lose that fleet, given the intent and orders of the Sho operation.

The second turning point of the war involved a purely American matter: the change in nature of the struggle from a combination of military and naval responsibility to one in which the military would assume ascendancy. The reason was that, with the Philippines invasion, for the first time the Americans came into a position where armies were to be used in assault, so large were the land masses involved. Before, the assaults had been carried by divisions. The marines were particularly quick and skillful in attacking small islands, and heretofore both the Central Pacific and South Pacific campaigns had been against relatively small land masses. Even in New Guinea only a small portion of the big island was involved. But in the Philippines at the time of invasion there were some 260,000 Japanese troops; in Okinawa there would be some 400,000 troops; in the Japanese islands there would be millions. This meant that tanks and other armor and army tactics would control. This, in turn, meant that the army would run the rest of the war in the Pacific. An argument could be made that whatever American failure existed in the battles of Leyte, from a naval point of view it can be traced back to this problem, too—the matter of overall command of the operation. Up to the time of the Philippines there was divided command, and that divided command hurt the American war effort in several ways. General Douglas MacArthur always held out for a single command with himself as commander. The latter part of the argument helped defeat the former until the exigencies of the Philippines operation shoved affairs in the "right" or single-command direction. After the Philippines battle there could be no further argument with MacArthur's contention that one man had to be in charge. Iwo Jima was a navy show; in Okinawa the army soon took control, when they could support themselves. Admiral Halsey, by the way, supported this thesis throughout—the matter of single control.

The reason for dual control at Leyte was the nature of the war itself. The war had begun in the Pacific as a naval war. The Japanese had tried to destroy our fleet, and when we went to stop them in their advance at the line drawn in the Solomon Islands, the stopping had to be done by ships of the fleet, supporting men ashore. The Japanese had control of the air in those days, except in local situations such as a carrier attack. Because it was a naval war in the early days, because General MacArthur sat in Brisbane and waited for supplies and men that did not come, and then came slowly and sporadically, Admiral Nimitz at Pearl Harbor had charge of the Central Pacific fighting, as General MacArthur had charge of the Southwest Pacific. There was a never-never land in the South Pacific itself, but Admiral Halsey occupied that land, as Commander of the Third Fleet and cooperator with MacArthur—and Halsey cooperated so well with MacArthur that there was no real trouble. But, in the end, MacArthur got his own navy, with Admiral Thomas Kinkaid in charge of it—and it was here that the trouble, or the root of it, was located.

The Philippines operation had been opposed strategically by the U.S. Navy all the way along as unnecessary. Admiral Ernest King, Chief of Naval Operations and Commander in Chief of the Navy during the war, wanted to go to Formosa or the coast of China, bypassing the Philippines. The decision for the Philippines was made over his opposition. But at the time of the Philippines invasion, strategists were still discussing the next moves. General MacArthur, of course, wanted to be in charge from then on, and let the navy come under his command. Admiral King, and Admiral Nimitz, were resisting. Thus it was that Admiral Halsey's orders were written the way he wanted them—so that he had a strategic responsibility stated, and a tactical one implied. He was supposed to *support* Admiral Kinkaid. He did so by blasting the Okinawan, Philippine, and Formosan airfields and shooting down so many planes that the Sho operation was doomed from the beginning. (We know that now through wonderful hindsight.) He did so by smashing Admiral Kurita's force in the Sibuyan Sea on October 24. But Admiral

Halsey's orders also directed him, if he had a chance, to engage the Japanese fleet: he was to do so above all else. Now, of course, in the Sho operation the Japanese divided their forces. So the words "engage the Japanese fleet" could have applied to engagement of Kurita's force at San Bernardino Strait as well as to Admiral Ozawa's decoy force coming down on the outside of the Philippines. Except for one thing: carrier doctrine.

World War II in the Pacific had resulted in the glorification (quite properly) of the aircraft carrier as the principal offensive weapon of sea war, at least the principal tactical weapon, the submarine proving itself absolutely to be the major strategic weapon in that sea war before the army and navy planes could get into the Japanese air sphere. With that emphasis on carriers, every American admiral worth a command had an emphasis on carrier doctrine in his own mind. And when the Ozawa force came down south with its carriers, and when the Kurita force, badly mauled, moved backward into the Sibuyan Sea without any carriers, Admiral Halsey came to a conclusion that seemed natural (to his enemies, too) and moved against the force with the carriers, because the carriers were always a clear and present danger. Planes could be flown off a carrier at any point (given decent weather). Planes could be flown *to* a carrier under the same conditions. The carrier in being was a constant threat to all other vessels, and to armies ashore as well.

Because of his orders, then; because of the jealousy between army and navy forces at the highest levels; because this was the moment of change in approach to the Pacific war although the change had not yet taken place; because of all these things, the second turning point of the war after Leyte came about, and the result of Halsey's decision to go north after Admiral Ozawa was as important in determining the future course of the war as was General Holland Smith's relief of Major General Ralph Smith in the Marianas a few months earlier. In the Smith vs. Smith controversy General Marshall swore that no Army general would again serve under a Marine general. After Leyte, Admiral Halsey was among the first to state that, in any naval situation, there ought to be a single command. Historically speaking, this is the importance of Leyte from a strategic point of view.

From a purely naval point of view, the battles of Leyte illustrate some interesting points about warfare. First, an awesome matter, is the notable degree to which communications and chance played roles in that battle. For example, Japanese communications among the fleets and between the fleets and the air bases and air commands of the Philippines were simply frightful. The only messages that ever seemed to get through were the ones from the fleets to Tokyo, and these were then parceled out among the other fleets. The Americans did not have this problem. Indeed, Admiral Kinkaid's eavesdropping on Halsey's messages not meant for him caused Kinkaid to jump to a wrong conclusion (perhaps proving the truth of the adage that the great American indoor sport is jumping to conclusions).

From the Japanese point of view, one might say that the first terrible tactical mistake in the Sho operation was the decision by Admiral Toyoda's staff, while he was grounded on Formosa, to commit the carrier air force of Ozawa's ships to the land battle. The planes were lost and Ozawa's carriers lost their teeth.

In fact, Halsey's smashing victory over the Japanese in Formosan air colored the whole battle. Admiral Kurita could not get the air support he demanded at any time, and he was mauled, and his assessment of the situation changed hour by hour, dropping ever lower. When by good luck he found himself in precisely the position Admiral Toyoda had hoped for, the conditions were such and his state of mind was such that he could not take advantage of his opportunity.

But look at it from Kurita's point of view. He set out on what was obviously a desperate mission. The orders were changed so many times that it was unnerving (Shima in particular). Kurita went into the Sibuyan Sea and found it full of sharks; he lost 2 cruisers and was banged up before he got past the Dangerous Ground, a long way from San Bernardino Strait—and he did not get any air cover. Next day, October 24, he was hit all day long by American planes and did not get any help from Japanese air that should have been all around him. For the most part he could not even get a message out of land-based air telling him what was going on. Then, when Kurita was ready to go through San Bernardino Strait, he was out of communication, except to have a strong message from the combined fleet. He was attacking the Americans very successfully, when he learned that the southern half of his pincers movement (Nishimura and Shima) were not going to help—and he could gather easily enough that for the most part they were not ever going to arrive anywhere again. Unnerving—no less. And he discovered so many ships (two sets of carriers were known to him, but he did not know their types) and he knew of so many other ships to his south and his east, that he was unnerved again. He delayed, and then he was too late to take after whatever he thought was the force to the east, and so he went home again.

Some historians say he turned tail. His conduct has been carefully ignored by Japanese strategists for the most part; on the high seas many of his subordinates disagreed with his action, Admiral Ugaki, for one. Perhaps Kurita was one of those Japanese commanders who disagreed with that part of Bushido, the philosophy of the samurai, which calls upon a man to give his life when there seems no other course than defeat. There were definitely two schools of thought: throughout the war, some admirals went down with their flagships and some swam to safety. When the *Atago* was sunk at the beginning of the Sho operation, Kurita swam for it, and was rescued by a destroyer. That's not conclusive, but it is an indication of his thinking. In any event, he took the *Yamato* and the lesser ships home, and put the finish to a distinguished naval career.

As for the other Japanese commanders, Shima and Nishimura suffered from personal differences, bad communications, and Shima from orders that were changed too many times. There was no sense in sending two forces down through the Sulu Sea to Surigao Strait. It probably would have made no difference, however, had they joined, because Admiral Oldendorf was ready and waiting—so calm and confident that he did not even make a minor change in his battle orders after the enemy was identified and enumerated going through. He smashed Nishimura and he could have smashed Shima as well at the same time.

Admiral Ozawa did precisely what he was told to do, and he did it very well. He was to lure the Third Fleet north, and be sacrificed. He was. His sacrifice was not total only because of Admiral Nimitz's interference in the action, and Halsey's quick reaction (which he ever after regretted) caused Halsey to break off the incipient surface action that would have smashed the *Ise*, the *Hyuga*, and the other ships. Well, Halsey smashed most of them later at Kure anyhow. It might have been more romantic to smash them off Cape Engano, but the Kure bombing was no less effective.

Speaking of the Japanese, the land-based air commanders might have been a little more considerate of their seagoing fellows. Japanese air suffered from the worldwide disease of conflict of interest between naval and army arms; the Army air simply did not know the first thing about naval engagement and air responsibility, and did not care. The Army air at Leyte was effective in bombing some ships around the beaches, but that was almost all its effectiveness as far as the naval action was concerned. But Naval air did not give the Japanese admirals even the rudimentary intelligence they needed—which is surprising because the battle reports of the American forces indicate the almost constant presence of "snoopers" everywhere. The failure lay, apparently, in base communications and in base-to-fleet communications. It was a drastic failure.

Speaking of the Americans, a number of commands were involved. First was General MacArthur, in command of the total operation. Actually at this stage of the operation, whatever failures there might have been in that command were not apparent. Halsey later complained that under the MacArthur setup, Army, Navy, and Air Corps commanders never seemed to know what the others were doing, and did not cooperate fully. MacArthur was responsible for fighting the Battle of Leyte. Under him Admiral Kinkaid was responsible for protecting those troops who had been gotten ashore, and their lifelines and ability to continue to fight. The responsibility for what happened was clearly in the naval sphere. From Admiral Kinkaid's point of view it was very simple, and just as it had been in the Central Pacific operations and all the Southeast Pacific operations until this point: the naval commander was in charge until the Army took over (or the ground troops, if it was Marines).

Therefore, from Kinkaid's point of view the total responsibility of all naval forces in the Philippines was to protect those people and those lines. That meant the Seventh Fleet, the parent fleet. It also meant the Third the army took over (or the ground troops, if it was marines).

To Halsey, as noted, the mission was quite different. He had a chance to get the Japanese fleet and he took it, thus creating one of the great controversies of wartime. Yet it is not really so much of a controversy, because naval historians and admirals line up almost entirely on one side: Halsey was wrong to have deserted San Bernardino Strait with the Japanese in the Sibuyan Sea. Naturally, Admiral Kinkaid has always thought so. But so have many of Halsey's admirals and other officers. Admiral Gerald Bogan was particularly outspoken in his feeling that Halsey should have left Admiral Lee and the fast battleships and Admiral Bogan's task group at the San Bernardino entrance.

It was an absolute gesture. There was nothing halfway about it. Halsey might have told Kinkaid that he was going (he did). But Kinkaid thought Halsey had formed Task Force 34 (the fast battleships) and did not pay any attention to the implication. Because of that feeling of security about San Bernardino Strait, Kinkaid did not send out enough scouts soon enough—but if he had, the result might not have been much different. The Japanese force could make perhaps 30 knots, and the American force of escort carriers perhaps 19.

Admiral Halsey never liked being blamed for San Bernardino Strait, and the loss of one escort carrier and 3 destroyers and escorts, but he never denied making a mistake. "Hell, yes," he would say, "I made a helluva mistake. But given the same information and the same conditions I would do it again." And he would have. That was the strength of the man, the reason that he was responsible for some of the notable victories of World War

II in the Pacific, from the Solomons to the smashing of the Japanese fleet at Kure Naval Base, those last beleaguered remnants of a once mighty navy.

But in the final analysis the battles of Leyte were won by the overwhelming might of American arms in October, 1944, against the slender, diminishing resources of the Japanese. The battles are tales of the courage of many men, and the bad luck of some. As exhibitions of the strength of the human spirit in self-sacrifice, whether the cause be deemed right or wrong, they are worth the telling. But the fact is that in October, 1944, Japan hadn't the ghost of a chance to win the war. It was too bad there was no easy way to stop the killing, when the Japanese fleet was cut to pieces at Leyte.

WAR BOOKS FROM PLAYBOY PAPERBACKS

GREAT BOOKS OF ADVENTURE AND SUSPENSE

J.D. HARDIN

"THE MOST EXCITING WESTERN WRITER SINCE LOUIS L'AMOUR"
—JAKE LOGAN

GREAT WESTERN YARNS FROM ONE OF THE BEST-SELLING WRITERS IN THE FIELD TODAY

JAKE LOGAN

___16702	ACROSS THE RIO GRANDE	$1.50
___16736	BLOODY TRAIL TO TEXAS	$1.75
___16722	THE COMANCHE'S WOMAN	$1.75
___16622	DEAD MAN'S HAND	$1.75
___16678	FIGHTING VENGEANCE	$1.75
___16939	HANGING JUSTICE	$1.95
___16795	HELLFIRE	$1.95
___16740	IRON MUSTANG	$1.75
___16741	MONTANA SHOWDOWN	$1.75
___16742	NORTH TO DAKOTA	$1.75
___16664	OUTLAW BLOOD	$1.50
___16585	RIDE FOR REVENGE	$1.75
___16866	SHOTGUNS FROM HELL	$1.95
___16744	SLOCUM AND THE WIDOW KATE	$1.75
___16738	SLOCUM'S GOLD	$1.75
___16841	SLOCUM'S GRAVE	$1.95
___16565	SLOCUM'S HELL	$1.50
___16526	SLOCUM'S REVENGE	$1.50
___16936	SLOCUM'S SLAUGHTER	$1.95
___16745	SLOCUM'S WOMAN	$1.75
___16648	WHITE HELL	$1.50